William Fraser

Egypt today; the first to the third khedive

William Fraser

Egypt today; the first to the third khedive

ISBN/EAN: 9783337229740

Printed in Europe, USA, Canada, Australia, Japan

Cover: Foto ©Andreas Hilbeck / pixelio.de

More available books at **www.hansebooks.com**

EGYPT TO-DAY

The First to the Third Khedive

BY

W. FRASER RAE

LONDON

RICHARD BENTLEY AND SON

Publishers in Ordinary to Her Majesty the Queen

1892

CONTENTS

EGYPT TO-DAY

CHAPTER I.

THE FIRST KHEDIVE.

THE Sultan of Turkey ordered his Grand Vizier
to despatch two telegrams on the 26th of June,
1879. The one was addressed to " Ismail Pasha,
ex-Khedive of Egypt ;" the other to his son,
Mehemet Tewfik Pasha. In the first telegram it
was stated that " His Imperial Majesty the Sultan,
as a result of a decision of his Council of Ministers,
has decided on appointing to the post of Khedive
his Excellency Mehemet Tewfik Pasha, and the
Imperial *iradé* on the subject has just been issued."

While the father was reading the document from
which the foregoing sentence has been taken, the
son was reading another, which contained the following words : " His Imperial Majesty the Sultan has
named you by Imperial *iradé* Khedive of Egypt,
and the Imperial firman will be delivered to you
with the customary ceremonial. Ismail Pasha, by
another despatch, has been invited to withdraw from
the affairs of Government. Consequently, upon
receipt of this telegram, convoke all the Ulemas,

1

EGYPT TO-DAY

the functionaries, the chief men of the country, and
the Government employés ; communicate to them
the stipulations of the Imperial *iradé* relative to
your nomination, and begin the direction of the
affairs of the Government."

Ismail was in Abdin Palace, and his eldest son
was in the palace at Koubbeh, when the telegrams
reached Cairo. The deposed Khedive telegraphed
at once to Constantinople that he submitted to the
commands of his sovereign lord the Sultan. His
son Tewfik visited him in the palace of which he
had ceased to be the master, and Ismail greeted his
successor with the phrase, " I salute my Effendina,"
kissing his hands afterwards. The son and father conversed together for a short time, and then the father
busied himself with preparations for leaving Egypt.
What is most remarkable in this sudden change in the
relative positions of the two is the circumstance of
the deposition of the father, and the elevation of the
son to sovereign rank in Egypt, having been effected
through the medium of the electric telegraph. Queen
Scheherazade never imagined a greater marvel.

Three days after his deposition, the ex-Khedive
sailed from Alexandria for Naples. He did not
depart empty-handed. Though he had hoped to
remain in power, chiefly through the bribes which
Talaat, his agent at Constantinople, was commissioned to dispense on his behalf, yet he was prepared for an adverse decision before the receipt of
the fateful telegram.

He had several palaces and many concubines ;
his palaces were treasure-houses, and his concubines

possessed stores of precious stones. He caused all
the portable articles of value in his palaces to be
packed up, and it was estimated that the whole was
worth £800,000. He compelled his concubines to
hand over their jewellery, and thus he obtained a
vast quantity of property which could easily be
converted into a large amount of money. He
selected seventy concubines to accompany him,
leaving the others to their fate, a prospect which
they did not relish, and they showed their displeasure by smashing mirrors and other fragile
articles, the damage done being reckoned at £8,000.

Seldom, since the days of Moses, had the Egyptians been spoiled as they were by Ismail while he
ruled over them and immediately after his deposition.
His reign had been an orgy of despotic plunder,
and when he had no throne to sit upon, or palaces
to occupy as master, he appropriated and carried off
as much of the Khedivial property as he could. On
the 30th of June a long luggage train, which he had
engaged, conveyed from Cairo pictures and cabinets,
dinner-services and rare carpets, bronzes and silver
candelabra, plate of solid gold and inlaid with jewels,
to Alexandria, where they were shipped on board the
gorgeous steam-yacht *Mahroussé*. Ismail followed
in a special train, with two of his sons, a small suite
and his harem, and as soon as the valuable freight
and the passengers were on board the yacht, it
steamed in the direction of Naples.

Ismail ruled over Egypt for sixteen years. Said,
his predecessor, contracted the first Egyptian loan,
the amount being about three millions and a half

sterling, and he bequeathed this, as well as a floating debt, to his nephew and successor, the whole liability being equal to ten millions. When Ismail ceased to be Khedive, the public indebtedness of Egypt exceeded a hundred millions sterling, the sum actually received by the country having been less than half this amount, while the lenders had obtained back in principal and interest the greater part of what they had personally advanced. He had borrowed money recklessly and spent it lavishly ; but the punishment which befell him came from a quarter where misdeeds like his had been committed with impunity. Ismail might have pleaded in his defence that, in burdening Egypt with debt, he had followed the example of his Suzerain, nor can it be denied that, if he had possessed funds wherewith to bribe on a gigantic scale at Constantinople, he might have checkmated his opponents. He had bribed his Suzerain before with £900,000.

The manner in which the Egyptian Fellaheen were taxed under Ismail was not more atrocious than that which was common in many parts of the Ottoman Empire over which the Sultan exercised direct supremacy. It is true that cases frequently occurred of the Fellaheen being compelled to pay their taxes more than once, and of being tortured till they handed over the last coin in their possession. These long-suffering tillers of the soil in Egypt were the patient victims of intolerable cruelty. They and their fathers before them had been subjected to a treatment which makes us wonder how they could continue to exist under it. If it were

true that abuses become more respectable with age,
then those which have been the curse of Egypt are
ancient enough to satisfy the most ardent admirer
of whatever has antiquity on its side. A poem can
be read on the walls of the great temple of Luxor
which was composed in laudation of Rameses the
Great. The author was Pentatour, who flourished
three thousand years ago. A letter written by him
to Ameneman, the monarch's chief librarian, has
also been preserved, and runs thus : " Have you ever
represented to yourself in imagination the state of
the rustic who tills the ground ? Before he has put
the sickle to the crop the locusts have blighted part
thereof ; then come the rats and the birds. If he
is slack in housing his crop the thieves are on him.
His horse dies of weariness as it drags the wain.
The tax-collector arrives ; his agents are armed
with clubs ; he has negroes with him who carry
whips of palm branches. They all cry, ' Give us
your grain,' and he has no way of avoiding their
extortionate demands. Next, the wretch is caught,
bound and sent off to work, without wage, at the
canals ; his wives are taken and chained ; his
children are stripped and plundered."

This gloomy picture of life in Egypt during the
reign of Rameses the Great might have been painted
when Ismail was its ruler. The methods had not
changed after the lapse of three thousand years,
the rest of the world having been transformed during
the interval.

If Ismail had been allowed to continue on the
throne, the iniquitous system which he fostered

would have existed for a few more years. He has been defended by some persons on the ground that his worst deeds have been blazoned forth and his best disregarded, and that he was not more blame-worthy than some other rulers over Egypt, while many Sultans of Turkey could keep him in coun-tenance. This line of defence is equivalent to the schoolboy's allegation that if he did anything wrong he was justified because his companions had set him the example. In the modern history of the Ottoman Empire there are abundant examples of Sultans who have been as vicious men and ruthless rulers as Ismail, the ex-Khedive of Egypt. The Turkish tax-gatherer has nothing to learn from any Egyptian colleague. Not even in Egypt has anything been done of a more tyrannical character than what happened when the sheep-tax was collected in another province of Turkey, where the tax-gatherer levied 9,000 piastres, which was the amount due, and on returning and recounting the sheep he levied 14,000 piastres on the plea that his first figures were inaccurate. He came for the third time and called for a second payment of 14,000 because the owners of the sheep could not produce a receipt for the former payment, no receipt having been given !

A much stronger plea on behalf of Ismail has been advanced by those who assert that, if he had not succumbed to the temptations held out to him to borrow money, he would have been a much more re-putable ruler. Baron de Malortie, who knew him per-sonally and possesses an intimate acquaintance with

Egypt, has presented this view of the matter in one
of his many interesting and useful works. Ismail is
depicted by him as resembling the gentleman farmers
who obtain great results, but who never calculate
the cost of production : " Generous and open-
handed, his mania was giving ;—his great fault
never to think of the liabilities incurred. In accepting the financial aid of the Continent, he did not
discern the political consequences, nor the jealous
intrigues which were to turn his monetary difficulties
into a source of international meddling and encroach-
ment.

" Blindfolded, Ismail allowed himself to fall into
the hands of money-lenders ; from high to low, all
Continental usurers threw themselves upon Egypt
as an easy prey. So long as he had securities to
offer, the ante-rooms of his Ministers were overcrowded with bankers anxious to lend him millions
at a percentage prohibited by penal laws in their
own country. Even after the Porte had put in a
veto, the money-lenders were equal to the occasion,
by finding means to evade a distasteful prohibition ;
they continued to push him to take their gold, and
to mortgage Egypt, to pawn his State and his
private properties up to their utmost value, renewing
greedily his bonds until they found it more advantageous to liquidate the estate. Cringeing as long as
they could hope to get something out of him, they
became as threatening and impudent as we know
the money-lending tribe to be with insolvent debtors.
Had this been the case of an ordinary mortal, a
court of law would have reduced the outrageous

claims to fair and just proportions. But then he was a sovereign, and his creditors were the kings of Jews, or rather the Jews of kings, and powerful enough to bring to bear the authority and pressure of their respective Governments to enforce their claims by every means available."*

Baron de Malortie adds to the foregoing statement the fact of Riaz Pasha, one of the most capable and respected among Egyptian statesmen, having told him that he estimated at twenty millions sterling the imaginary claims which were wrongfully exacted from Egypt by means of the Mixed Tribunals and foreign pressure. It was an aggravation of the state of things then existing that, while the foreign creditors received the sums which they demanded, the native creditors were sent empty away; the foreign bondholders could cash their coupons, while Egyptian clerks, soldiers and officers were denied the money for which they had toiled.

The people of Egypt, who had to bear the load of Ismail's extravagance, received less consideration than the bondholders and other creditors. A debt exceeding one hundred millions sterling was saddled upon Egypt. While interest had to be paid upon this gigantic sum, the amount of capital received was not more than the half. The contractors with whom Ismail arranged for the execution of public works obtained 80 per cent. profit; some of the bankers from whom he borrowed money charged 28 per cent. for a temporary advance.

When the credit of Turkey was exhausted and

* " Egypt: Native Rulers and Foreign Interference," pp. 131, 132.

the settlement of obligations which had been incurred could no longer be postponed by a fresh
issue of bonds, the Sultan quietly repudiated the
debts which he was unable to discharge. His
creditors grumbled, but they did not obtain any
redress, and thus they were punished for their
credulity in accepting Turkish promises to pay.

The foreign creditors of Egypt invoked the assistance of their respective Governments, and these
Governments set themselves to wring from the impoverished Egyptians the sums necessary to pay the
interest upon the public debt. Ismail refused to be a
convenient tool in their hands, and his deposition was
the penalty of his contumacy. His subjects had no
reason to regret his fate. He had been a harsh and
remorseless master. Partly by purchase and partly
through compulsion, he had become the possessor of
one-fifth of the cultivable land in the country, and
it seemed as if his ultimate object was to enter
into possession of the whole. He had not dazzled
them with military glory ; on the contrary, he was
worsted in his contest with Abyssinia, and he
wasted both treasure and lives in an expedition
thither which was a shameful failure.

In a review of Ismail's reign an event is sadly
conspicuous which has never been explained, and
which no one has attempted to defend. His most
trusted adviser was Ismail Sadyk Pasha, who was
his foster - brother, and who for twenty years had
filled the office of Moufettish, or inspector. Ismail
kept no secrets from Sadyk. He had countenanced
and possibly enriched his servant, who, beginning life

in poverty, left behind him property which was believed to be worth three millions sterling. That the Moufettish had accumulated wealth by practising rigid economy has never been asserted, and the method by which he heaped up treasure remains nearly as great a mystery as the manner in which he left the world.

He was in power when Mr. Goschen and M. Joubert arrived in Cairo as agents commissioned by certain foreign bondholders to negotiate with the Khedive on their behalf. The Commissioners proposed a scheme which was unwelcome to the Moufettish. They asked for information which the Khedive was either unable or unwilling to give. The Moufettish could have told them everything if he had chosen, and it is possible that some of the things which he might have divulged would have been discreditable to his master.

It was no secret in Cairo that the Moufettish looked with disfavour upon the mission of Messrs. Goschen and·Joubert, and declined to help them in any way. If he had been removed from office and if a more pliable and complaisant man had been appointed in his place, no one would have been surprised ; but what astounded the public was an article in the *Moniteur Egyptien*, to the effect that Ismail Sadyk Pasha had resigned, that he had been plotting against the Khedive, and had been condemned to undergo close imprisonment at Dongola. When this announcement appeared, Sadyk had probably been dead for thirty-six hours.

Mr. McCoan, who was in Cairo at the time, and

who collected all the particulars and rumours which were current, has set them forth in his *Egypt under Ismail*, and the general result is as follows : He had dined with Sadyk on the 7th of November, and heard from his lips a distinct condemnation of the scheme put forward by Messrs. Goschen and Joubert, and very uncomplimentary expressions concerning one of the Commissioners. On the following evening Mr. McCoan was the guest of the Khedive in Abdin Palace, where Sadyk was present, and on the most cordial terms with his master. The following day he resigned his office, and on the evening of that day the Khedive was again surrounded by guests on the balcony of his palace, and in excellent spirits, joking with each in turn and being in his most jovial mood. Sadyk was not present. Mr. McCoan heard the next day that he had been given into arrest by the Khedive for high treason. He at once went to the palace, was admitted to an audience, and learnt from the Khedive's lips his version of what had occurred. This was to the effect that early on the previous day he had received a letter from Sadyk tendering his resignation and denouncing the scheme of Messrs. Goschen and Joubert. " He must have been drunk when he wrote it," added the Khedive ; "the letter itself was never published," is Mr. McCoan's comment.

He said to the Khedive : "Well, Monseigneur, at least I earnestly hope he will not die, as his death would be interpreted only in one way in Europe."

"What does it concern me," was the reply, "whether he lives or dies ? He will probably drink himself to death, and I will let him have all the brandy he wishes."

Many versions of what happened to Sadyk have been circulated, but as they differ they cannot all be equally authentic.

What cannot be gainsaid is, that on the morning of the 10th of November, 1876, the Khedive invited Sadyk, as was his custom, to join him in a drive, and the latter accepted, possibly thinking that his master might wish him to withdraw his resignation. The two men sat in an open victoria, smoking and laughing as they were driven along. The coachman had received orders to proceed to the palace at Ghezireh ; on arriving there he drove up to the main doorway. Ismail stepped out at once and ordered the officer of the guard to arrest Sadyk, who laughed, thinking it a joke. However, he found the whole to be grim earnest when he was taken across the entrance-hall and locked up in a small room, outside of which a sentry was posted. Ismail returned to Abdin Palace, leaving his son Prince Hassan at Ghezireh. It is not known that Sadyk ever left this palace alive.

It had been asserted, however, that he was put on board a steamer which sailed up the Nile, and that two eunuchs strangled him there and threw his corpse into the river. Immediately after this statement was circulated an official contradiction appeared, with the addition that Sadyk was alive, and that he was drinking brandy to excess on board the steamer, which was bound for Assouan. A further official statement, and one which was as worthy of credence as any other, announced his arrival at Dongola and death there, the certificates of his death from an Italian physician being adduced as confirmatory evidence.

Thus the matter remained in doubt till after the deposition of Ismail, when Ishak Bey, who had been a soldier in Cairo at the time Sadyk disappeared, and had received a pension which was cancelled when Tewfik became Khedive, confessed that he was the executioner of Sadyk. He stated that an hour after the latter's arrest he was ordered by Prince Hassan to take his life by breaking the bones in his body so that he might die without any external mark of violence being visible. In the struggle for life, Sadyk bit off his executioner's thumb, and Ishak Bey was able to display a hand without a thumb in corroboration of his story. The body of the murdered man was wrapped in canvas, to which weights were attached, was placed on board a steamer, and cast into the Nile a few miles above Cairo.

These are the stories of how Ismail's confidential servant came to his end, and, whichever be correct, it appears indisputable that Ismail must have been privy to his disappearance. This is the most atrocious deed which has been laid to his charge, yet it may not be the only infamous one of which he is guilty. His son Tewfik informed Mr. Butler that when his female slaves refused to submit to his will they were punished with one hundred, and sometimes two hundred, strokes on the soles of their feet.

" People in Europe," said the Khedive, " would

be astonished if they knew Ismail's real character and history."

" Yes," I said ; " he is thought to be extravagant and selfish, but otherwise polite, clever and enlightened."

" But," said Tewfik, " thank God, those barbarous times are over."*

Ismail consoled himself for Sadyk's death by taking possession of his property. He selected the choicest members of his harem and added them to his own. Others he presented to officers in his army, and the remainder he sold as slaves. The youngest of the dead man's children, who was the adopted daughter of the Khedive's mother, was separated from her husband, to whom she had been married a few months before. The pecuniary gain to Ismail was estimated at nearly three millions sterling. Like Catiline, he was greedy of other people's riches and lavish of his own.

He was feared but not beloved, and when he took his departure from Egypt he left it on the verge of bankruptcy and the people on the brink of famine. These things gave him no concern. Though Ismail was indifferent to the condition of those over whom he ruled, he was apprehensive concerning his own safety. Indeed, according to the statement which Tewfik made to Mr. Butler, he lived in terror of the assassin, "and would never allow a stranger or a native to come near him, if he could avoid it, for fear of a dagger up the sleeve. He had no heart or affection ; his sensuality had ruined that."†

* " Court Life in Egypt," by Alfred J. Butler, p. 205.   † *Ibid.*

Ismail had the mania for building which is not uncommon among despots, and which has been the distinctive mark of those who have governed Egypt. Not one of the palaces which he built at a vast outlay is an architectural masterpiece. The city of Cairo in its modern aspect is more likely to perpetuate his name. He transformed it from a city of narrow alleys and gloomy houses into one with broad and airy streets lined with palatial mansions. He deserves great credit for having supported Nubar Pasha in his laudable and untiring efforts to establish international Courts of Justice, and it is even more honourable to have acquired the reputation of lending the weight of his authority in opposition to the slave trade.

He relinquished power at the command of his Suzerain, but it was long before he relinquished all hope of returning to Egypt as its ruler. It has been shown already that he took with him enough property in money and kind to render him independent. In addition to what he had appropriated, the Egyptian Government allowed him £86,000 a year for himself, and £30,000 for his family. He considered this insufficient. He held, moreover, that he had received an inadequate sum for his private estates, and he made repeated applications on the subject to the Government. He failed to obtain attention or redress till he secured the services of Sir William Marriott, Judge-Advocate-General in the Adminis-tration of Lord Salisbury, through whose advocacy he was paid two millions sterling—"in final satis-faction of his own and his family's claims upon the

Egyptian Government." The payment made to his advocate was proportionately as large as that made to him, the fee being £35,000.*

Years were passed by Ismail Pasha in vain attempts to be restored to the Khediviate. He visited London, Paris and Vienna, and implored the statesmen in these capitals to espouse his cause ; but he received no encouragement from them. With the money which he could still distribute he bribed some venal journalists to afford him a worthless support in worthless newspapers.

Weary of fruitless efforts, he finally resolved to inhabit his palace on the Bosphorus ; and having obtained the Sultan's consent, he transferred his harem and his servants to Emirghan. He met with several refusals before leave was given him to take up his abode there. Now he cannot leave his own palace, and he is a prisoner in a gilded cage, being forbidden to receive visitors, newspapers or letters. No surprise would be manifested at Constantinople if the ex-Khedive Ismail Pasha were to disappear as suddenly and as strangely as his confidant the Moufettish, Ismail Sadyk Pasha.

Ismail might have lived a more honoured life, and Egypt would have been a more prosperous country, if he had followed the sage counsel which the first Caliph gave to his son : " Beware of money-lenders, and devote one-third of thy income to making canals."

* " Egypt under Ismail," pp. 267, 296.

CHAPTER II.

A DECREE from the Sultan of Turkey cast down Ismail Pasha from his high estate and elevated his eldest son Tewfik to the position of Khedive of Egypt. Nothing could be in closer accord with immemorial custom in the Morning-land. It is still possible in Oriental real life, as it was in the imaginative and romantic scenes of *The Arabian Nights*, for a pipe-bearer to be suddenly raised to the high rank of Grand Vizier, and for a Grand Vizier to be dismissed with contumely simply because his master had grown tired of him.

The power of the Sultan of Turkey over Egypt had gradually declined during recent years, and it appeared as if Egypt would soon acquire the independence which Mehemet Ali longed for, and strove vigorously, but in vain, to achieve. When England and France requested the Sultan to depose Ismail and raise Tewfik to the throne of Egypt, the Sultan did not hesitate, and it was probably a pleasure to demonstrate that he was the supreme Lord over the Valley of the Nile. In this respect the change was a misfortune to Egypt ; yet, despite

2

its drawbacks, it could not have been averted unless the Great Powers had displayed the courage collectively with which any one of them may fairly be credited when acting alone.

The special drawback consisted in the false position of the new Khedive. Nominally an autocrat like his predecessors, he was devoid of power in reality, and, while he had to bear the blame of all miscarriages in the conduct of public affairs, others were lauded when the machinery of government worked smoothly and well.

Mehemet Tewfik, who was born on the 15th of November, 1852, was the son of a peasant girl. He had never been the favourite of his father, Ismail. Owing to his entrance into the world, his mother was recognised as Ismail's fourth wife, the other wives not then having any living sons. After his birth Ismail had another son by his second wife. This son became his favourite, and his mother, Princess Djenajar, intrigued as strenuously as her husband when the latter was engaged in obtaining the Sultan's consent to change the order of succession and proposed naming his favourite son his heir. The right was acquired at a cost of three millions sterling, and after the 9th of June, 1866, the day on which the desired firman was issued, Ismail was prepared to appoint Ibrahim Hilmy Pasha to rule over Egypt when he himself should have been gathered to his fathers. Then it was that the Great Powers and the Sultan informed him that he must nominate his eldest son, and he reluctantly followed the counsel, which was equivalent to a command.

While Ismail sent his other sons to England and France to complete their education, he kept Tewfik at home till he was eighteen, and then he permitted him to visit Europe. Tewfik had not been absent many weeks, and he had not gone farther than Vienna, when he was recalled and appointed to an office in the Government. He was married in 1872 to a daughter of El Hemy Pasha, who was a grandson of Mehemet Ali; and he was installed in a palace at Koubbeh, near Cairo, with an allowance of £30,000 a year. He had a small estate, which he cultivated with care, and gained the character of a good landlord. He was an affectionate husband and an indulgent father. Though a devout Muslim, yet he never used his right to give rivals to his wife in the persons of other wives or their handmaidens. He interested himself, moreover, in the education of children, establishing a school in his palace where 120 pupils were educated at an expense to himself of £4,000 a year, the pupils being orphans and many of them sons of officers. Indeed, his private life was exemplary, and he seemed to prefer being regarded as a private gentleman rather than as heir to the throne.

His father would not give him credit for abstaining from intrigue. An illustration of this has been given by Mr. Edward Dicey, who writes that he was at a ball in the Ghezireh Palace in 1878, when "An Anglo-Egyptian official, not celebrated for his tact or discretion, seized hold of my arm with the words, 'I want to present you to his Highness Prince Tewfik!' I turned round, and saw a stout, heavy-looking young man, seemingly very ill at ease. The cause of his discomfort was obvious enough. His father was standing near us, and was watching us with his sharp, sleepy eyes, which always reminded me of a cat shamming sleep. I have seldom seen a man so manifestly anxious to cut short an interview as Tewfik was on the occasion of which I speak. He stammered, hesitated, spoke a few words of halting French, and uttered an audible sigh of relief as I bowed and passed on. . . . He was always suspected at Court of being in league with his father's opponents; and though I doubt whether Ismail Pasha really believed this, yet to have intrigued so much was so exactly what, in like circumstances, he would have done himself, that he could never shake off the suspicion."*

Mr. Butler records, on the authority of Tewfik himself, that his movements were watched and reported to his father. Many overtures were made to join in intrigues, but he always rejected them. When he was Regent during his father's absence in Europe, he received "a letter from a then Minister offering him the services of all the land and sea forces, and promising to sink Ismail in the harbour of Alexandria, on his return to Egypt. Tewfik rejected the offer, not once but twice over; but he kept the letters." At this time he lived in daily dread of being poisoned. " I assure you," he said to Mr. Butler, " those were dreadful times for me ; I can never forget what I suffered. It was only the

* *Nineteenth Century* for February, 1892, p. 236.

strength of a good conscience and the resolve to do right that kept me up."*

Few events in the history of modern rulers are more striking and dramatic than the sudden substitution of Tewfik for Ismail. The way in which the transfer took place has often been told, but curiosity has been as often displayed concerning what passed between the two men immediately after Ismail had sunk to be a subject and his son had risen to be a sovereign. Tewfik's account of what then occurred has been overlooked by many investigators. He told the story to Mr. Butler, the principal facts being the following :

" When at last I came to the throne, I received the news without any joy. Sympathy with my father's fall, and the great sense of responsibility, left me no room for rejoicing." After his father had bowed to fate, had kissed his son's hands and cheeks, and exclaimed, " I salute my Effendina !" the private talk took this form : " My father heaped reproaches upon me, and accused me of having intrigued at last successfully. I then produced the letters which the Minister had written, offering me the army. My father read them, was much moved, and kissed me, saying, ' Forgive me, my son, forgive me !' "

The father and son differed widely in their religious views, though both were Muslims. Ismail's religion sat lightly on him, and he never allowed it to interfere with his tastes or fancies. Tewfik, on the contrary, was a thorough believer in the faith of the Prophet. He was abstemious in

* " Court Life in Egypt," pp. 206, 207.

other things than wives, never smoking tobacco or
drinking anything stronger than coffee. His father
had as little scruples about abstaining from fasting
in the manner that the founder of his religion had
enjoined as he had in giving way to any of his
appetites. He used to jeer at his son for the strict-
ness with which he discharged his religious duties,
telling him that he ought to adopt European modes
of living and thinking. On one occasion he gave
him this advice, which certainly did him no credit :
"When you come to the throne, pretend to be a
good Muslim like me ; the natives will like you for
it ; it is good policy."

When Tewfik did succeed to the throne, at a time
and in a fashion which his father had never anticipated, he was careful to carry out his own views
concerning religious observances. The day of his
accession was a Friday, which is the holy day in
the Muslim world. Tewfik then went in state to the
mosque. His father had remarked on hearing of his
intention to do so : "What! Still determined to
play the Muslim ?" His son dutifully replied :
" Yes, sire, more than ever."

It is difficult to imagine a more arduous position
than that which Mehemet Tewfik occupied on
becoming Khedive of Egypt. I have already
intimated that he was supreme in name only. All
his training had led him to regard the office which
he held as one in which absolute power was
exercised. During his father's reign a Minister of
State had threatened him with condign punishment
if he did not conduct himself differently, his reply

being : " He is my father and my sovereign, and can fling me into the Nile if he wishes." He had examples from his father of autocracy in its most extreme and repulsive type. Ismail really believed that the people of Egypt had been sent into the world to minister to his wants, and that, if he treated them tenderly at times, it was for the same reason that he would not overwork a horse. If a horse is not allowed to rest, it dies ; if the Fellaheen were not permitted to accumulate some money, they could not meet the demands of the taxpayers. His personal view was given in a conversation with Mr. Rivers Wilson, who remonstrated with him on account of his exactions. He deprecated the good advice which had been offered, saying in substance : " These people are mine, their land is mine, and all they have, and I must have the use of what is my own."

Omar Loutfi Pasha, one of the governing body, expressed the opinions which his fellows entertained, and upon which they had acted. When subjected to examination before a commission of inquiry, he admitted that he had been a party to many atrocities, and excused himself by alleging that he had obeyed the orders of the head of the State. He was further asked :

" But if a superior order commanded you to squander public funds for the Khedive's personal use, would you defend it ?"

" Certainly," he answered, " if I have my master's order."

" Were the Fellaheen ever unjustly taxed ?"

" How could they be ?   All they had belonged to the Khedive."

" But if it were against the law ?"

" The law!   What other law is there but the Khedive's superior orders ?"

Though chief ruler of Egypt, and anxious to use his authority in the interests of his people, Tewfik found himself as helpless as Gulliver when he was bound hand and foot by the Lilliputians.   Each cord which surrounded Gulliver was small and weak, but the number of them sufficed to hinder him from regaining the use of his limbs.   Thus it was with the Khedive.   His hands were pinioned by the Dual Control which the representatives of France and England exercised.   He could complain, but he could not shake himself free from it.   His Ministers, of whom, Riaz Pasha was the chief, had more of their own way than any who had served his father. Baron de Malortie, writing with an intimate know-ledge of the facts, says of the Khedive at this time :

" He complained to his Ministers of the Con-trollers, to the Controllers of his Ministers, and to his surroundings of both."

However little real power Tewfik could display, he was regarded by his people as the master of their destinies.   To quote from Baron de Malortie again :

" All grievances, home or foreign, were addressed to him ; he was made responsible for all wrongs ; he was the centre of all reproaches, and on his head were accumulated the discontent and hatred of the aggrieved."*

* "Egypt : Native Rulers and Foreign Interference," p. 159.

There was sufficient reason for discontent. While the Controllers were desirous that the greatest economy should be exercised in the Administration, and reductions were effected in all departments of the Government, the saving thereby caused meant poverty, if not slow death by starvation, to thousands of the Khedive's subjects. He was quite ready to remedy abuses, and he gave many examples of his desire to lop off superfluous and ruinous expenditure. Having been a careful administrator of his private estate, he continued this habit when he ascended the throne, and one of his earliest cares was to examine the palace accounts. He then learnt, as he told Mr. Edward Dicey, "that in his father's time some ten thousand inmates or hangers-on of the palace were lodged, boarded, and clothed at the expense of the State."*

He got rid of these useless mouths without closing them. Being hampered in the exercise of power, he made enemies without gaining friends. In Egypt, as in other countries, the ruler who distributes places and pensions is always surrounded with eulogists, whereas the ruler who is an economist of his own money and that of his subjects must expect to be reproached as a niggard and denounced as incompetent.

A spirit of insubordination had been manifested by the officers of the Egyptian army before Tewfik's accession in June, 1879. In February of that year four hundred officers had menaced Sir Rivers Wilson and Nubar Pasha at the Ministry of Finance,

* *Nineteenth Century* for February, 1892, p. 237.

and put their lives in danger, the two Ministers
being saved from a horrible fate by the personal
intervention of Ismail.   These were but four hundred
out of two thousand five hundred officers who were
in the like plight and of the same mind.   While the
European Powers were using the utmost pressure
upon the Egyptian Government to pay the European
bondholders the interest on the foreign debt, the
officers in the Egyptian army were left unpaid, and
many of those who were entirely dependent upon
their pay died for lack of food.

On one occasion an army officer appeared at the
Ministry of Finance with his dead child in his arms,
praying for some of the money due to him that he
might provide decent burial for the little one.   For
one case of the kind that was made public, hundreds
may have been borne in private.   There were other
cases which could neither be concealed nor ex-
tenuated.   When the strain to find money wherewith to pay the bondholders was greatest, the crops
failed in Upper Egypt, and it was intimated that
hundreds of persons had perished of hunger.   Those
who died had a happy release from the exactions of
the tax-gatherer, while the faces of those who sur-
vived were ground still more shamefully.

The joint part which France and England played
in Egypt occasioned confusion and discontent.
Nothing more effective than the Dual Control could
have been invented if the object had been to insure
failure and mischief in the conduct of public affairs.
The first Controllers were both excellent men, M. de
Blignières representing France, and Major Baring

England, in a manner which could not be excelled. It happened, however, that the former became unpopular with his countrymen, and the latter left Egypt to occupy a post in India at a critical stage in the evolution of the new Government. If these two men had remained longer in office, some of the subsequent complications might have been averted, while it is certain that if the Dual Control were to work efficiently, this was possible only when the direction of affairs was in hands such as theirs. They were not only most capable men, but they worked in harmony, and one of the reproaches levelled at M. de Blignières was that he did not quarrel with his English colleague. He gave offence to his countrymen by thinking more about putting the Egyptian finances upon a solid basis than about obtaining places of emolument or concessions which would prove remunerative to them. Hence it was concluded and asserted in France that he had sold himself to the English. It is true that he had given a certain number of his countrymen a specific ground for complaint by declining to aid them in getting a contract which he considered injurious to Egyptian interests, and these men united with others in signing petitions for his recall. One of the signatories asserted that he had seen a cheque drawn in M. de Blignières' favour, and signed " Beaconsfield, Premier Ministre d'Angleterre." If all the statements of the petitioners were as ludicrously false as this one, then they must fill a conspicuous place in the annals of mendacity. The misfortune was that M. de Blignières, while standing aloof from all censurable practices by which his countrymen might benefit at the expense of the Egyptians, afterwards took a more active part in Egyptian politics, with a result which was detrimental to his office.

Everything which was done in Egypt by France and England led to rendering the country more dependent upon foreigners, and the Khedive more and more of a figure-head. The Commission of Liquidation which was appointed in April, 1880, at the instance of the Great Powers, effected reductions of expenses and other financial arrangements in the interests of the bondholders, and further lessened the Khedive's authority. A large reduction was made in the army, against which the Egyptian officers rebelled, and their riotous, if not outrageous, conduct led to the obnoxious order being rescinded, the army being increased and the pay of the soldiers and sailors in the Khedive's service augmented to the amount of nearly £60,000 a year.

In the history of Egypt many pages can be filled with the narrative of events beginning with the rise of "Achmet the Egyptian" (who is better known now as Arabi Pasha) from an obscure position to be the leader of a revolt among his fellow-officers in the Egyptian army, to be the head of a revolution having the predominance of a national party as its professed aim, to be a military dictator for a time, and then to be a convicted rebel to whom mercy was extended, and whose later years have been passed as an exile in Ceylon. At several points in this changing scene it appears as if the Khedive displayed a lack of firmness, yet more than once he was as heroic as any man can be at a moment of imminent peril. He was one of the last of the non-combatants to leave Alexandria before it was bombarded, saying, when implored to take refuge on board his yacht or a man-of-war: " I am still Khedive, and I remain with my people in the hour of their danger!" While he and his wife were in the palace at Ramleh, three miles distant, they were in constant danger for two days, and it is a marvel that they escaped with their lives. He was Sovereign by firman of the Sultan, but whenever he attempted to exercise his authority he was made to feel that it existed on paper only. When material help was indispensable, he telegraphed to the Sultan for the aid of twenty battalions of Turkish troops. For so doing he received a reprimand from Lord Granville on the part of England, and from M. Barthélemy St. Hilaire on the part of France. Both France, as represented by M. Waddington, and England, as represented by Lord Salisbury, had called upon the Sultan to raise him to the position of Khedive, yet while the Sultan's power was invoked to give Egypt a head, it was not to be exercised to give Egypt peace. In these circumstances, it is not only difficult but preposterous to find fault with Mehemet Tewfik for being deficient in firmness and resource.

Whether some adverse criticisms of the Khedive's conduct may or may not be justified must remain undetermined, seeing that conclusive evidence cannot be obtained now. It is beyond all question, how-ever, that a man of the greatest genius might have

found it difficult to thread his course through such
a labyrinth of doubts and misfortunes as that in
which the Khedive was placed. In the autumn of
1882, after the insurrection headed by Arabi had
been crushed, a Mahdi, or Saviour, arose in the
Soudan and began a crusade against the Egyptian
Government there, while almost simultaneously
cholera raged throughout Lower Egypt between
Cairo and the sea. The disease was less widespread
and fatal at Alexandria, where the Khedive was
staying. He considered it his duty to return to
the capital, and he did so, accompanied by his wife,
against the wish of his advisers and greatly to their
dismay. He personally visited the hospitals at
Cairo; he helped the bereaved with money from a
purse which was not overflowing; and he inspired
an amount of confidence by his conduct which
proved serviceable to the sick, as well as set an
example which was of inestimable value.

The plague of cholera proved to be a less
formidable foe to Egypt than the Mahdi. All the
efforts designed to rescue the Egyptians in the
Soudan miscarried, despite the aid afforded by Great
Britain, and the Soudan itself, which Mehemet Ali
annexed to Egypt, was detached from it under
Tewfik. Many episodes in the story of which this
was the ending cannot be contemplated without
painful emotion, the untimely death of Gordon at
Khartoum being the climax of vacillation in London
and blundering in Egypt.

From the time of the deposition of Ismail to
the revolt of Arabi and his followers, Egypt was

nominally governed by Tewfik, while the representatives of England and France really directed the
chariot of State. But when the insurrection was
quelled and the ringleader sent into perpetual exile,
the Dual Control ceased, and the Egyptian Government re-acquired most of the authority which it had
lost. A force of British soldiers remained in the
country to hinder a relapse into anarchy.

The massacres at Alexandria had shown that, in
addition to the predatory element which exists in all
cities, there was an amount of Muslim fanaticism
which would make no terms with foreigners, provided they were infidels. Sir Donald Mackenzie
Wallace remarks in his work on *The Egyptian
Question* that Mehemet Ali and his immediate
successors oppressed people of all creeds with perfect
impartiality, the native Christian and the Muslim
concentrating all their hatred upon their governors,
and tolerating the religious views of each other.
Under Arabi Pasha the fanaticism of the Muslims
was again allowed vent ; indeed, while proclaiming
himself the leader of a national party, he did not
mean that any Christians should be enlisted under
his banner. Writing from personal knowledge acquired at the moment, Sir Donald adds : " Nearly
all the native and foreign residents . . . are convinced that their lives and property are safe only so
long as the British troops remain in the country."*

It was unavoidable, and a necessary result of the
Dual Control, that the Power which had aided the
Khedive to retain his throne should continue to

* " Egypt and the Egyptian Question," p. 38.

give him advice and support. The Earl of Dufferin, the British Ambassador at Constantinople, was ordered by the Home Government to visit Cairo, to examine the state of affairs there, and to make what suggestions he deemed advisable in the circumstances. The report, dated the 6th of February, 1883, which he made to Earl Granville at the conclusion of his mission, is a document as comprehensive as it is able, and it is classed among the most remarkable State papers of this age.

All that concerns the future and well-being of Egypt is touched upon by Lord Dufferin in a masterly fashion in that document, and a complete scheme for reorganizing the Government of Egypt is there set forth in clear and graphic terms. The survey and recommendations embrace the army, the police, the establishment of a Legislative Council and a Representative Assembly, the administration of justice, public education, irrigation and the slave trade. The Khedive expressed to Earl Granville his appreciation of Lord Dufferin's services, and intimated his " sincere satisfaction at the manner in which the Earl of Dufferin has afforded to me and to my Government the assistance of his great experience and high capacity in the reorganization of different departments of the Egyptian Administration, and, above all, for the creation of institutions calculated to enable the nation, in accordance with my wishes, to participate progressively, and to a reasonable degree, in the administration of the country, and thus interest every Egyptian in the prosperity of Egypt."

The Khedive afforded practical proof of the sincerity of his declarations by issuing a decree constituting the " Egyptian Charter," which provided for the creation of Provincial Councils, a Legislative Council, a General Assembly and a Council of State. This Charter is dated the 1st of May, 1883, and since then it has amply justified the wisdom and forethought which presided over its birth. Many feared at the time that Lord Dufferin was too sanguine in some of his forecasts and premature in some of his suggestions. Yet the results which he hoped for have been attained in a measure beyond his expectations, and experience has proved him to have been as shrewd and practical when framing a Constitution for Egypt as he was bold and dexterous when conducting a negotiation.

After the recovery of Egypt from its depression and calamities many inquired whether the country could not stand alone and the British occupation terminate. The Khedive did not relish being under a sort of tutelage, and it would have been discreditable to him if he were satisfied with his lot. His feelings were as keen as they were natural, and as patriotic as any of his subjects could desire. One of his Ministers told Mr. Edward Dicey that His Highness " once pointed to a British sentinel standing in front of the Abdin Palace, and said in a sudden outburst of irritation :

" Do you suppose that I like this ? Why, every time that I pass a British soldier in the street I long to get out and take him by the neck !"*

* *Nineteenth Century* for February, 1892, p. 239.

His Suzerain, the Sultan of Turkey, regarded the British occupation with a dislike equally keen and genuine, his constant dread being lest it might be prolonged indefinitely and lest his power to meddle in Egyptian affairs should be ended for ever. The French were indignant as well as annoyed at having ceased to exercise what they considered to be their legitimate rights in Egypt. The claims of France to have a preponderating voice in Egyptian affairs have been urged with greater pertinacity than those of the Sultan of Turkey, and a legend has been formed in favour of the French contention.

No one denies that one Frenchman, Mariette Bey, has done more for Egyptian archæology than any other European since Belzoni, and that another Frenchman, M. de Lesseps, has earned the glory of having connected the Mediterranean and Red Sea through the medium of a navigable canal. Many Frenchmen have been in the service of the rulers of Egypt, and many remunerative concessions have helped to fill French pockets ; but these unquestionable facts hardly establish the claim on the part of France to be paramount in Egypt. Neither would the claim be strengthened, even if well founded, by the further fact that several Egyptians have been educated in France, and that much good French is spoken in Cairo and Alexandria.

The French long ago cast covetous eyes upon the Valley of the Nile. Shortly before the beginning of this century, and in the year VII. of the first French Republic, a French naval officer named Sonnini, who had travelled through Egypt, published the result of his experience and observations, his work being among the best in the copious and dreary literature of Egyptian travel. When he gave his conclusions to the world the expedition to Egypt under the command of Bonaparte had been resolved upon, and, in view of the anticipated result, Sonnini wrote in his preface that Egypt may recover her ancient lustre, and that, transferred into the possession of a people as " renowned as that which was once the boast of antiquity, this celebrated country, which ages of unrelenting destruction have completely disguised, will reassume her departed glory. The men as well as the soil, the territory as well as its inhabitants, are hastening to wear a new aspect." When Sonnini voyaged to Egypt he passed Malta, which was then in possession of the Knights of St. John ; when his book was published the island had been conquered by Bonaparte, and this caused him to write : " The French Republic, which, in the space of a few years, has hurried through ages of glory, has just put an end to the existence of the Order ; it has looked down with disdain on the advantages which that institution procured to France, and the hope of concord of which it opened a glimpse to the nations. Speculations like these were too narrow for the immensity of her power. Mistress of the Mediterranean, by means of the conquest of Malta and Gozzi, she has extended her Departments as far as the seas of the Levant, and thus appropriated to herself the commerce of it ; while by her intimate alliance with the nations which can no longer have an interest separate from hers, she has accomplished the great work of social order, the fraternization of mankind."*

The attempt to promote fraternity by force, and to add Egypt to the Departments of France, was a costly and sanguinary failure. Little remains that is worth mentioning about the French invasion of Egypt except a grandiose phrase, the reports of men of letters and science and the Egyptian Institute. That learned body, though transformed in 1859, when Said was Viceroy, is the existing embodiment of the best service that France has rendered to Egypt.

While it is impossible to instance any adequate achievement, or any intimate association conferring upon France greater rights over or in Egypt than any other nation may have, it is indisputable that her policy in the East has been based upon the assumption that such rights exist. The French are as much convinced of this as the Russians are that they should rule supreme on the Bosphorus and in India. Lord Dalling remarks, in his *Life of Palmerston :* " There is, in fact, a policy dating far back in the traditions of the French Foreign Office, which would assign to France the possession of or patronage over Egypt. Napoleon's expedition indented this policy deeper into the French mind. It was a policy natural for France if France were the enemy of England ; but it was a policy impossible for France if there were to be a sincere alliance and friendship between the two countries, because the mistress of India cannot permit France to be mistress directly or indirectly of the road to her Indian dominions."†

* " Travels in Upper and Lower Egypt," pp. 82-84.
† " Life of Viscount Palmerston," vol. ii., pp. 292, 293.

Baron de Malortie, after commenting on this passage, adds the remark made by Prince Metternich, that all governments in France agree in regarding Egypt as an assured conquest, and he also supplies the following piece of personal experience :

" In speaking in the month of April, 1881, with a well-known French Envoy, he told me that England had no interests in Egypt, that they could at any rate not be compared to those of France, and that in less than half a century the English flag would no longer be permitted to float in the Mediterranean."*

However difficult it is to argue this question in the abstract, and however easy it might be to treat the rights of any nation to influence Egypt in the spirit that Burke treated Tom Paine's *Rights of Man*, yet I confine myself to dealing with facts, among which the most important is that British influence preponderates in the Valley of the Nile. Another fact is, that British statesmen, without distinction of party, have declared against absorbing Egypt into the British Empire. Yet the policy of annexing or permanently occupying the country has some strenuous supporters in England. To them the words of Franklin, when he heard that General Howe had occupied Philadelphia, might appropriately be recalled. With a slight change, they would run, in the event of a permanent occupation of Egypt being resolved upon : " It is not Great Britain that has taken Egypt, but Egypt that has taken Great Britain."

Mr. Charles Royle writes in his able work on the

* "Egypt : Native Rulers and Foreign Interference," i. 273.

Egyptian Campaigns, that in March, 1883, a petition in English, French, Italian and Greek, urging the permanent occupation of the country by a European force, was prepared, and that nothing more was heard of it after its presentation to Lord Dufferin.   This is an error, as its terms were laid before Parliament, along with a despatch from Lord Dufferin.   A still more remarkable document, emanating from the American missionaries in Egypt, was also presented to him and noticed in his despatch.   A summary of that despatch will supply information to those who may not find it convenient to turn to the blue-book in which it is printed.

The Earl of Dufferin begins by informing Earl Granville he had told the petitioners that the permanent military occupation of Egypt by a British force could not be favourably entertained, and that he had referred the petitioners to the declarations on the subject made in the House of Lords and the House of Commons by his Lordship and Mr. Gladstone, "as an authoritative exposition of the views and intentions of Her Majesty's Government on the great subject."

He added that neither the Consul-General, Sir Edward Malet, nor he had countenanced the petition ; that, on the contrary, each had regarded such a demonstration as "unnecessary and inopportune." He had to admit, however, that the document cannot be regarded as other than the "genuine and spontaneous expression of the convictions and wishes of the European colony in Lower Egypt."

The signatures amounted, in round numbers, to

2,600, of which 1,600 were those of Greeks, 350 of Englishmen, 177 of Italians, 21 of Germans, 10 of Frenchmen, 6 of Austrians, and 255 of persons belonging to other nations. What impressed Lord Dufferin the most was the petition placed in his hands about the same time by the members of the American Missionary Society. As the sentences in which he records what he thought of it cannot be abridged without detriment, I give them in full :

" The society to which these gentlemen belong has, as your Lordship is aware, been for many years past established in the East, and has won for itself a very high and honourable position. Its college at Constantinople is one of the noblest educational institutions in the Levant ; and in every part of the Sultan's dominions its endeavours to promote the cause of justice, humanity and religion have been universally recognised. When I heard that the petition referred to above was being signed at Alexandria, I thought that it might be advisable to compare its conclusions with that of the American missionaries, who at that moment happened to have come up to Cairo to attend the General Assembly. I was all the more disposed to attach importance to what they might say, from the fact that there are as many as fifty-two different mission stations in Egypt; that all the members of the society speak Arabic ; that they have been long resident in the country ; that they have as fair a knowledge of the disposition and feeling of the people as any foreigners are likely to acquire ; that they have no personal, mercantile, or political interests to subserve, and that by the very

obligations of their profession they are bound not to
be over-anxious for their personal safety. . . . It
will probably surprise your Lordship as disagreeably
as it did me, to find that the unanimous and deliberate opinion of the gentlemen in question was
very much in accord with that of the European community in Alexandria.   They assure me in the most
positive and uncompromising terms that they consider that nothing but the continued presence of a
British force for some time longer can assure the
tranquillity of Egypt, or prevent the recurrence of
disturbances.   They state positively, that had it not
been for the fortunate intercession of the British
army and the victory of Tel-el-Kebir, massacres
upon a large scale would have been perpetrated, in
spite of the exertions of Arabi to prevent them,
throughout the Coptic villages of Upper Egypt, and
that the feelings of animosity, engendered by recent
events between the two sections of the native population, are not yet assuaged."

In the speech from the Throne delivered at the
opening of Parliament on the 15th of February,
1883, it was said that "the British troops will be
withdrawn from Egypt as promptly as may be
permitted by a prudent examination of the country."

Many years have elapsed since then, yet, though
the number of the British troops there has been
greatly reduced, a certain number still remain to
afford a physical support to the Khedive in the
exercise of his regal functions and to enable him
to act without hesitation in the best interests of his
country and people.   What Sir Henry Bulwer wrote

to Lord Palmerston from Constantinople on the 30th of July, 1838, applies to Cairo at the present day : "The whole source of influence here, then, is strength, and the fear which follows it. . . . The two things which the Turks [and Egyptians] best understand and reverence are power and justice."*

If the prolonged occupation be a grievance, the blame rests upon the Sultan of Turkey. A Convention was framed by Sir Henry Drummond Wolff, as special Commissioner, which was intended to set a limit to the occupation; and the Grand Vizier signed it on the 22nd of May, 1887, by command of the Sublime Porte. The essential provision in it was an undertaking that all the British troops were to leave Egypt at the end of three years, provided the country's peace would not then be jeopardised, and the proviso was added that, if danger arose from internecine dissensions or external attack, they were to return. Owing to pressure exercised by Russia and France, who were inimical to this Convention, it was not ratified by the Sultan.

Though the Khedive might have been pleased if the Convention had been ratified, he did not manifest any displeasure at having to govern his country with the co-operation of the Great Power which had kept him upon the throne. The results of personal investigations on the spot as to the manner in which the country had been administered, and the nature of the changes which have been wrought since the second Khedive ascended the throne of Egypt, will be set forth in the succeeding chapters.

* "Life of Viscount Palmerston," vol. ii., p. 279.

CHAPTER III.

FROM THAMES TO NILE.

THE late Edmond About visited Egypt nearly a quarter of a century ago, and recorded his impressions in a book called *The Fellah*. He had been so hospitably entertained by His Highness the Khedive that he shrank from making such a return as the production of a work on contemporary Egypt, which should be written in the spirit of his *Contemporary Greece*, under King Otho, or of his *Contemporary Rome*, under Pius IX. He doubtless felt that he could not write the truth about Egypt, as, indeed, he implied in the dedication to his friend Gérome, the great painter, without making enemies of the Egyptians in the same way that he had made many Greeks and Romans his mortal enemies. He contented himself, then, with writing a romance, of which Achmed, the hero, is a Fellah who has no parallel in the Valley of the Nile, while the heroine, Miss Grace, is an English girl such as has never been seen in England.

About's purpose in visiting Egypt was more admirable than the book which he wrote after returning home. Many travellers who preceded him had looked upon the land simply as one in which discoveries of antiquities might be made, and their minds were so intent upon restoring or revivifying the Egypt of the past that they were comparatively indifferent to the Egypt before their eyes. About's curiosity had been excited concerning the condition of the people and the nature of the country at the present day, throughout a thousand miles which are watered by the Nile. For him the ancient land of Isis and Osiris, the museum of gigantic monuments and mysterious hieroglyphics, had far less interest than the modern Egypt, with its mud-built villages, in which the tillers of the soil live and labour in the hope of earning a scanty livelihood and satisfying the tax-gatherer. It is as taxpayers that the real Egyptians have the strongest claims for notice and pity.

While Egypt as a country is the oldest on the globe, as a community it is one of the newest. Modern Egypt has been created in the course of the present century. Mehemet Ali is its founder. He was born in the same year as Bonaparte and Wellington, and, like them, he was destined by his natural qualities to rise to the top. When a young man he prepared himself for afterwards ruling over the Egyptian Fellaheen by compelling the inhabitants of a Turkish village to pay taxes against their will.

Owing to his cunning and his courage, he contrived to become Viceroy of Egypt in 1805, and he would have made himself absolute Sovereign of the country, and perhaps Sultan of Turkey, if he had not been thwarted by the European Powers. He had extended the dominion of Egypt over Nubia and the Soudan, and he would have retained the advantages of his other conquests, which were due to the generalship of his son Ibrahim, and opened the road to the possession of Constantinople, if diplomacy had not caused him to forego the fruits of his most remarkable victories. He did succeed, however, in being recognised as the virtual master of Egypt, the obligation to his Suzerain being confined to a yearly payment of tribute.

His successors profited by his energy and relentless policy. They had no Mamelukes to dread, for he had slaughtered them all; they had no apprehension of interference from Constantinople, for he had made it clear that the best policy for the Sultan was to leave Egypt alone. They did not display his thirst for conquest, being ambitious only of resting upon his laurels. They gathered in the taxes as conscientiously as he had done, and expended them with even more lavish hands. In their eyes, as in those of the Pharaohs of olden times, the tillers of the soil were mere human machines for yielding revenue. If the Fellaheen refused to pay taxes, they were flogged till the last coins in their possession were delivered up, and if they expired under the lash, or of starvation afterwards, their deaths were regarded with no more human sympathy than the break-down of a steam-engine is regarded by its owner. In the bad old days, when slavery was not considered a disgrace or a curse, European or American slave-owners might flog their human chattels for indolence or disobedience, but they fed

them for reasons of prudence. These slaves had a
few pleasures in life, but the Egyptian Fellaheen
had no relief from toil and misery save in the grave.
When Edmond About visited Egypt with the
laudable intention of studying the people, he failed
to record the actual state of the tillers of the soil
under Ismail, who was treating his guests with
unbounded hospitality at the expense of his long-
suffering and harshly-used subjects.

I saw these people after Ismail had been succeeded by his son, Mehemet Tewfik, and I think a
statement of facts about them and the country itself
will be as serviceable to those in quest of useful
information as the successful romance called *The
Fellah*. The changes in Egypt since About visited
and wrote about it are not greater, though they
are really more wonderful, than the changes in its
floating population. The journeying Nilewards
every year of Europeans and Americans is as remarkable a phenomenon in Egyptian history as the
Exodus itself. The two differ from each other in this
important particular, that the Israelites despoiled the
Egyptians before their departure, while the winter
visitors now enrich the Egyptians during their
sojourn, and they leave the country lighter in purse
if not much wiser than when they entered it.

A trip to Cairo is as commonplace as it is easy.
A man or woman can dine in the capital of Egypt a
week after having done so in London or Paris,
Berlin or Rome, Vienna or Madrid. There is no
more difficulty, and but little more romance, in
ascending the Nile to the first cataract, than there

is in a trip on the Seine or the Thames, the Spree
or the Danube. The tourist who desires to reach
the Valley of the Nile and traverse it without trouble
or fatigue can do so by making a payment to Messrs.
Thomas Cook and Son. In comparatively recent
days the traveller through Egypt could bring back
with him novel facts as well as new impressions.
At present the principal facts are set forth in guide-
books, and the majority of tourists take impressions
at second-hand as well as facts, not venturing to
form opinions of their own.

The attraction which the Valley of the Nile has
long exercised over the people of Europe and
America has increased at an accelerated rate during
the last twenty years. So much that is of deepest
interest to the Christian world being associated with
Egypt, it is natural that a longing should be excited in
countless breasts to see the country which is hallowed
by sacred traditions to an extent but slightly inferior
to the Holy Land. Yet even pilgrims of the present
day, however greatly they may be filled with religious enthusiasm, are reluctant to run any risks
when travelling, and they object as strongly to
suffering the slightest hardship. The mere sightseer
is desirous of living in comfort when moving about.
He does not enjoy a monument unless he has had,
or can look forward to having, a good dinner, and
he much prefers an uninterrupted night's rest to
visiting the most historic or picturesque spot by
moonlight or at sunrise.

Indeed, the people of the present day are both
restless when at home and reluctant to start if they are

expected to rough it when away. Discomforts had
to be borne and lives risked by those who made a
voyage up the Nile when the nineteenth century
was young ; now that the century is approaching its
close, the chief danger of the trip is an attack of influenza or catarrh. Among the tourists of various
nationalities who are to be seen in Egypt during the
winter months, the most boisterous are those who
represent the United States. The Riviera and Italy
have heretofore been the favourite winter resorts in
Europe of citizens of the Great Republic, but the
Valley of the Nile has now the preference in their
estimation. No one who has made the acquaintance
of the better class of Americans can desire pleasanter
travelling companions, while the society of the others
is as objectionable as that of the most offensive
British tourist. Those who encounter Americans of
any class on this side of the Atlantic wherever the
climate in winter is more balmy than that of Northern
Europe, must be puzzled to hear them repeat, as
they do with tiresome iteration, that no winter climate
is comparable to that of California or Florida. The
citizens of the United States, who, on their own
showing, possess a country which surpasses every
other in natural charms, and is filled with cities
which science has rendered more habitable than
those of the Old World, display an abnegation which
is almost unparalleled in leaving it at all. It may
be a consolation for them when enduring privations
in the Old World to recall and brag about the un-
surpassable attractions of the New. Certainly the
Americans whom I had the pleasure of meeting in

Egypt appeared happiest when they were eulogizing
the beauties and comforts of America.

It appears to have been forgotten that the journey
from Europe to Egypt and the ascent of the Nile—
which can now be accomplished at a moderate
outlay and within a reasonable time—could have
been undertaken by our forefathers at a smaller cost
and more speedily than might be supposed. The
particulars of such a journey are given in the introduction to Baron Denon's *Voyage dans la Basse et
la Haute Egypte*, which appeared in London in
1809. Denon, as is well known, was one of the
body of artists, men of letters and science that
accompanied Bonaparte when he went to annex
Egypt to the territory of the French Republic.
M. Peltier, a French refugee, whose name survives
owing to the splendid defence made of him by Sir
James Mackintosh when he was charged with
libelling Bonaparte, was the editor of this edition.
In the introduction he inserts a communication from
a man of letters concerning the expense and the
time required to travel from London to Thebes and
back. The details are so curious as to deserve re-
production ; but I must remark that to sail up the
Nile from Cairo to Thebes in ten days is a feat which
can be performed in exceptional circumstances only.
Five days are allowed by him to go from London to
Paris ; five from Paris to Lyons ; five from Lyons
to Marseilles, partly by the Rhone ; eighteen from
Marseilles to Alexandria ; four from Alexandria to
Cairo by the canal and the river : and ten from Cairo
to Thebes. Allowance being made for twenty-four

days being spent at Thebes, Cairo, and Alexandria. the time taken for the journey to and fro, including this sojourn, would be one hundred and twenty days, The outlay is put at £80. The traveller who should now pass the same number of days in the like manner would have to pay double that amount, so that travel has not been cheapened so much as many fancy, though it has been immensely accelerated, and rendered many times more comfortable.

It is noteworthy that M. Peltier's correspondent had the intention of establishing a hotel on the European model at Thebes. What was a project in 1809 was realized in 1877, when a hotel was opened in the part of Thebes which is now known as Luxor, under the management of M. Pagnon, and a second has been built since then. Those who are pressed for time can now journey from London to Cairo in nearly as short a time as their parents could proceed from London to Paris. This implies a journey by rail through France and Italy, and embarking at Marseilles or Naples, Trieste or Brindisi for the passage by sea. Those who can spare four or five days more can be transported nearly the whole way by water from the Thames to the Nile.

I chose the sea route, and had many reasons for satisfaction that I was a passenger by the fine P. and O. steamer *Sutlej*, under the most efficient command of Captain Worcester, whose popularity is as undisputable as his seamanship. Edmond About sailed from Marseilles, and he made his first acquaintance with the Land of the Pharaohs in the

4

mud of Alexandria; mine began in the mud of Port Said.   Alexandria has the attraction of a past filled with noteworthy events in the history of the world, and reaching back 300 years before the Christian era, while Port Said is but thirty years old, and its most interesting association is connected with the Suez Canal.   This town, which is the youngest among those of Egypt, is built on a spit of land separating Lake Menzaleh from the Mediterranean, and its growth has been rapid, the population now numbering 37,000.   Port Said has a resemblance to those cities in North-Western America which spring up with the rapidity of a mushroom and decay as rapidly.   At the outset they are styled shanty cities.   Should they possess an element of stability they are gradually transformed from the original log-huts and rude tents into houses of brick and stone, yet some time elapses before the houses are comfortable and the streets paved.   The last stage is drainage, and, as this is frequently imperfect, the last state may be worse than the first.   Port Said is in the second stage of a prosperous shanty city.   Many of the houses have been constructed to last and to please the eye, while the streets are filthy and fever is rife.

Several large ocean steamers stop here daily to coal, and the passengers are glad to land and escape from the din of the process and the plague of coal-dust.   The shopkeepers of Port Said shrewdly count upon finding customers among those who go on shore after several days' confinement on board ship. Men who thought only of stretching their legs by walking along the muddy or dusty streets are allured by the temptation to buy cigarettes, being victims of the common delusion that Egyptian cigarettes are unrivalled, though the tobacco and paper with which they are made have been imported. Ladies always long to buy something after an enforced abstinence from shopping. The male passengers who resist the temptation to buy anything may not be equally virtuous when they see a café or other place where they can enjoy what the Americans call a "good time."

Though the Egyptian Government has prohibited public gaming, the laws against it are not rigidly enforced, owing, it is said, to the opposition of the representatives of certain Foreign Powers. When I visited Port Said it was easy enough to find a roulette-table in operation. The strains of a band attracted the passers-by to halls wherein such tables were placed. No method of losing money at play is more certain than that of staking it at roulette, and this is true even when the game is played with perfect fairness. According to the rules, the chances are necessarily in favour of the bank, although the player need have no fear of being cheated. While watching the game as played at Port Said, I felt convinced that the bank had opportunities for winning which were not legitimate. After the stakes had been laid upon the table and the ball was spun round in the cylinder, a cover was placed over it, and the result was announced as soon as the cover was removed. This was literally playing in the dark, and the man who risked his money at such a game was more than ordinarily foolish. Several persons

won, but I should be greatly surprised to learn that
they were not in league with the croupier, who spun
the ball and proclaimed the winning number. The
sight recalled one which I witnessed at Ogden in
the early days of the first railway which had crossed
the North American continent. During the stoppage
there, and the transference of the passengers and their
luggage from the cars of the Union Pacific to those of
the Central Pacific Railway Company, the passengers
were offered the relaxation of a game at three-card
monté, a game which has a close resemblance to
thimblerig. The smallest stakes were gold pieces
of twenty dollars. Men whose dress betokened
extreme poverty staked these pieces with the indifference and recklessness of a mad millionaire, and
they won with a regularity which excited the cupidity
of the bystanders, and induced them to try their
luck. At Port Said, as at Ogden, the only winners
were those whom I regarded as the accomplices of
the keepers of the table.

There is a small but highly respectable element
in Port Said, its members being the agents of the
leading steam-shipping companies, the managers of
banks and partners in mercantile firms of the best
class. The French and the Greeks are in a majority,
and a considerable number of the Israelites, whose
ancestors fled from the house of bondage, must
have returned to it and taken up their abode in
Port Said. I landed there with curiosity, and I
left it without regret. As a place of residence it
appears to be an excellent one to avoid. The
day may come, however, when it is drained and

rendered less pestilential, and when, united by rail
with Cairo, it may grow into greater importance.
Moreover, the day may be at hand when Lake
Menzaleh shall be drained and the 1,000 square
miles, which are now covered with water and are
the abode of fish and pelicans, shall again be the
fertile tract of dry land that it was in ancient days.
Just as the Dutch have pumped the water out of
Lake Haarlem and added the soil which formed its
bed to the cultivable area of Holland, so may the
beginning which has been made for rendering Lake
Menzaleh dry land have a consummation as greatly
to be desired. Egypt's decline from being pre-eminent
as a garden or granary is largely due to some of the
reservoirs of water having been restored to the
hungry desert, and to much of the prolific land
having become a morass. When the reservoirs shall
be refilled and the morass cultivated, a new face
will gladden the eyes which look upon Egypt, and,
when thousands of industrious Fellaheen are growing
crops upon the site of Lake Menzaleh, the city
of Port Said will then expand and attain a rank
which it can never reach as a mere station at
which steamers call for coal, and where passing
visitors indulge in wild freedom, to the profit of
shopkeepers who have few scruples and the keepers
of gaming-houses who have none.

I did not anticipate enjoying a romantic spectacle
when passing through the Suez Canal on board the
Sutlej. A canal is more prosaic than a railway, and
a canal through the desert might be supposed to be
as dull as a ditch. I do not mean to detract from

the importance of the work as an engineering achievement and a link between two seas. Its designer has made his mark in history. He had to contend against many obstacles which were as hard to overcome as those of a purely physical kind. M. de Lesseps accomplished what had been the dream of centuries. His credit is not lessened owing to the idea which he put in practice being devoid of novelty, a similar water-way having existed in bygone ages. But the successful piercing of the Isthmus of Suez places Sir John Bowring in the first rank of modern prophets. As long ago as 1839, he thus wrote to Lord Palmerston : "A port immediately in contact with Suez would be one of the greatest of *desiderata*. It is yet to be ascertained whether the old port of Pelusium is beyond the reach of reconstruction ; in which case, whether no other point can be fixed on to become the terminus of a canal across the Isthmus of Suez. There is little doubt that in some future time a communication will be opened between the Red Sea and the adjacent part of the Mediterranean, either by again excavating the ancient canal, or by fixing on some other more convenient locality."*

Though the Suez Canal is not more picturesque by day than the Rhine below Cologne or the Thames below Richmond, yet at night, when the moon sheds a glamour over the water and the expanse of sandy desert on either side, and when the electric search-light of a large steamer like the *Sutlej* flashes an illumination equal to forty thousand candles far in

* "Report on Egypt and Candia," p. 70.

front, the sloping banks glisten like new-fallen snow, and the buoys which mark the channel resemble huge cones of frosted silver. The effect is marvellous; but it palls after it has been beheld for several hours, and the most impressionable spectator is not sorry when the steamer anchors in Lake Timsah during the chilly hours which precede the dawn. Here a steam tender carries the passengers to Ismailia whose destination is Cairo.

Ismailia is another mushroom town which shot up while the canal was being cut, and which has lost vitality since its completion. When Ismailia ceases to be a halting-place for travellers to Egypt, as must happen after Port Said is connected with Cairo by rail, its decay will be as rapid as its growth. At present, however, it is worth a visit, and makes a most pleasing impression upon the visitor. When wide alleys, lined with trees and bordered with gardens, are traversed, it is hard to believe that many years have not elapsed since this spot was a part of the desert. The villa built by M. de Lesseps, which was the first, is still the most attractive, while the palace hastily constructed to house the Khedive's guests when the canal was opened is desolate and falling into ruin. There are two hotels, in both of which there is good accommodation. The view of the blue waters of Lake Timsah, upon the margin of which Ismailia lies, is as charming as the breeze from it is refreshing. Indeed, the whole prospect is delightful, and the place might be supposed to be healthful though dull. I was told, however, that a low fever is prevalent, owing, it is

supposed, to the exhalations from the banks of the
sweet-water canal. As a station for the officers and
the pilots of the Canal Company this place will continue to subserve a purpose, but the days of its
prosperity are numbered.

The route from Ismailia to Cairo by rail was
formed long after that from Alexandria to the
capital. However, the Ismailia railway-station was
the first which I had entered in Egypt as a passenger,
and there I saw, what I have since noticed in other
Egyptian railway-stations, the Oriental character in
striking and sudden contrast, passing abruptly and
for no apparent reason from an apathy which was
almost absolute to an activity which was formidable
and feverish. An armed policeman was on duty,
and he had a whip in his hand, this being the courbash of which so much has been written and with
which so much torture has been inflicted. In the
hands of this policeman it was rather a symbol of
authority than an instrument of punishment, and
when used by him against an unruly mob of Arabs,
who swarmed in places where they had no right to
be and annoyed the passengers, the policeman
seemed to be doing his duty in the only effective
way.

The line runs through the desert, and some of the
smaller stations are built upon and surrounded by
sand. Though the prospect is not fascinating, it is
not more monotonous than that of the desert in the
heart of the North American continent. Here, as
there, a dull green plant is seen at intervals. In
the wilder parts of Kansas, Nebraska, and Wyom-

ing, the first settlers live in "dug-outs," these being
rude dwellings excavated in the slope of a rolling
prairie ; the Scotch crofters and poorest Irish peas-
ants live in miserable cottages, and an Arab village
is an agglomeration of habitations as rude and
wretched in appearance as the worst places of abode
in the United Kingdom and the United States.
The Egyptian tillers of the soil are as poorly clad
as they are housed. Some of them wear a single
garment only, and their bodies are as well venti-
lated as those of the wearers of Scottish kilts.

When Ismailia has been left behind, and Tel-el-
Kebir is reached, the desert dwindles in area and
green crops and palm-trees begin to brighten and
variegate the landscape. I was surprised to see
many pools of water in a country which I had been
taught to consider as rainless. I was told that, if I had
arrived a day earlier, I should have seen rain falling
as it does in the tropics and flooding the greater
part of Cairo. Communications had then to be maintained by boats in some quarters of the city. Outside
the railway-station there was a mud-hole such as I
had often struggled through in Manitoba, being
about a yard deep and many yards in area. One
advantage of travel is to learn something new and
to meet with something which it is well to avoid.
The capital of Egypt is a place to be shunned in
the rainy season.

A familiar sight, and one wholly un-Egyptian, impressed me. It gave great offence to a Frenchman,
who was a fellow-passenger, and who, like myself, was
visiting Egypt for the first time. This was several

privates of the Dorset regiment walking along the pavement. My companion said, "That is a disgraceful spectacle!" Then I asked him, "Would you object if they had red trousers instead of red jackets?" "Certainly not," was his answer; and he added, "Your soldiers have no business here."

CHAPTER IV.

CAIRO PAST AND PRESENT.

SINCE Alexandria has been rebuilt, after being bombarded and burnt, it has lost much of its Oriental appearance, yet this change for the worse, from a picturesque point of view, is still more marked in the capital. Ismail created a new Cairo, just as Napoleon III. created a new Paris. The Khedive of Egypt had as great a passion for building as the Emperor of the French, and both may be remembered as the transformers of the capitals of their respective countries.

The external changes which Cairo has undergone in the course of the last few years are greater than those which had been effected during a century previously, but they are not the most noteworthy. I had read much about the city before I saw it for the first time, and I doubt whether those who are not acquainted with its past history, irrespective of the information they may have obtained from guidebooks, can realize how different a stranger's lot is there at present, when contrasted with what it was in bygone days. A foreigner now feels himself as much at home in Cairo as he can do in any

European city, and he can be accommodated in
hotels which are as luxurious and well managed as
the best in Berlin or Vienna, in London or Paris.
I doubt, indeed, whether there is to be found in any
of these capitals a hotel with so many comforts and
attractions as Shepheard's, one of the oldest and
best of them all. When Richard Pococke visited
Cairo in 1723, he had a different story to tell about it.
He was struck with the narrowness of the streets
—"the widest would be looked upon as a lane
in Europe." He considered that "the city is
exceedingly well regulated for its security, more
especially by night ; for most of the streets, or at
least each end of every district or ward, has a gate
and porter to it, who shuts up the gate as soon as it
is dark, and to every one of these wards is a guard
of two or three or more janizaries, so that no idle
people can go about the streets at night." The
gates and the janizaries have disappeared long ago,
and those who choose to walk about after dark may
do so—in streets which are silent and deserted by
pedestrians. They will find that the chief obstacle
to locomotion is the number of persons who have
made their beds on the pavement, where they pass
the night. They do not dread noise or chills.
Thick coverings guard their ears from sound and
their skins from dew.

It is as true still as it was when Pococke wrote,
that "there is a great mixture of people in Cairo,
the city being composed of original Egyptians,
among whom are the Coptic Christians, of Arabians,
of the people of Barbary and the western parts of

Africa, and the Berberines of the parts of Nubia, a great number of their men coming here to offer themselves as servants. . . . There are likewise in . Cairo some Greeks, a few Americans, and many Jews. Of the Europeans, there are settled here only the French, English, and some Italians from Venice and Leghorn."*

Twenty-five years after Pococke visited Cairo, it was the halting-place of James Bruce on his journey to Abyssinia, his final object and his ambition being the discovery of the source of the Nile. He was dissuaded against going farther by those in Cairo to whom he communicated his purpose. The Egyptian Government of that day was opposed to an enterprise such as that upon which he was bent, and, in order to avert a formal prohibition, he intimated that India was his destination. But he emphatically remarks, what he might repeat if he were in Cairo to-day, "this intention was not long kept secret (nothing can be concealed at Cairo) ; all nations, Jews, Turks, Moors, Copts and Franks are constantly upon the inquiry—as much after things that concern other people's business as their own." Bruce tried to baffle curiosity by seldom appearing in public, and also by disguising himself when he did, being then considered "as a fakir, or dervish, moderately skilled in magic, and who cared for nothing but study and books."

There has never been a dearth of magicians in Cairo ; at present many of them come from India, and they are all well satisfied if public perform-

* Pinkerton's "Collection of Travels," vol. xv., pp. 188, 195.

ances on the terrace before Shepheard's hotel should
be sufficiently remunerative to pay their expenses and
leave them something to carry home.

The passage in which Bruce describes the
French quarter is instructive reading now. As he
does not mention any other European merchants
than those of France, it may be inferred that they
were the most numerous and, probably, the most
important of the foreign merchants in his day.
"The part of Cairo where the French are settled is
exceedingly commodious and fit for retirement. It
consists of one long street, where all the merchants
of that nation live together. It is shut at one end
by large gates, where there is a guard, and these
are kept constantly closed at the time of the plague.
At the other end there is a garden tolerably kept, in
which there are several pleasant walks and seats ; all
the enjoyment that Christians can hope for, among
this vile people, reduces itself to peace and quiet ;·
nobody seeks for more. There are, however,
wicked emissaries who are constantly employed, by
threats, lies, and extravagant demands, to torment
and keep them from enjoying that repose which
would content them instead of freedom or more
solid happiness in their own country. I have always
considered the French at Cairo as a number of
honest, polished, and industrious men by some
fatality condemned to the galleys ; and I must own,
never did a set of people bear their continual vexa-
tions with more fortitude and manliness. Their
own affairs they keep to themselves, and, notwithstanding the bad prospect always before them, they

never fail to put on a cheerful face to a stranger, and protect and help him to the utmost of their power; as if his little concerns, often ridiculous, always very troublesome ones, were the only charge they had in hand. But a more brutal, unjust, tyrannical, oppressive, avaricious set of infernal miscreants there is not on earth, than are the members of the Government of Cairo."*

Since Bruce's visit to Egypt, the changes in the Government there are as marvellous as any in the city itself. The Turkish system of misrule, which excited his wrath, has long passed away, the predominance of the Turk being as purely historical as that of the Pharaohs. The ruler of Egypt and his Ministers are now as civilized as any visitors.

M. Sonnini, to whom I have already referred, visited Cairo ten years after Bruce, and wrote about it in terms resembling his. The Egyptian capital bore on likeness, in his opinion, to any European city. He considered it a disagreeable place of abode for a foreigner: "In fact," as he writes, "the mass of the people in no place could be more barbarous than at Cairo. Foreigners, persecuted and even illtreated under the most frivolous pretexts, lived there in perpetual fear." They did not appear in public in the attire of their own country; if they had ventured to do so, "they would infallibly have been knocked on the head or torn to pieces." He held that it was specially unsafe for them to leave the quarter in which they were ordered to live. When the French merchants made an excursion elsewhere,

* Bruce's "Travels," vol. i., pp. 100, 101, 102.

"fear was their close companion. They were obliged to be attentive to the persons before and behind them. If a Mameluke, a priest, or a man in office appeared, they made way for him, alighted, placed the right hand on the breast as a token of respect, and durst not pursue their way till the rigorous and haughty Mussulman was gone by, and then only to repeat the same ceremony a few minutes afterwards. If their attention were otherwise employed, so as to make them neglect these degrading duties of slavery, they were reminded of them in a cruel way. A set of domestics, called cavasses, armed with stout sticks six feet long, and clothed in a black robe, the sleeves of which are tucked up under the arm-pits by means of a cord crossing at the back, attended men in power on foot, and gave the Franks notice of their inattention by smart blows. One French merchant whom I knew at Cairo had his leg broken in this manner, and another, whom I knew likewise, his neck.

"It is easy to conceive how disagreeable and dangerous a residence at Cairo, where fatal apprehensions and alarms were incessantly succeeding each other, must be to Europeans, and how culpable and disgusting its monstrous government was. To foreigners it was truly a place of desolation, dread, and danger, hence Hasselquitz, in his letter to Linnæus, dated Cairo, the 7th of September, 1750, as truly as wittily said that, if a man were guilty of any crime, he could not expiate it better than by going to reside a little while at Cairo."*

* Sonnini's "Travels in Upper and Lower Egypt," translated by Dr. Hunter, vol. ii., pp. 263, 265-267.

The unhappy Europeans, whose sad fate Sonnini depicts in the foregoing terms, had a fresh humiliation to bear while he sojourned in Egypt. Having been forbidden to ride on horseback, they rode on donkeys as a makeshift. They kept animals of the best breeds, and this was brought to the notice of the Government in 1779. Sonnini records that "it was deemed indecorous for foreign merchants, abominated on account of their religion, to ride upon animals superior even to those kept for the wives of the Beys themselves. This was sufficient to bring upon the European merchants a forced contribution, an *avanie* of four or five hundred thousand francs, which they were obliged to pay, for having kept fine donkeys."

Volney, who is famous as a traveller and observer, visited Cairo three years after his countryman Sonnini, and Volney was struck with the large number of stray dogs in the streets, and of kites hovering over the houses. The stray dogs are not painfully conspicuous now, owing, probably, to a great diminution in their number; but the kites are still as plentiful and as useful as they were a century ago. Volney's narrative agrees with that of Sonnini; however, he enters into greater detail. He records that the French Consul was removed in 1777 from Cairo to Alexandria for reasons of economy, and that the French merchants remained in Cairo at their own risk. He adds: "Their situation, which is unchanged, is much the same as that of the Dutch at Nagasaki—that is to say, being shut up in a large blind alley, they live together

5

without frequent communication with the outside ;
indeed, they fear leaving it, and go out as seldom as
possible, so as not to be exposed to insults from the
people, who hate the name of Frank, or to the outrages of the Mamelukes, who compel them to get
off their donkeys in the streets.   In this species of
virtual imprisonment they live in constant dread
lest the plague should oblige them to shut themselves up in their houses, or a riot lead to the pillage
of their quarter, lest the commandant should make
a demand for money, or finally lest the Beys should
compel them to furnish supplies, which always entails
risk.   Their business does not give them less concern.   Obliged to sell on credit, they are seldom
paid at the appointed time.   Even for bills of
exchange there is no legal provision, no remedy in a
court of justice, because going to law is worse than
bankruptcy ; every transaction is a matter of conscience, and recently this conscience has deteriorated ; .
payments are put off for years ; sometimes they are
not made at all, and nearly always they are cut
down.   The Christians, who are their principal correspondents, are more treacherous in this respect
than the Turks themselves.   It is curious that the
character of the Christians is inferior throughout the
whole empire to that of the Muslims, yet it is neces
sary to have everything done through their inter-
mediary.   Add to this that the capital sum cannot
be realized, because the only way of recovering a
debt is to give credit to an increased amount.   For
all these reasons Cairo is the most precarious and
unpleasant place of commerce in the whole Levant ;

fifteen years ago there were nine French houses of business here ; in 1783 they were reduced to three, and soon there will not be a single one left."*

Many French travellers had described Cairo, and several French merchants had carried on business there before a French army arrived, on the 26th of July, 1798, to take possession of it. Several houses were burnt to the ground before the con-querors were able to settle down quietly, and even when they thought that all opposition had been extin-guished, they were subjected to a cruel disappoint-ment. The army had been told to bear hardships in view of the reward which would be found at Cairo ; but both private soldiers and general officers soon ascertained that the enchantments of the capital of Egypt were idle dreams. General Kléber wrote as follows to General Damas : "We have arrived at last in the land for which we have longed. It is far removed from what the most moderate imagination could have depicted.

" The horrible straggling city of Cairo is inhabited by a lazy rabble, seated cross-legged all day in front of their wretched hovels, foul-smelling, swallowing coffee, eating melons and drinking water. One can easily lose himself for an entire day in the filthy and narrow streets of this famous capital. The only habitable quarter is that of the Mamelukes."

General Dupuy, who was appointed Governor of the city, wrote to a friend in the same strain : " This city is detestable ; the foul streets smell of the plague ; the people are horrible and brutish. Though

* "Voyage en Egypte," pp. 181-183.

I work like a horse, I cannot get to know this city, which is larger than Paris, but different in all respects."

Neither the occupation nor the evacuation of Cairo by the French is an event of such baleful memory as the assassination of General Kléber there on the 14th of June, 1800. He was one of the best officers in the army which held temporary possession of Egypt. Had it not been for this tragedy, and for many miscarriages, the destiny of Cairo might have been changed. The object of Bonaparte in proceeding to conquer Egypt, as avowed in his memoirs, was to checkmate the English in India. He looked forward to becoming the master of India, when the English least expected it, after firmly establishing himself in Egypt. Even if the English and the French continued rivals as they were before, the former would, in his opinion, soon be beaten in the race. Bonaparte looked forward to the reconstruction of the Suez Canal, and he was firmly convinced of the commercial advantages which the French would reap from having a monopoly of it. He was convinced that the commerce with India by sea would be annihilated when it was open. Such was Bonaparte's dream, as set down in the memoirs which were written during his enforced solitude in the peaceful island of St. Helena.

The failure of the French to retain possession of Egypt, and the success of the British force in compelling them to evacuate it, had a marked and unforeseen influence upon its subsequent relation to foreigners.

Mr. Hamilton bears testimony to this in his *Ægyptiaca*, a work designed to give a fuller account, with illustrations, of Egyptian antiquities than any which had previously appeared ; a work which, in his opinion, "ought at least to be one of the effects of the very active concern taken by Great Britain in the affairs of that country when it was thought necessary to rescue it out of the hands of the French." He was in the country during the years 1801 and 1802. Our action there at that time was inspired with a determination to maintain the power of the Sultan in Egypt, while at a later day it was to maintain the authority of the Khedive. Much unfavourable criticism has been passed upon our conduct in the latter case ; it was as unfavourably regarded by Mr. Hamilton in the former, his decision being : " Having sown the seeds of indecision, we have reaped the harvest of disgrace and loss."

The facts which he records are more valuable than the opinions which he expresses, and among them is the following piece of trustworthy informa- tion relative to the changes in the capital. Mr. Hamilton writes : " Before the French invasion, no Frank or European traveller was permitted, except by very especial favour, to mount horses in Cairo. In general they were reduced to go on foot, or to make use of asses, when they paid their visits or went in search of curiosities. When we were there this distinction had for some time been laid aside, and Europeans thus mounted were not afraid even of meeting a Bey or a Turk ; a presumption which, a few years ago, would have been attended with some unpleasant consequences. However, not even now did those who had long resided in the country as merchants under the protection of European Powers venture to profit by this relaxation in the sight of the ostentatious police of the ruler of Cairo. They reflected that the time might come when things would be restored to their former footing, and that then they would be made to pay for this among other advantages which they had taken of the preponderating influence of the Christians."*

While the temporary occupation of Egypt by a French army had changed the attitude of the rulers to Europeans in the manner which Mr. Hamilton noted, the change might have proved as fleeting as the European residents predicted and feared, if it had not been for the rise of Mehemet Ali to the office of Viceroy. This occurred in 1805, and from that time the position of Europeans in Egypt has never returned to the ignominious state of earlier days, with the exception of the brief space during which Arabi Pasha usurped the office of ruler.

A farther change in the position of Europeans in Egypt began after Mehemet Ali became its chief, and it was perfected under his successors. He was a most remarkable and unscrupulous man. Mr. De Leon says of him that " he found Egypt a chaos and left it a country," while Lane remarked with equal truth that, " under Mehemet Ali's rule, the Egyptians exchanged anarchy for tranquillity." Belzoni was at Cairo in 1815, and he learnt then

* Hamilton's " Ægyptiaca," pp. 330, 331.

that Mehemet Ali was ready to welcome Europeans, and also to protect them against the fanaticism and brutality of his soldiers. At that time, however, the custom still prevailed of having a quarter set apart for the Franks, and closed by gates against intruders. On one occasion Belzoni had an adventure which clearly demonstrated that a Frank could no longer be maltreated with impunity. He was riding on a donkey in a narrow street when a loaded camel appeared, the result being that there was barely room for the donkey to pass. Then a major, heading a detachment of soldiers, approached and, "seeing that it was a Frank who stopped the way, gave me a violent blow on my stomach. Not being accustomed to put up with such salutations, I returned the compliment with my whip across his naked shoulders. Instantly he took his pistol out of his belt. I jumped off my ass ; he retired about two yards, pulled the trigger, fired at my head, singed the hair near my right ear, and killed one of his own soldiers who by this time had come behind me. Finding that he had missed his aim, he took out a second pistol ; but his own soldiers assailed and disarmed him." Belzoni hastened to Mehemet Ali and related what had occurred, and he ordered the officer to be apprehended. Belzoni "never heard or knew anything more about him."* In earlier days anyone acting as Belzoni did would have been the victim.

Seventeen years later Mr. J. Augustus St. John printed his experience of Egypt and of its capital

* "Narrative of Operations in Egypt and Nubia," vol. i., pp. 31, 32.

under the rule of Mehemet Ali. He was impressed
by the difference between the country as he saw it,
and that which his reading had led him to expect.
After avowing this in the introduction, he adds :
" Without knowing why or wherefore, the bigoted
Turk and ignorant Fellah had ceased to exhibit, in
their intercourse with Europeans, that brutal contempt which is the most offensive characteristic of
barbarians ; taking their tone, perhaps, from their
ruler, who, it matters little whether from partiality or
policy, openly evinces on all occasions a respect for
enlightened foreigners."

Another matter which received Mr. St. John's
attention was still more worthy of note. Preceding
travellers had written in the most uncomplimentary
terms of the Cairo streets, and that he had been impressed with their statements is shown in the following passage : " I have not been many days in Cairo,
and yet I discover that many changes have taken
place in its appearance even since the descriptions
of the very latest travellers were written. The
streets, formerly disgustingly filthy, are now remarkable in general for their cleanliness, being all swept
three times a day. Ibrahim Pasha, a few years ago,
issued an order commanding every householder to
cause the space before his own dwelling to be swept
as above. The dust is collected into heaps, and four
hundred carts, drawn by bullocks, are employed in
conveying it out of the city. All the dust thus collected is passed through a kind of sieve, and the
straw, leaves of vegetables, and every sort of com-
bustible matter, are used for fuel. The remainder,

when carried out of the city, is not thrown, as formerly, into heaps, but is employed in filling up the pits, hollows, and inequalities which are found in the environs. In the meanwhile all the old mounds of rubbish are clearing away at a vast expense, and the land thus gained is laid out in gardens and olive plantations."

It is sixty years since Mr. Augustus St. John penned this account, and the process of street-cleaning has not become perfect during the interval. On the contrary, there are many of the older streets in which the householders clear nothing away, and which foot-passengers find most noisome. Yet in the days when some of the streets in Cairo were almost impassable on account of filth, those of Paris and London were not much better, and even now there are streets in Marseilles and Naples which are as obnoxious to those who are not born and bred in the South as any in Cairo. Madame de Stael was never happier than when she lived in the Rue de Bac, and that street, with a gutter in the middle, would now be pronounced a disgrace to a civilized capital. As late as the middle of the eighteenth century there was no systematic plan for keeping the streets of London clean, and Benjamin Franklin, when he lived in Craven Street, paid a poor woman out of his own purse to sweep it regularly.

Lord Lindsay was in Cairo two years later, and, though as much impressed as Mr. St. John had been with what he saw, he found more to criticise in the city. He thus expresses himself: " Viewed from any of the neighbouring eminences, she is still

Grand Cairo, but the narrowness of the streets, a perfect labyrinth of alleys, and the general air of decay, forbid one's application of the epithet to the interior of the city." He, too, bears testimony to the alteration in the treatment of foreigners, saying : " The insults Christians were formerly subject to are now unknown. Whatever be one's opinion of the Pasha's domestic policy, travellers owe him much, for throughout his dominions (in Egypt and Syria, at least) they may travel in the Frank dress with perfect safety. What would old Sandys or Lithgow have said, had anyone prophesied in their days that two Britons would, in 1836, walk openly through Cairo, preceded by a native servant clearing the road before them by gentle hints indiscriminately administered to donkeys and Moslemin, to get out of the Giaours' way ?"

Lord Lindsay and his friend Mr. Ramsay were presented to the Pasha by Colonel Campbell, then. Consul-General for the United Kingdom, and they were struck with the minuteness of Mehemet Ali's acquaintance " with everything which concerned his dominions." But they doubted whether his reforms would prove stable. An extract from Mr. Ramsay's journal supplies evidence that Mehemet Ali's misfortune was to depend too much upon others who were unworthy of his confidence. After stating that Mehemet Ali had drained the country of money in order to produce striking results, Mr. Ramsay adds : " It is to the unprincipled roguery and ignorance of his European advisers and officials that most of this waste and expense is to be charged. His counsellors consist of all the needy emigrants from France and Italy, who are scouted or in bad odour at home, and who have the assurance to pretend to be what they are not here, where detection is diffi-cult, and where success is their fortune for life."*

I have quoted enough from the narratives of several visitors to show how great has been the im-provement in the lot of Europeans in Cairo since the beginning of this century. Yet, when these narratives were written, the city still remained sub-ject to the plague, which was as greatly feared by the foreigner and the native as the worst tyranny of any ruler. In 1824, as many as 50,000 persons were smitten with it. In 1835, as many as 30,000 died. When it is remembered that the season during which the plague raged began in December and ended with May, these figures appear the more ghastly and terrible.

No writer has given a more striking picture of Cairo during the plague than Kinglake, and his ac-count is one of the passages in *Eothen* which, when read, can never be forgotten. Since it was written, the cholera and influenza have caused consternation and mourning in Cairo, yet neither is dreaded in our day with the same intensity of despair as the plague was in the days of our forefathers. After the plague had ravaged Cairo at the time of Kinglake's visit, prayers were offered up in the mosques, not that it might cease, but that it might be transferred to another city. The Muslims of Cairo did not deny

* "Letters on Egypt," by Lord Lindsay, pp. 25, 27, 29, 30.

that the plague was a fatality, but they preferred
that others might be the victims of it.

Kinglake was warned against visiting the plague-
stricken city, yet he voluntarily chose to run the risk ;
he was told, moreover, that contact with a sufferer
was certain to lead to an attack, yet he braved
danger, and he did so with impunity. His description of the streets of the city tallies with that of
others who visited it shortly before and after him :
" The streets of Cairo are not paved in any way, but
strewed with a dry sandy soil so deadening to sound
that the footfall of my donkey could scarcely be
heard.   There is no trottoir, and as you ride
through the streets you mingle with the people on
foot ; those who are in your way, upon being
warned by the shouts of the donkey-boy, move very
slightly aside, so as to leave you a narrow lane
through which you pass at a gallop.   In this way
you glide on delightfully in the very midst of crowds,
without being inconvenienced or stopped for a
moment ; it seems to you that it is not the donkey,
but the donkey-boy, who wafts you on with his shouts
through pleasant groups, and air that feels thick
with the fragrance of burial spice."

When Kinglake arrived in Cairo the deaths from
the plague numbered five hundred daily ; they
numbered twelve hundred before his departure. He
had been seven days there before he perceived a
change in the appearance of the streets ; he then
first observed " that the city was *silenced*. There
were no outward signs of Despair nor of violent
terror, but many of the voices that had swelled the

busy hum of men were already hushed in death, and the survivors, so used to scream and screech in their earnestness whenever they bought or sold, now showed an unwonted indifference about the affairs of this world ; it was less worth while for men to haggle, and haggle, and crack the sky with noisy bargains, when the Great Commander was there, who could ' pay all their debts with the roll of his drum.' "

Kinglake narrowly escaped the fate of the banker who cashed his letters of credit, and of the Italian physician who treated him for a sore-throat, both falling victims to the plague. He cured himself of the menacing symptoms by swallowing deep draughts of hot tea. The state of Mysseri, his servant, gave him anxiety, and he wished to procure medical aid for him. All the European doctors had either fled or died, with the exception of an Englishman in the medical service of the Pasha, and whose name, I regret to say, is not preserved. He was an honour alike to his nation and to his profession. Though told that this doctor did not engage in private practice, Kinglake wrote a note, in the hope that he might make an exception in this case: "The doctor instantly followed back my messenger, and was at once shown up into my room. I entreated him to stand off, telling him fairly how deeply I was ' compromised,' and especially by my contact with a person actually ill, and since dead, of Plague. The generous fellow, with a good-humoured laugh at the terrors of the contagionists, marched straight up to me and forcibly seized my hand, and shook it with manly violence. I felt grateful indeed, and swelled with fresh pride of race, because that my countryman could carry himself so nobly. He soon cured Mysseri, as well as me, and all this he did from no other motives than the pleasure of doing a kindness, and the delight of braving a danger."*

Eliot Warburton, who saw Cairo in 1843, was struck with the first glimpse which he got of it when emerging from the lanes of Boulac. " Never yet," he wrote, " did fancy flash upon the poet's eye a more superb illusion of power and beauty than the ' City of Victory ' presents at this distance." He is not the first who has been impressed with the spectacle of the city sloping up to the citadel, where two slender minarets are conspicuous in the clear air, while the range of the Mokattan mountains forms a picturesque background. Neither was he the first to feel, as he entered the city itself, that much of the impression produced depended upon the point of view.

Warburton's own description deserves to be quoted as a vivid picture of Cairo fifty years ago : " And now we are within the city ! Protean powers ! what a change ! A labyrinth of dark, filthy, intricate lanes and alleys ; in which every smell and sight from which nose and eye revolt meet one at every turn (and one is always turning). The stateliest streets are not above twelve feet wide ; and, as the upper stories arch over them toward one another, only a narrow serpentine seam of blue sky appears between

* " Eothen," pp. 297, 307, 318.

the toppling verandas of the winding streets. Occasionally, a string of camels, bristling with faggots of firewood, sweeps the streets effectually of their passengers; lean, mangy dogs are continually running between your legs, which afford a tempting passage in this petticoated place ; beggars, in rags quivering with vermin, are lying in every corner of the street ; now a bridal or a circumcising procession squeezes along, with music that might madden a drummer ; now the running footmen of some Bey or Pasha endeavour to jostle you against the wall; unless they recognise you as an Englishman—one of that race whom they think the devil himself can't frighten or teach manners to."*

Nothing did so much to revolutionize Cairo, and to affect Egypt generally, as the establishment of the Overland Route. This brought the Valley of the Nile within the sphere of English interests. Lieutenant Waghorn, who was the promoter of the route, did not obtain all the credit which he deserved. It was considered a great feat when, on the 31st of October, 1845, he accompanied the mail to London which had left India on the first of that month. What he began was perfected by the railway after his death, and the Suez Canal has superseded the railway in turn, yet as a pioneer Waghorn achieved a success which was wonderful.

Mr. Samuel Bevan, who was in his employment for a time, wrote a graphic account of the manner in which passengers from India to Europe or from Europe to India were transported across the desert

* "The Crescent and the Cross," pp. 184, 185.

In his book there is a curious narrative of Mr. Raven's experience of the plague, Mr. Raven being the agent of Lieutenant Waghorn in Cairo. The passage is valuable as a supplement to that which I have quoted from *Eothen*. Mr. Raven "remembered being shut up for six months in a house at Cairo, without once being permitted to cross the threshold, the doors being sealed, and a watchman constantly on the look-out. Provisions were drawn up in baskets, and paid for in money let down in a bucket of water. These precautions were rendered necessary by the critical state of one of the household, who was attacked with the plague, but eventually recovered. Poor Raven aired himself on the house-top, and almost got by heart every book in the place, until the seals were knocked off and he was suffered to escape; but, as may well be imagined, the remembrance of his captivity and its horrors is not easily to be effaced, and he will scarcely suffer himself to be entrapped a second time."*

As worthy of perusal as any of the notices of Cairo in bygone days is the account given of it by Thackeray in 1844. He looked upon the scene before him with an artist's eye. Where others groaned about smells and filth he saw material for the pencil, and he expressed his feelings in the following enthusiastic strain: "How to describe the beauty of the streets to you! The fantastic splendour; the variety of the houses, and archways, and hanging roofs, and balconies, and porches; the delightful accidents of light and shade which chequer

* "Sand and Canvas," pp. 97, 98.

them; the noise, the bustle, the brilliancy of the crowd; the interminable vast bazaars with their barbaric splendour! There is a fortune to be made for painters in Cairo, and material for a whole Academy of them. I never saw such a variety of architecture, of life, of picturesqueness, of brilliant colour, of light and shade. There is a picture in every street and at every bazaar-stall."

Before Thackeray had written the foregoing passage he penned another, depicting his life in the Hôtel d'Orient, where "Lieutenant Waghorn is bouncing in and out of the courtyard full of business."

A description of the dinner in that hotel follows, and Thackeray adds : " This as an account of Cairo, dear M——, you will probably be disposed to consider as incomplete; the fact is, I have seen nothing else as yet. I have peeped into no harems. The magicians, proved to be humbugs, have been bastinadoed out of town. The dancing girls, those lovely Alme, of whom I had hoped to be able to give a glowing account and elegant, though strictly moral, description, have been whipped into Upper Egypt, and as you are saying in your mind. . . . Well, it *isn't* a good description of Cairo ; you are perfectly right. It is England in Egypt. I like to see her there with her pluck, enterprise, manliness, bitter ale, and Harvey sauce. Wherever they come they stay and prosper. From the summit of yonder Pyramids forty centuries may look down on them if they are minded; and I say those venerable daughters of time ought to be better pleased by the examina-

6

tion than by regarding the French bayonets and
General Bonaparte, Member of the Institute, fifty
years ago, running about with sabre and pigtail.
Wonders he did, to be sure, and then ran away
leaving Kléber to be murdered in the lurch—a
few hundred yards from the spot where these
disquisitions are written.   But what are his wonders
compared to Waghorn ?   Nap massacred the Mamelukes at the Pyramids : Wag has conquered the
Pyramids themselves, dragged the unwieldy structures a month nearer England than they were, and
brought the country along with them.   All the
trophies that ever were brought to Roman triumph
were not so enormous and wonderful as this.   All
the heads that Napoleon ever ordered to be struck
off (as George Cruikshank says) would not elevate
him a monument as big.   Be ours the trophies of
peace !"*

If Thackeray could re-visit Cairo he would find
little to alter in the foregoing passage at the present
day.   He probably would substitute Shepheard's
Hotel for the Hôtel d'Orient, and he would certainly substitute Mr. John M. Cook for Lieutenant
Waghorn.   He would be impressed still more now
than he was formerly with " England in Egypt,"
and he would record with cordial feelings that it was
largely mixed with " America."

While he might not miss anything which gave
him pleasure before, he would take a patriotic pride
in observing the transformation which is in progress
under the guidance of his countrymen.   He would

* Thackeray's Works, vol. xii., pp. 312, 322.

observe with unalloyed satisfaction that the presence of the British troops did not denote conquest, but that these troops were in Cairo to uphold the Khedive's legitimate authority. After making minute inquiry into the working of the Government, and after learning the nature and extent of the reforms which had been effected, he would have still greater reason and satisfaction than he formerly had in closing his narrative with the words, "Be ours the trophies of peace!"

CHAPTER V.

THE CAPITAL AND ITS SUBURBS.

LORD LINDSAY wrote in 1836 : "With English hotels at Alexandria and Cairo, and floating palaces at command for navigating the Nile, what is to prevent our English ladies and their beaux from wintering at Thebes, as they have hitherto done at Paris and Rome? A hotel in the city of Sesostris would in that case prove a profitable speculation." This suggestion has been acted upon during many years, and thousands who cannot appreciate or endure an English winter now proceed to Egypt in quest of that ideal climate which is as hard to find as the Holy Grail.

Those who delighted in the Cairo of many years ago may now declare that it is altered for the worse. The phrase applied to it by Thackeray has not ceased to be pointed and appropriate, the city still being " magnificently picturesque." Some Oriental characteristics have gone the way of other vestiges of the past. The wide streets, bordered with arcades like those of Turin, are in striking contrast to the narrow alleys of an earlier day. Purchases can now be made in shops as spacious as any in London or

Paris, and in the best of them the prices affixed to goods approximate to their value. The seeker after novelty can still haggle in the native and malodorous bazaars for articles which appear to have the impress of native workmanship. Several years may yet lapse before the bazaars are supplanted by shops in airy streets, and before Cairo is still further modernized and improved. The day may even arrive when sewers shall be constructed, and then many Oriental smells in the "City of Victory" will have vanished. With the admission of more air into the older streets, and the removal of things from them which offend the senses, the death-rate of the city will fall low enough to satisfy the most exacting sanitary inspector. At present, it is 46 in the thousand. What this means can best be realized when a comparison is made with other cities which are not better planned than it, or more favoured by Nature for the conservation of human life. In Marseilles the average rate is 26 in the thousand, in Berlin and Paris it is 23, and in London it is 17. The difficulty of draining Cairo is not much greater than that which had to be overcome in the case of London; there is little doubt that if the drainage of the capital of Egypt were nearly as thorough as that of the capital of England, the rate of mortality in the two cities would be on a par. Thousands now die young in Cairo who, if they saw the light in the less balmy air of London, might reach the average age of civilized man.

A pleasant place of abode is valued as highly as

a healthy one, otherwise the winter resorts in the French Riviera would be as much avoided by strangers in the cold months of the year as they are in the warm ones. Invalids frequent Cannes, Nice, and Mentone, despite warnings from competent persons that the mortality from chest affections is as great in all of them as in the northern parts of France and England. The bright blue sky and the blazing sun appear to them natural specifics, and they disregard warnings from those who are aware of the drawbacks, from a sanitary point of view, of the places which seem to be paradises in miniature. This is as true of Cairo as it is of any health-resort in Southern France, from Hyères to Mentone ; but the new-comer who first sees Cairo in mid-winter is apt to fancy that it has all the charms of the Garden of Eden, with the superadded advantages of Christian churches and capital hotels, fine shops and some well-paved streets.

It is true that the rainfall in Egypt is much less than in Europe, and that the sunshine, while not less powerful, is far softer and more genial than in the southern villages or cities of France and Italy. The Egyptian sun warms without scorching ; it can be borne with ease in a city, but when the yellow sands of the desert are traversed, then the glare is insufferable.

Everything, from the temperature of the air to the temperament of the people, runs to extremes in a southern clime. There is either too much sun and too little water, or else too much moisture as well as too much sun. There may be not a trace of vegetation, or it may be so rank as to impede locomotion. In Upper Egypt and in Nubia a shower of rain is a rarity, and the lack of sufficient rain is as great a mischief there as a continuous Scottish mist is in other places. Those who are disappointed with the climate of Cairo in winter may have expected too much, and, if they are invalids of the worst type, no place or air will suit them. To cross the sea and change the sky, instead of availing to cure an ailment, may aggravate the dangerous symptoms, and the sufferer who hoped to regain strength in a strange land passes away there.

A health resort is best fitted for the healthy, and this is as true of Cairo as of many places in high repute for their climate. Those who can enjoy life at all, enjoy it the most when the surrounding conditions are delightful. The dryness of the air is one of the reasons why the climate of Cairo is exhilarating. There the mean annual degree of humidity is 58, while in Algiers it is 70, and 87 in London. Statistics have been preserved of the rainfall in Cairo during each year since 1798, and the largest number of rainy days in any one year has been 15, and the smallest 9. While not raining often, neither does it rain much, the quantity falling not exceeding $1\frac{1}{2}$ inches. Formerly the amount was but $\frac{1}{2}$ inch, according to Dr. Sandwith,* but it is possible that the old-fashioned rain-gauges gave incorrect results in Egypt, as they are known to have done elsewhere. It is difficult to realize the smallness of a rainfall of an inch and a half, and nothing but comparison will

* "Egypt as a Winter Resort," p. 36.

convey a notion of the truth.   If that in the three
capitals of the United Kingdom be taken, the con-
trast is remarkable, the mean annual rainfall in
Dublin being 30 inches, in Edinburgh 26, and in
London 24.   It is 39 in Naples, 30 in Rome, 28 in
Brussels, and 22 in Paris.

Some cities in the New World are not far
behind the worst in the Old as regards the rainfall,
48 inches being registered in Boston and 38 in New
York City.   In Hindostan the rainfall is as astounding as the fauna and flora, it being 110 inches in
Bombay and 81 in Calcutta.   If Dr. Sandwith had
quoted these figures, those which he prints would
appear even more significant, the mean average at
Hyères being 28 inches, Bournemouth 28, Nice 31,
Torquay 39, Pau 43, and Montreux 50.   During
the season at Cannes and Mentone, that is, from
November till April, the rainfall at the first is
32, and at the second it is 17 inches.   I have given
round numbers in each of the above cases, and I
agree with Dr. Sandwith when he adds that " the
absence of rain and umbrellas does not necessarily
make a country suitable for invalids, but it enables
them to count with certainty upon the morrow,
and removes at least one element of risk and depression."

It is more wonderful that Cairo should be so
healthy than that the rate of mortality should be
so high.   The air must be as full of death-dealing
organisms as the water of the Nile.   The water is
purified by artificial filtering, while the air is purified by the chemistry of Nature.   The proportion

of ozone in the air during the winter months is often
as much as 12, the maximum of the ozometer being
14. Indeed, it is discreditable that man has omitted
to second Nature in rendering Cairo one of the
healthiest cities in the world ; yet this wicked neglect is not likely to continue. Since the British occupation, if not actually in consequence of it, all the
streets in the city have been regularly swept and
watered. Till 1885 the cleansing process was confined to the European quarter. It is nearly half a
century since the plague visited Cairo, and it is hoped
that such a scourge will never again cause panic and
exceptional mortality. Other epidemics, of which
cholera and influenza are the most fatal, have raged
here as in places where the conditions are quite
different, and it is preposterous to expect that Nature,
even when most ably seconded by Art, can ever
hinder the advent of an epidemic, though it is quite
possible to remove the hotbed wherein it thrives
in deadly luxuriance.

Visitors to Cairo who carefully follow the programme laid down for them in guide-books, and
surrender themselves into the doubtful hands of
dragomans, refrain from going to Boulac now that
the famous collection of Egyptian antiquities has
been transferred from that suburb to the palace
at Gizeh. Yet this part of Cairo should not be
neglected. Many things there possess an interest
owing to their historical associations. At one time
the traveller from Alexandria to Cairo by water
landed at Boulac after a trip in a sailing-boat
lasting four days and nights. At a later time

steamers made the trip in twenty-four hours, and now the journey can be accomplished by rail in less than five hours.

Boulac has fallen from its high estate since Eliot Warburton thus wrote of it : " Toward the river, it is faced by factories and store-houses; within, you find yourself in a labyrinth of brown, narrow streets, that resemble rather rifts in some mud-mountain than anything with which architecture has had to do. Yet, here and there, the blankness of the walls is broken and varied by richly-worked lattices, and specimens of arabesque masonry. Gaudy bazaars strike the eye and relieve the gloom, and the picturesque population that swarms everywhere keeps the interest awake."*

Many of the buildings which Warburton saw were the factories which had been established by Mehemet Ali with a view to render Egypt independent of European manufactures, and in which 30,000 men were employed. Sir John Bowring visited them in 1838, and was dissatisfied with the waste due to the mismanagement which prevailed. However, it gratified the Viceroy to have factories in which carpets were made, and silk and cotton were spun and wrought into fabrics, to have an iron foundry, an arsenal, and a printing-office. His successors considered that the cost of the factories was excessive and far greater than Egypt could afford to pay, and one factory after another was closed. The arsenal, the foundry, and the printing-office remained in operation after the others had been shut

* " The Crescent and the Cross," p. 29.

up. Ismail was smitten with a fancy for establishing
a paper-mill here, which should produce all the paper
which was used in Egypt, and possibly leave a
surplus for exportation. Buildings were erected at
Boulac, and machinery of the newest pattern and
the costliest kind was placed in them. The mill had
to be abandoned, as it was found that paper-making
could not be carried on except at a heavy loss.
This dismantled paper-mill, covering an area of
20,000 square yards, recently passed into the hands
of Messrs. Thomas Cook and Sons, who are the
largest employers of labour in Boulac.

Their workmen put together vessels which have
been constructed in sections on the Clyde for service
on the Nile. The iron and brass work required in
ship-building or repairing is here cast and wrought
into shape in foundries and machine-shops, while the
woodwork is executed by carpenters, many of whom
are natives and skilled artisans of the highest class.
A floating-dock, which was constructed on the spot,
is the latest addition to the shipping plant of the
Messrs. Cook. Formerly it was necessary to despatch a vessel to Alexandria if the hull needed
repairing below the water-line, the cost of the trip to
and fro being not less than £300. This can now be
saved, since a floating-dock enables the mechanic at
Boulac to effect repairs as easily as his fellow-work-
man could do in the dry dock at Alexandria.

While an English firm has largely contributed to
restore the departed glories of Boulac, the German
landlord of a hotel near the Pyramids has brought
them within easy reach of dwellers in Cairo by

means of a mail-coach. Formerly a trip to the
Pyramids involved some toil and a little risk. It
was necessary for the sight-seer, who desired to go
and return the same day, to rise at daybreak, to
ride on a donkey from his residence in Cairo to the
right bank of the Nile, to be ferried across the river
in a flat-bottomed boat, and to remount a donkey on
the left bank. After a fatiguing ride he would reach
the Pyramids, at which he could take but a hasty
glance, as no time could be wasted before starting
on the return journey in order to reach Cairo before
sunset. The more adventuresome traveller who had
plenty of leisure and money might pass some time
at the base of the Pyramids, provided he took a
tent, a cook, and provisions with him, as well as a
guard of Bedouins for protection against robbers.

At present, the visitor can drive in a mail-
coach from Shepheard's Hotel, in Cairo, to the
Mena Hotel at the base of the Great Pyramid, take
luncheon there, and return in time for dinner. The
river is spanned by the Kasr-el-Nil bridge, which is
one of the most creditable and useful works executed
while Ismail was Khedive. He caused two Ethiopian lions to be set up in bronze at each end of the
bridge, in disregard of the Muslim prejudice against
images or portraits of living things. At the Kasr-
el-Nil barracks there is a sight which gives intense
annoyance to all who hate England. A regiment
of red-coats is quartered here, the barracks having
formerly been a palace, which was the abode of Arabi
during his brief dictatorship. In the large parade-
ground the soldiers who are not on duty are playing

at football or cricket, and numbers of native spectators always watch them with curious eyes. Once the bridge is crossed, a road, shaded with trees on either hand, runs for six miles, till the desert is reached. The Prince and Princess of Wales were the visitors to the Pyramids who first passed over this road.

Those who now cross the Nile bridge and drive along the road will find it hard to believe that there ever was a time when the Pyramids were inaccessible. Yet Chateaubriand records that in November, 1806, he could not approach them, first, because the Nile was not high enough to allow of a boat reaching their base; and secondly, because the land was too deep under water for a horse to find a footing.

That the desert can be entered at a short distance from Cairo is a blessing to all the residents in the city. Whether sight-seeing or business be pursued, the visitor to Cairo whose health is good soon feels languid and eager for change, while the invalid is frequently told that he will not get well unless he exchange the air of the streets for that of the desert.

The Mena Hotel owed its foundation to an Englishman, whose story has been told by Dr. Sandwith, and it may be thus summarized. Being afflicted with consumption, he desired to try the effect of the desert air, and he bought from the Egyptian Government, in 1884, three hundred acres of sand upon which a small house stood. He took up his abode here with his wife. The improvement in his physical condition was marked; the worst symptoms disap-

peared, and his lost strength returned. Two winters
and a summer were passed in his desert home. He
was persuaded to try the mountain air of Cyprus
during the summer for a change; he did so and
died. Had he lived longer, he would have built a
sanatorium for sufferers like himself.

After his death, an Englishman resident in Cairo
bought this property, added to the house which he
had occupied, and opened it for public use as the
Mena Hotel. Herr Adolf Düringer, who now
keeps it, is also the landlord of the Cur-Haus
Hotel in Kreuznach. Those who are not invalids
find a new sensation and a rare pleasure in spending
several days or weeks within a few yards of the
Pyramids, and with the Lybian desert stretching
away to the horizon. To such persons the Pyramids
and the Sphinx become fraught with impressions such
as cannot be felt by the hasty tourist who visits them
as an interlude between his luncheon and dinner.
They can be seen at all times from the hotel, and
under varied conditions, and the dwellers in it can
count upon being left in peace by the donkey-boys and
guides, who are nearly as much dreaded by the casual
visitor now as the brigands were in the olden days.
Though plagues, the guides are not robbers or
murderers. No one runs the risk that Kinglake did
when a man in a soldier's uniform proposed to the
Arab Sheikh to put him to death when in the interior
of the Great Pyramid and to share the booty with
him. On this coming to the knowledge of
Kinglake he exclaimed : " Fancy a struggle for
life in one of those burial-chambers, with acres and

acres of solid masonry between one's self and the daylight !"*

When Harriet Martineau ascended and entered the Great Pyramid early in 1847, she was the subject of a miracle. Her own belief in the supernatural was faint, yet few Catholic saints could tell a more wonderful tale of personal experience than that which she pleasantly tells about herself. She apologizes for narrating the anecdote on the ground that it shows the engrossing interest of the Pyramid on the spot ; this was unnecessary, however, as she was the last person in the world to note down and reproduce anything which was utterly trivial or uninstructive. I give the story in her own excellent words : " The most precious articles of property I had with me abroad were two ear-trumpets, because, in case of accident happening to them, I could not supply the loss. I was unwilling to carry my trumpet up the Pyramid, knocking against the stones while I wanted my hands for climbing. So I left it below in the hands of a trusty Arab. When I joined my party at the top of the Pyramid, I never remembered my trumpet ; nor did they : and we talked as usual, during the forty minutes we were there, without my ever missing it. When I came down, I never thought of it ; and I explored the inside, came out and lunched, and still never thought of my trumpet, till, at the end of three hours and a half from my parting with it, I saw it in the hands of the Arab, and was reminded of the astonishing fact that I had heard as well without it as with it, all the time. Such a thing

* " Eothen," p. 324.

never happened before, and probably never will again : and a stronger proof could not be offered of the engrossing interest of a visit to the Pyramid."*

Before visiting the Pyramids I had listened to the speculations regarding them of Mr. Cope Whitehouse, an ingenious and scholarly American who has an extensive and profound acquaintance with the Egypt of history and the Egypt of the present day. He broached the theory that the builders of the Pyramids had availed themselves of mountains to form the body which they shaped and faced with stone. I was impressed with the plausibility of the notion. Since then I have seen many mountains in Nubia which require but a slight dressing to present the appearance of artificial pyramids. When Lord Lindsay first saw the Pyramids of Gizeh he noted that they towered in the distance "like mountains cut down into their present shape."

There is little that is accepted as new which is not old. It may be that even Mr. Cope Whitehouse was unaware that his hypothesis had been first advanced by James Bruce. After gazing upon the Pyramids in 1768, Bruce wrote that he thought it extraordinary that travellers should repeat what they had been told rather than make use of their own eyes. "Anyone," he adds, "who removes the sand on the south side will find the solid rock hewn into steps ; and in the roof of the large chamber where the sarcophagus stands, as also in the top of the chamber in the gallery, as you go up into that chamber, you see large fragments of the rock, affording an unanswer-

* "Eastern Life : Present and Past," vol. ii., pp. 64, 65.

able proof that those Pyramids were once huge rocks, standing where they now are ; that some of them, the most proper for their form, were chosen for the body of the Pyramid, and the others hewn into steps to serve for the superstructure and the exterior parts of them."*

The visitor who has beheld the Sphinx and the Pyramids only when the sun is high in the heavens, can have no conception of the solemn weirdness and extraordinary variety of the spectacle which they present at sunrise, at sunset, and when they are transfigured under the light of the moon. The moonbeams veil their decay and give softness to their outlines. Then it is that the sandy waste in which they stand has a beauty alike strange and incomparable, and the beholder feels himself unable or reluctant to agree with Sir Thomas Browne's remark that " Pyramids, arches, obelisks, were but the irregularities of vain-glory, and wild enormities of ancient magnanimity."

The Sphinx still remains the most mysterious among many marvellous relics of the past. Sand no longer hides the greater part of it from view, but the meaning of the gigantic figure remains an unsolved problem. Its antiquity is the one thing about which there cannot be any doubt. Those who gaze upon the inscrutable features of the huge head can admire what Kinglake wrote, after so doing, without agreeing in every particular with his conclusion :

" Upon ancient dynasties of Ethiopian and Egyptian kings—upon Greek and Roman, upon

* " Bruce's Travels," vol. i., p. 115.

Arab and Ottoman conquerors, upon Napoleon
dreaming of an Eastern empire, upon battle and
pestilence, upon the ceaseless misery of the Egyptian race, upon keen-eyed travellers—Herodotus
yesterday and Warburton to-day—upon all and more
this unworldly Sphinx has watched, and watched
like a Providence with the same earnest eyes, and
the same sad, tranquil mien.   And we, we shall die,
and Islam will wither away, and the Englishman,
leaning far over to hold his loved India, will plant a
firm foot on the banks of the Nile, and sit in the
seats of the Faithful, and still that sleepless rock will
lie watching, and watching the works of a new and
busy race, with those same sad, earnest eyes, and
the same tranquil mien everlasting."*

* " Eothen," p. 327.

CHAPTER VI.

THERE is fascination in the phrase, "an oasis in the desert." The reader pictures to himself a spot where clusters of graceful palm-trees and patches of rich vegetation form a delightful contrast to the savage barrenness of the surrounding waste. Above all things an oasis is blessed with springs ; indeed, its existence and attractiveness are due to the presence of sweet water.

Helouan is an oasis, but, as it is easily accessible, it differs from any other which the wearied and parched traveller hails as a haven of refuge and repose. The journey thither by rail from Cairo occupies forty minutes. Some of the poetry of an oasis vanishes when it is possible to reach it in a train. Helouan is not such a spot in the desert as that for which the camel pants and the traveller sighs when the supply of water has run short, and when both animal and man are threatened with death from thirst. Three miles from Helouan the Nile flows along, and the water of that yellow river is conveyed to the dwellers in the oasis. There is an abundance of water in Helouan, which is highly mineralized, and much of it closely resembles that of Aix-les-Bains, in Savoy. The mineral springs of the Heluan have been its chief attraction during many centuries. The place itself is to Egypt what Carlsbad is to Austria, Aix-la-Chapelle to Germany, and Aix-les-Bains to France.

A small Arab village has long existed near the spot where the modern town of Helouan stands. This town was the favourite resort of Mehemet Tewfik, when reigning Khedive of Egypt. He built a palace there in which he lived during the greater part of each year. One of the mineral springs was discovered by him. He and his family often bathed in the waters. His death, after a short illness, and as the consequence of unskilful treatment, took place in his palace at Helouan. This palace, which was his favourite place of abode in the winter months, appears destined to decay. The rulers over Egypt have a foolish prejudice against inhabiting a palace where a relative has died, and an uninhabited one is neglected and soon becomes a ruin. The palace erected at Ismailia has been untenanted for years, and it is now falling to pieces.

Whether it be a palace or a tomb, the tooth of Time is permitted to do its worst in Egypt as soon as the interest in either ceases. The Egyptians care more about building than about repairing and preserving; hence their country is as emphatically the land of ruins as of hope. There are no marks of antiquity in the streets of Helouan; on the contrary, the town seems to have been built yesterday, being as new as it looks, and yet it has much of the same attrac-

tion for the lover of antiquities that leads many to
visit Resina. Both stand upon the sites of ancient
cities, and the remains below the surface have
greater charms than the finest building upon it.
Helouan, or rather Helwan, was named after a king
of old Egypt, about whom little else is known. No
mention is made of this place in any hieroglyphics
yet discovered, nor in any of the Greek and Latin
accounts of Egypt. Al Makrizi, the voluminous
Arab historian, who flourished in the early part of
the fifteenth century, devotes a portion of his work
on Egypt and Cairo to an account of Helouan, in
which he records that the village is said to have
derived its name " from Helouan, who was the son
of Babylon, who was the son of Amrou, who was
the son of Emir-el-Keiss, kings of Egypt, and that
Helouan lived in Syria as the chief of the advanced
guard of Braha."

It is less important, however, to learn why a
town or village is called by a particular name, than
to obtain trustworthy particulars of its rise and
growth. Two other historians supply this information about Helouan in a stinted but probably
authentic measure. One of them is Abd-el-Hakem,
who writes that "when the plague broke out in
Fostad [that is, Old Cairo] Abd-el-Aziz, who was
the son of Marouan, left the city and settled at
Helouan, in the desert, at a spot named Abuker-
kurah, where he caused a well to be dug, and led
the water to the date-palms which he planted in
Helouan."

The other historian is El Kendi, who narrates

the same occurrence at greater length and with additional details : " The plague broke out in Egypt in 690, and Abd-el-Aziz, who was the son of Marouan, left the city, turned his face eastwards and went to Helouan. The locality pleased him ; he remained and established his soldiers, guards, and police there. Abd-el-Aziz caused many mosques and other buildings to be erected ; and he peopled the land and planted many date-palms and vines, which were celebrated by poets. Having planted date-palms and eaten their fruit along with his soldiers, Abd-el-Aziz often walked through the garden and stopped beside the spring. When Marouan, the father of Abd-el-Aziz, left Egypt in the month of Regheb, in the year 67 (687 A.D.), his son exercised authority over it. Marouan died in the month of Rhamadan, his son, Abd-el-Malek, succeeding him in the government of Syria, and his brother, Abd-el-Aziz, continuing to govern Egypt in accord with him. Abd-el-Aziz sickened and died on the 13th of Gamad Avel, 86 (706 A.D.) ; his remains were conveyed across the Nile from Helouan to Fostad, and buried there. His reign lasted twenty years, ten months, and thirteen days. There was then a ferry at Helouan, by which men and boats were transported from east to west." This ferry is still in use.

It is quite clear from the writings of the Arab historians that springs were found in the desert nearly twelve hundred years ago, and that Abd-el-Aziz caused the water from them to be brought to the village of Helouan. There is no doubt also that splendid baths were erected by Abd-el-Aziz,

but it is a mystery why these baths were destroyed, or were suffered to fall into decay. That
fire played a part in effecting their destruction is
probable, as large quantities of charred remains
have been found on the spot where the baths and
houses once stood. When explorations were made
there it was found that the covering of rubbish
and sand was twelve feet thick. The structures
which were laid bare seemed to have been the
works of giants, every part of them being on a
colossal scale.

The very existence of the place which had once
been famous for its mineral springs was forgotten
during many centuries, and its site became a mound
in the desert. Very little that was worthy of notice
in Egypt escaped the attention of the men of science
who accompanied Bonaparte, and drew up most
exhaustive and valuable reports ; but no mention
was made in them of the mineral springs of Helouan,
neither was the place itself indicated in the maps of
the country which they compiled. However, the
springs continued to flow undisturbed throughout
centuries, and a sulphurous odour floated in the air
above the swampy ground, in which they slowly
evaporated under the hot sun.

No exact account is extant of the rediscovery of
the springs, neither has the name been preserved
of him who again brought them into use. All that
can be affirmed with confidence is that the map of
Egypt prepared by Linant de Bellefonds Pasha in
1830. by command of Mehemet Ali, contains the
indication, "springs of mineral waters," on a spot to

the east of the village of Helouan.   Linant Pasha
had carefully examined this locality, and he had
verified the presence of mineral springs over a large
tract of land on both banks of the Nile.   Many
poor and ailing inhabitants of Cairo had been accustomed to encamp near the source of the mineral
water and bathe in it.

During the viceroyalty of Abbas Pasha, wooden
huts were built for the accommodation of patients at
Helouan, and the springs themselves were enclosed
in a wooden chamber.   Though the arrangements
were primitive, the baths were gladly used by ailing
Arabs and Copts, Syrians and Greeks, who went to
Helouan for health, and sometimes found it.   The first
Khedive was impressed with what he heard about
the mineral water, and he ordered Professor Gastinel
Bey to report upon it, the report afterwards appearing with the title, "*Étude Topographique, Chimique
et Medicale des Eaux Sulphureuses et Salines de
Helouan-les-Bains.*"

A well-appointed bathing establishment was
erected by order of the first Khedive, and during
the excavations which were then made the large
bath was discovered that Abd-el-Aziz had caused
to be constructed in the seventh century, as well as
ruins resembling those which are attributed to the
fabulous Cyclops.   The Grand Hotel was opened
in 1873, and its management was entrusted to Herr
Heltzel, whose small work in German on Helouan,
published there, contains the best sketch of its history
which I have met with.   I am chiefly indebted
to it for the particulars which I have given above,

and which I have translated from the last and
enlarged edition of it.*

Ismail visited Helouan with his first wife, and
bathed in the mineral water. His eldest son,
Tewfik, took a strong liking to the place, and, as
I have already said, he discovered a spring there.
Shortly after becoming Khedive he built himself the
palace in which he died in the prime of his years
at a time when his life was most precious to his
country.

In 1876 Helouan was connected with Cairo by
rail. So long as the place had no communication
with the capital, save by road or river, its frequenters
were chiefly invalids, and few in number. The railway added to its popularity and led to its increase. A
well-built town arose, which presented a remarkable
contrast to the rude hamlet of earlier years, and high
hopes as to its future were entertained by those who
were interested in its progress. Dr. Reil Bey was
entrusted with the charge of the rising watering-
place. For some reason which has not been dis-
closed, he was removed by the Khedive Ismail, and
Franz Pasha, who was appointed to succeed him,
performed the good service of causing the morass
in the neighbourhood of the baths to be drained.
However, this energetic man was transferred to fill
another office, and the Government undertook the
management of the hotel and the baths. There are
many duties which a government can discharge
better than any private company. No private com-

* "Die Schwefelthermen von Helouan, von Em. Heltzel,"
pp. 10-17.

pany, for instance, whether limited or unlimited, can be an efficient manager of a prison. If a profit is to be made out of keeping prisoners, either the latter will be victims or the public will suffer. It is equally absurd for a government to keep a hotel. Prison-cells may be filled, if the number of malefactors is sufficient, but no one can be condemned to live in a hotel against his will. The hotel in Helouan remained empty while the Egyptian Government acted as landlord.

Helouan appeared in 1879 to be gradually returning to the state of nature from which it had so slowly emerged ; no strangers were seen in its dusty streets ; building was suspended ; the physician, whose livelihood depended upon having patients to treat, left a place in which patients were unknown, and the depth of depression was reached when the single apothecary in Helouan put up his shutters and closed his door. Physicians are not necessary to the enjoyment of life. There are many tracts of the habitable globe where human beings increase and multiply, pass in slow succession from the uncomfortable cradle to the peaceful tomb without a physician having exercised any control over their movements. But the number of those is small who never take medicine, while the number is enormous of those who think that, unless they take it, their lives will be embittered or shortened. For these reasons Helouan was regarded as uninhabitable when the opportunity of obtaining drugs there was at an end. Owing to the place being shunned by patients and visitors, the railway company diminished the number

of trains by one half. The oasis near the capital of
Egypt had ceased to attract.

Though the tide of prosperity in modern Helouan
had ebbed rapidly, it began to flow with a suddenness
which was startling. Madame de Lex, the wife of
the Russian Consul-General at Cairo, used her influence with the Khedive in favour of Helouan, and
she could do this with the greater effect because the
Khedive who then occupied the throne was a warm
friend to the place. The Government gave up the
thankless and ruinous task of hotel-keeping and the
superintendence of mineral baths for which there
was no demand, entrusting Dr. Engel with the
medical care of the bathing establishment, and appointing Herr Heltzel to the management of the
Grand Bath Hotel for a term of ten years. The
public appreciated the change, and the numbers of
visitors increased so largely that the hotel had to be
enlarged.

Since this revival of Helouan it has continued to
grow in prosperity and size. A fine new hotel was
opened recently, and houses are erected at short
intervals. Patients flock to it from all parts of the
world. The bathing arrangements are as good as
in any European bath, and they are infinitely superior,
as regards comfort and cleanliness, to those in any
other Oriental bath which I have visited. In rheu-
matism, rheumatic gout, in gout itself, and in certain
maladies of the chest and stomach, the mineral waters
of Helouan are accounted sovereign remedies.

The mineral springs of Helouan are not panaceas
for suffering humanity; yet, being medicines of a

powerful character, they cannot be taken with benefit except under medical advice. I can vouch for the completeness of the appliances, and I have found, when bathing as an experiment, that nothing is wanting that can be found at baths of a like kind, of which those of Aix-la-Chapelle and Aix in Savoy are the best examples.

Alike in France or Germany, in England or Austria, the season for deriving benefit from bathing and drinking in mineral waters is that period of moderately good and not always inclement weather which begins when May opens and ends when September closes. The doors of the most renowned European baths are shut during winter, or, if they remain open, few but semi-lunatics ever pass within them. Fine weather is regarded as a con-comitant of the best mineral water, and what is called "a cure" cannot be followed with advantage during the bleak months of a European winter. In contradistinction to the baths of Europe, those of Helouan can be taken by the invalid throughout the year. The climate of this oasis in the desert is a serviceable adjunct to the treatment at all seasons. Custom, fashion, or both may have ordained that Helouan should be most crowded during the winter months, but this is due to the fact that winter in the Arabian desert is the twin-brother of summer in Northern Europe.

In reality, then, there is no season, in the Euro-pean sense of the word, at Helouan as there is at watering-places on the Continent, the baths being available and curative all the year round. Tonic and aperient waters from sources not far distant can be prescribed to the patient who is taking courses of sulphur baths, and in this respect Helouan has as many advantages as Harrogate. The value of these baths was strikingly illustrated in 1883, when many of the English troops quartered in Cairo fell victims to malarial fever. The horses, as well as their riders, were laid low with this malady. Both were sent to Helouan and put under canvas while undergoing treatment. The mortality ceased at the end of a few weeks, and the malady disappeared at the end of a few months. Though the value of Helouan as a health-resort is insufficiently appreciated in Europe, the information supplied concerning it being scanty, yet statistics show it to be rapidly rising in popularity.

In 1881 the number of baths taken was 8,000. Owing to the civil convulsions in the following year the numbers fell to 6,000. They rose to 10,000 in 1886, and they were 17,000 in 1890. Since then the increase has been continuous, while many dwellings have been built to house those who visit Helouan as patients or pleasure-seekers.

The houses are 140 in number, and building goes on rapidly. Trees line and shade the wide streets, and the patches of garden around each house are gay throughout winter with flowering shrubs which in northern climes are seen in hot-houses alone. The town is laid out according to a plan approved by the late Khedive. His own house is now desolate ; though styled a palace, it is not more imposing than many private dwellings. Though the patronage

of the present Khedive may not be extended to
Helouan, yet the place has received an impetus
which should suffice for its further development.
There are many inducements to build here, the
greatest being that a site is granted for nothing
to anyone who erects a house upon it within two
years.

Amusements are provided for the visitors ; many
excursions can be made to places of historic interest
in the neighbourhood, and those who delight in sport
can hunt hyenas, wolves, and jackals, without going
far afield.   When water-melons and dates are ripe
in the gardens, these wild beasts approach the town
to feed upon them.

If such an oasis in the desert as Helouan were
in Southern Europe, it would be as crowded as Aix,
Carlsbad and Wiesbaden are when the season is at
its height.   Now that Egypt is as accessible to the
English and American invalid as many a watering-
place on the European continent, the inducement is
great to frequent the mineral springs of Helouan.
Those who seem to enjoy life the most when they are
undergoing " a cure " might take a course of waters
here during the winter, and another in the spring or
summer at a European health-resort.   There is no
impropriety or temerity in predicting that an increasing proportion of the visitors to Egypt will spend
several weeks in one of the villas or hotels of
Helouan, will drink and bathe in its healing springs,
and return home with many pleasant reminiscences,
and rejoicing at having left their ailments in the
Arabian desert.

NOTE.

I subjoin the analyses of the springs at Helouan, which were made by Professor Gastinel Bey, and are quoted in Herr Heltzel's small work. In addition to translating the whole, I have given English equivalents for the foreign terms and quantities.

FIRST GROUP OF SPRINGS, COMPRISING TWO IN THE BATH HOUSE, AND TWO WHICH ARE ABOUT 330 YARDS DISTANT.

Temperature, 30° Cent., or 86° Fahr., where the water issues from the ground. Specific gravity, 1·0025. 1 litre, equal to $1\frac{3}{4}$ pints, contains :

Gaseous Constituents.

	Cubic Inches.	Grains.
Free sulphuretted hydrogen -	2·86	1·128
„ carbonic acid - -	3·72	1·851
„ nitrogen - - -	0·61	0·194
	7·19	3·173

Solid Matter.

	Grains.
Chloride of calcium - - -	2·900
„ magnesium - - -	27·928
„ sodium - - -	49·376
Bi-carbonate of lime - - -	12·344
Sulphate of lime - - -	3·240
Silica - - - - -	0·226
Nitrogenous organic matter - -	0·022
	96·036

ANALYSIS OF THE DEPOSIT, WHICH IS KNOWN AS BAREGIN, EVAPORATED TO DRYNESS.

100 grains contain :	Grains.
Sulphur - - - -	1·75
Iodine - - -	0·22855
	1·97855

Liquid State.

	Grains.
Sulphur - - - -	0·65152
Iodine - - - -	0·08509
	0·73661

SECOND GROUP OF SPRINGS, WHICH IS FROM 110 TO 270 YARDS
DISTANT FROM THE FIRST.

Temperature, 25° Cent., or 77° Fahr.   Specific gravity, 1·0362.

FIRST SPRING.

Gaseous Constituents.

	Cubic Inches.	Grains.
Sulphuretted hydrogen -	0·213	0·0786
Carbonic acid - -	0·360	0·1805
	0·579	0·2591

Solid Matter.

	Grains.
Chloride of calcium - - -	72·89
„ magnesium - - -	61·25
„ sodium - - -	566·97
Sulphate of magnesia - - -	39·90
„ alumina - - -	7·09
„ lime - - -	54·00
Bi-carbonate of soda - - -	16·51
„ lime - - -	41·04
Silica - - - - -	1·23
	860·88

SECOND SPRING.

Temperature, 26° Cent., that is, 78·8° Fahr.   Specific gravity,
1·0137.

Gases.

	Cubic Inches.	Grains.
Sulphuretted hydrogen -	0·692	0·263
Carbonic acid -	0·792	0·393
	1·484	0·656

Solid Matter.

	Grains.
Chloride of calcium - - -	0·308
„ magnesium - - -	9·103
„ sodium - - -	63·254
Sulphate of magnesia - - -	11·726
„ soda - -	12·498
„ alumina - - -	4·166
Bi-carbonate of lime - - -	13·169
„ iron - - -	0·308
„ soda - - -	1·234
Silica - - - - -	0·061
Organic matter - - - -	0·154
	117·215

THIRD GROUP. THIS COMPRISES TWO SPRINGS ABOUT 500 YARDS FROM THE KHEDIVIAL PALACE. ONE WAS DISCOVERED BY THE LATE KHEDIVE.

Temperature, 25° Cent., or 77° Fahr. Specific gravity, 1·0445.

Gaseous Products.

	Cubic Inches.	Grains.
Carbonic acid - -	1·586	0·786

Solid Matter.

	Grains.
Chloride of calcium - - -	25·453
„ magnesium - -	163·558
„ sodium - - -	574·921
Sulphate of magnesia - - -	36·260
„ alumina - - -	8·949
„ lime - - -	16·664
Bi-carbonate of lime - -	92·580
„ iron - - -	0·771
„ soda - - -	3·394
Silica - - - - -	0·154
Organic matter - - - -	0·462
	923·166

S

FOURTH GROUP. THIS STRONGLY APERIENT SALINE SPRING IS A MILE TO THE NORTH OF HELOUAN.

Temperature, 25° Cent., or 77° Fahr. Specific gravity, 1·0152.

Gaseous Products.

	Cubic Inches.	Grains.
Carbonic acid - - -	0·366	0·169

Solid Matter.

	Grains
Chloride of calcium - - -	2·468
„ magnesium - - -	47·987
„ sodium - - -	61·874
Sulphate of magnesia - - -	16·510
„ soda - - -	6·889
„ alumina - - -	6·480
„ lime - - -	0·308
Bi-carbonate of lime - - -	19·287
„ iron - - -	Trace.
Silica - - - - -	0·154
Organic matter - - - -	0·462
	162·419

CHAPTER VII.

SOME citizens of Colorado are credited with telling stories of doubtful authenticity and of a startling character. They delight to repeat one concerning what befell an Englishman when he visited their State for the first time. Soon after his arrival he took a walk with a companion and reached a river's bank. Though told that the stream was broad, he thought that he could easily leap across it, the result of his effort being that, instead of alighting upon the opposite bank, he fell mid-way into the water. Afterwards he came to a narrow ditch, and when his companion asked him to jump over it he declined, saying that the ditches in Colorado corresponded to broad rivers in England. The extraordinary translucency of the air had misled him when determining the distances and relative positions of objects. His eyes required a training on the spot.

If that Englishman were to visit Egypt with a view to study the problems of the moment, he would make serious blunders if he came with preconceived impressions, and he could only hope to succeed in even a partial measure if he were exceed-

ingly clear-sighted, cool-headed, and unprejudiced.
The political and social, as well as the physical,
atmosphere of the Valley of the Nile is peculiarly
Egyptian. There is nothing like it in Europe. It
is impossible, by previous reading or meditation, to
qualify one's self for understanding Egyptian problems without personal knowledge of the country.
Those who have looked at photographs of Niagara
or the Pyramids may feel, when in the presence of
either, that the spectacle is exactly what they have
expected to behold ; but the longer they actually
remain within the sound of Niagara, or the shadow
of the Pyramids, the more conscious do they become
that each is unique, and that it cannot be appreciated
till some time after it has been looked upon.

Heine wrote that every age is a sphinx which
sinks into the earth the moment its riddle is solved.
There is as little likelihood of the Egyptian problem
rapidly and for ever ceasing to cause discussion and
division of opinion as there is of the actual Sphinx
disappearing from view after having weathered the
storms of centuries and remained visible and imposing while the rolling sands of the desert have
covered other monuments of the past with oblivion.
The Egyptian problem has been more clearly defined
of recent years, during which the Sphinx itself has
been freed from the surrounding accumulations of
ages. It is of the first importance that any historic
puzzle should be distinctly presented to view. When
this has been done its solution may follow. I make
no pretension to solve the Egyptian problem, but I
hope in this chapter, as in others, to supply some

trustworthy details that may contribute towards making it understood.

Those who speak in the name of France, either as Frenchmen or French sympathizers, allege in writing or speech : ' Let Great Britain cease to be represented in Egypt by her troops, and then the Egyptian question will no longer give concern, or any occasion for argument.' I hold now, as I have done from the first, that it was a mistake for this country to have intervened in Egyptian affairs either to enforce the claims of usurious creditors or to defeat the predatory aims of Egyptians calling themselves Nationalists. International philanthropy is the most thankless of all tasks. A nation that cannot take care of itself, after it has been put in a condition to do so, does not deserve to exist. We lavished treasure as if it were dross, and blood as if it were water, to restore freedom to Spain and to seat a Bourbon king upon the throne of France, and in both cases our conduct was maligned.

Since British troops have been quartered in Egypt, and the representatives of Great Britain have exercised an influence over the Government, a new condition of things has arisen, and the real problem now consists in determining the degree in which the British occupation is beneficial to the Egyptian people while they are undergoing training for independence.

The result of an examination of the working of the Government may supply the answer to a question which merits serious attention, and I purpose setting forth a series of facts upon which a decision can be based. At present it is sufficient to state that the opinions which are current among those who are ignorant of Egypt differ materially from the conclusions which prevail when time is given to study the country itself, to converse with the people and to ascertain their present state.

The views and position of Sir Evelyn Baring, now Lord Cromer, the representative of Great Britain in the Valley of the Nile, deserve respectful consideration. They are those of a man whose capacity is marked, and whose experience is exceptional. Few Egyptians are more intimately acquainted with their own country than he, are better qualified for understanding its needs, and are more in unison with its aspirations. Lord Cromer has had a wide personal knowledge of the people in many countries ; he has discharged official duties in the Isles of the Ægean and the West Indies, in Hindostan and Egypt. Mere sentiment never weakens or obscures his judgment. He does not delight in keeping the beaten path, or in repeating the platitudes that betray the absence of thought ; but he diligently seeks for the true path, or that which he accounts as such, and then he walks in it, while his views are as unhackneyed as his expressions.

Those who maintain that the withdrawal of the British troops from Egypt would simplify and immediately settle the Egyptian question should peruse what he has written on the subject with a candour which inspires respect. In a despatch to the Marquess of Salisbury, which was forwarded from Cairo in 1891, he wrote : " I have never, as your Lordship

is aware, been a partisan of a British occupation of
Egypt. Indeed, during my early connexion with
Egyptian affairs, I did all that lay in my power to
prevent the creation of a state of things which would
render any foreign occupation necessary. If, at this
moment, I thought the evacuation of the country
a policy the execution of which did not involve
risks which no prudent Government should run, I
would not hesitate to recommend its adoption. It
is because I am convinced of the serious nature of
those risks that I am at present unable to recommend it. Whether it would have been possible to
have avoided any foreign occupation of the country
may be a matter of opinion. This question, however, only presents an historic interest. As matters
now stand, I venture to think that the Government
and the people of England cannot lightly throw off
the responsibilities, which they have not willingly
assumed, but which have rather been thrust upon
them by the force of circumstances."

When the Egyptian problem is studied in Egypt,
it appears, as I have said, to be vastly more complex
than when discussed by the light of available facts in
London. New conditions have been created since a
British force occupied the country and British officials
were entrusted with high and responsible duties in its
administration. These officials have brought order
out of chaos ; they have rendered the country self-
supporting, though not yet self-governing ; and they
have succeeded in their tasks because they had
material support at their backs. The work is still
in progress, and it is far from completion. Shall it

be carried on, or must the labour be lost? That is the main question which demands an authoritative answer. No answer can be conclusive which is not based upon an attentive survey of the various issues, and a careful consideration of the opinions which are entertained by natives as well as foreigners.

Sir Donald Mackenzie Wallace records that Nubar Pasha has declared the whole question to be one of irrigation. Others, who do not speak lightly or at random, consider it to be exclusively a question of finance; others, again, hold it to be one of education; while the number is considerable of those who maintain that all will be well whenever a purely native Government is in office, and the Khedive is freed from the necessity of listening to good advice, and from the intolerable tyranny of being expected to follow it. By a native Government is understood a Government which is wholly Egyptian. One of the greatest difficulties I met with in Egypt was to define "an Egyptian," and I still despair of finding a formula which can defy criticism.

I affirm, however, without fear of contradiction, that many who contend there should be no foreign element in any administration which the Khedive might fairly form or direct, really mean to exclude from office such men of note as administrators and statesmen as Nubar Pasha, Tigrane Pasha, Jacoub Artin Pasha, and others who, though Egyptians by adoption or birth, are Armenians or Syrians by descent, and Christians in religion. In Egypt, as in certain other places, religion sets men at variance. Though Christians are no longer treated there as

dogs, they are as obnoxious as they have ever been
to the fanatical followers of the Prophet. The dislike
may not be publicly avowed, yet it is none the less
keen though latent. It constituted the power of
Arabi Pasha, nor did it disappear from the country
when he was exiled to Ceylon.

The existing Government of Egypt is a spiritual
and material despotism, tempered by a Charter
which has been scrupulously observed during the
British occupation. If the natural development of
the country should not be impeded, then the Valley
of the Nile might become the only part of the globe
in which representative government has been introduced and has flourished without the Koran being dis-
carded or ceasing to be revered. The experimental
institutions which the Earl of Dufferin sketched, and
Tewfik Pasha sanctioned, proclaimed, and obeyed,
may grow into a form under which constitutional
rule will be exercised Time is required for this
growth; at present the seed which has been sown is
slowly germinating. It is, however, a great feat to
have got the seed into the ground. Egypt to-day
is a country with a magnificent future; the Egypt of
a few years ago was a country bereft of aspirations,
and living upon the soulless memories of a great past.

A quarter of a century ago the late Edmond
About made Achmet the Fellah say that "the
Consuls dominate in Egypt. They have watches
by which the sun rises and sets." Each of the
seventeen Consuls, who were then a great power in
the land, had a single eye to the interests of his
countrymen; he did not concern himself about the

Egyptians so long as his countrymen were suffered
to trade in peace and to their own profit. The
sphere of each was wider or narrower, and he was
supreme within it ; but no Consul or Consul-General
could then exercise any control over those who
belonged to a nationality other than his own. At
present the Consul-General and Plenipotentiary of
Great Britain is the man who possesses the most
authority in Egypt, after the Khedive. In theory,
the present Khedive is as autocratic a ruler as
Mehemet Ali, the founder of the existing dynasty,
or as any other of his predecessors. It is scarcely
open to doubt that the country suffered owing to
Mehemet Ali being checkmated by the Powers of
Europe when his ambition to render Egypt an independent State was on the point of being gratified.
Those who talk about the Egyptians being suffered
to rule in their own country, and who also praise
what Mehemet Ali did for it, may not lay sufficient
stress upon the fact that he was a Roumeliote.

Mehemet Ali rose to wield supreme power in a
country where he was an alien, and he did so by the
display of an energy which is as undeniable as his
ruthlessness. Those who faithfully obeyed him
found favour in his sight, while those who thwarted
or offended him were executed. His methods for
maintaining authority in Egypt are antiquated, yet he
died as recently as 1849. The stream of progress
in any country may seem very sluggish to those
who have no data from which to determine its
speed. The current in Egypt may appear to the
unscientific observer to be as languid as that of the

Nile, whereas those who try to stem the Nile soon
learn that they had miscalculated in supposing that
there was no resistance to encounter.

Some facts are set forth in Sir John Bowring's
Autobiographical Recollections which serve as land-
marks by which to note Egypt's advance in civilization. He wrote that the state of society under
Mehemet Ali "is such that there is no law but
the law of violence, and every master beats his
servants. The Minister of Public Instruction gave
2,300 blows on the feet to one of his dependents,
who died the next day ; but he paid £45 to the
family and the affair was hushed up. I saw a
young man take off his sash in the street, throw it
round the neck of an old man, and nearly strangle
him in the presence of the lookers-on. The Duftur-
dar, in order to punish a smith who had shoed his
horse badly, ordered the shoes to be taken off and
nailed to the feet of the smith, which was done."*

Such occurrences as these send a thrill of horror
through many Egyptian readers at the present day,
while their fathers would have regarded them as per-
missible. They excited little surprise half a century
ago; other outrages, which are as grievous though less
revolting, were perpetrated with impunity within the
last twenty years. The late Khedive set his face
against cruelty to man and beast, and it is due to
him that practices which received no check under his
father Ismail are now extinct. Some men in authority
under Ismail were not more squeamish about in-
flicting physical pain than those who served Mehemet

* "Autobiographical Recollections," p. 186.

Ali. The poor and the humble were flogged without
mercy at the bidding of their superiors in wealth
and social position, this being done either out of
revenge or to extort money. They had no redress.
If they complained to any judge, they would probably be punished with another flogging for their
audacity and impudence. At present a court of
law will do them justice in the improbable event of
their having been the victims of illegal treatment.
In bygone days the witnesses who declined to answer
questions, and the prisoner who asserted his inno-
cence, were flogged by order of the judge to teach
them better manners. Any judge who should now
act in the like fashion would be summarily dismissed
and punished.

The substitution of the restraints of law for
arbitrary violence is not popular among the governing class in Egypt. No man, nor any body of men,
can be expected to submit without murmuring to
the loss of a privilege. It is not strange, then, that
the governing class should look askance at reforms
which have curbed its power and diminished its
influence. Old residents in Egypt have assured me
that the British occupation would be less disliked by
this class if so many reforms had not been made
since it began, and are certain of being maintained
while it lasts. This class regards the abolition of
the indiscriminate use of the courbash, or whip, as
having been dictated by exaggerated and unpractical
notions of humanity. The iniquitous *corvée*, or
forced labour, which rendered the poor still poorer
and the rich still richer, has been ended, despite

opposition from France; and, as might have been expected, those who profited by the compulsory labour of their humbler brethren are inimical to the Power through whose influence the change has been made.

While the great are no longer permitted to flog the poor, and while the peasant is no longer torn from his village and compelled to labour at public works without pay, the crusade which has been carried on against corruption in high places, as well as in the lower spheres of government, promises to achieve the desired result. Heretofore, Egyptians were not taught to regard bribery as an offence, and it is hard to make them understand that the giver of a bribe is damnified as well as the taker. It is very difficult to instil into their minds that good government is impossible if persons in authority can be bribed to do that which is contrary to their duty as servants of the State. They remember that Ismail had to bribe the Sultan of Turkey with £800,000 in order that his eldest son might succeed him on the throne. As all the Englishmen in the Khedive's service have set their faces against bribery in any form, the result has been that official work is more faithfully done than it used to be, while the servants of the Government are acquiring a self-respect in which they were formerly wanting.

Improvements in irrigation, upon which the welfare of the agricultural population chiefly depends, have not been always acceptable to the governing class. In olden days the rich and powerful could get an undue preference in the distribution of water, and the crops of the man of rank and wealth would ripen when those of his poorer neighbours withered. At present there is no favouritism in irrigation, while the country as a whole benefits by the new system. Yet the individuals to whom the old and corrupt system was a source of gain denounce the new one and its introducers.

Neither rich nor poor in Egypt care anything for sanitation. They are as indifferent to bad smells as any Italian or Southern Frenchman. Tell them that the death-rate of their cities will fall when the latter are properly drained, and they will display utter scepticism and express themselves as being quite reconciled to the dirt with which they are familiar, and to the mortality which they deem inevitable. The optimistic philosophy of the Egyptians is a part of the Egyptian problem. Those of them who are resolute predestinarians consistently fold their hands before the threatenings of Fate, and reverently bow their heads in the presence of the Angel of Death.

It is true that all Egyptians are not Muslims. Nevertheless, the attitude of the Copts and other Christians as regards hygiene does not greatly differ from that of the devout followers of the Prophet. They both drink polluted water without dreading typhoid fever; and they appear to consider it superfluous, or worse, to aim at prolonging human life by observing the laws of health. The reformer in Egypt, whether he deal with finance or education, agriculture or sanitation, has a dense barrier of prejudice and apathy to pierce before he can accomplish his task; and unless he be able to count upon physical support,

till a generation shall have grown up and accepted
the new state of things as a part of the order of
Nature, he had better relinquish his task at the outset.

A good beginning was made under his Highness
the Khedive Tewfik to solve in practice the Egyptian problem. He took an intelligent interest in
seeing his native land adopt the more civilized
methods of Europe. Fortunately, the advisers who
surrounded and helped him were at once more competent and disinterested than those who urged
Mehemet Ali to sanction many extravagant schemes.
Though not a constitutional ruler by virtue of his
position, Tewfik was gradually adopting and acting
upon constitutional maxims. He listened with a
favouring ear to the recommendations of Lord
Cromer, and he was the more inclined to do so
because the representative of Great Britain had an
armed force at his back.

The Sultan of Turkey solemnly undertook to
redress grievances in Armenia ; but years have
passed away, and the condition of that country is no
better than it was when the Treaty of Berlin was
signed and ratified. The British Ambassador at
Constantinople frequently reminds the Sultan of his
omission to fulfil certain stipulations in that treaty,
and he is told in reply that the matter will receive
careful attention. If he could speak with the authority of the British Envoy at Cairo, the condition of
Armenia would be improved instead of being merely
considered.

The French people who read the fictions in
French newspapers labour under the delusion that

Great Britain is not disinterested in temporarily
occupying the Valley of the Nile, and the French
residents in Egypt scoff at the idea of British
philanthropy being other than a jest or a cloak for
villainy.   They feel certain, perhaps, that their own
country, if in occupation of Egypt, would never be
chargeable with the weakness of acting in a manner
from which no great and direct advantage was
reaped.   Though a paradox in terms, it is true in
fact that the work performed by Englishmen in the
Khedive's service is contributing in a marked degree
to render the country more capable of self-govern-
ment.   Their example is a political education.   It
serves as an object-lesson.

The Egyptians as a body do not resent the
supremacy of a foreigner so much as other races
might do.   They have been cradled in misgovernment, and now that they are under a sage and
considerate rule, they must feel their condition to
be novel.   Since the days of the Pharaohs, the
Egyptians have not been masters in their own land,
and they have placidly borne the successive domina-
tion of Persians and Greeks, of Arabs, both from
Arabia and Bagdad, of Tartars, Circassians, and
Turks.   The control which Great Britain now
exercises is not that of a ruthless conqueror, but it is
that of a Power which holds that the best interests
of each country are bound up in the prosperity of
the other; a Power which will rejoice when it
succeeds in rendering the Valley of the Nile the
home of an independent and self-governing nation.
The trade and commerce of the country are open to

all other countries, and Great Britain neither insists upon, nor would she accept, exclusive favours. Despite free competition, however, Great Britain does not suffer from rivalry. Two-thirds of the Egyptian exports find a market in the British Isles, while one-half of the imports come from Great Britain.

Other powers have their schemes for solving the Egyptian problem, the most notable among them being Turkey and France. It is no secret that the Sultan of Turkey is jealous of the semi-independence of Egypt. If he could reduce the Khedive to the lower rank of Viceroy, he would think that he had won a victory.

The days have departed in which a Turkish Sultan can convert most of his wishes into acts, and the utmost mischief which the present Sultan can do to Egypt is to cause annoyance. He has done so by retaining Mouktar Pasha there as his Commissioner, and by attempting to limit the jurisdiction of the reigning Khedive. Mouktar has earned renown as a soldier, and he bears the illustrious title of Ghazi, or the Victorious. A shrewd observer, holding high office, remarked to me that Egypt is not big enough to hold both the Khedive and the Turkish Commissioner. So long as the latter remains, the greater will the need be for the British occupation. France, like Turkey, desires the British troops to leave Egypt, for the reason that French influence cannot be fully exercised while they remain. But there is no greater necessity for the Valley of the Nile passing under the rule of France than for its reverting to the rule of Turkey.

French residents in Egypt consider themselves
deeply injured by the fact that their country plays a
secondary part on the Egyptian stage. Their views
are faithfully represented in the newspapers printed
and published at Cairo in their native tongue. I
shall advert to these newspapers in a future chapter.
It will suffice for the present to quote two sentences
from an article which appeared in a number of *Le
Sphinx* in December, 1891, beginning : " The principal thing wanted is the evacuation of Egypt by the
English troops ; the corollary is the dismissal of the
Englishmen in the service of the Khedive." The
writer adds that " The Britannization of Egypt
cannot be effected without the presence of the 'red
and blue jackets' on the banks of the Nile."

By " Britannization " the writer apparently means
the introduction and maintenance of reforms which
have lightened the Fellaheen's burdens, which have
insured the fair imposition and just collection of taxes,
which have provided for the impartial administration
of justice—reforms which have contributed to change
the administration of the country from a despotism
which was almost absolute, and frequently cruel, into
a system of government approximating to constitutional rule.

In ascertaining and recording the opinions of all
classes in Egypt, I have not forgotten Talleyrand's
cynical advice : " Distrust first impressions ; they
are generally good." The more pleasing these impressions are, the greater may be the mistake in
acting upon them as if they were accurate and conclusive. There is no rashness, however, in affirm-

ing that the chief requirement of Egypt is a lasting
peace. Uncertainty as to what may occur in the
country's immediate future depresses the spirits and
hampers the energies of the truest Egyptian patriots.
Even French writers and French sympathizers
agree in recognising that diplomatic worry does the
country an injury, and they, too, pray that tranquillity may prevail, with the proviso that the golden
era cannot begin till they have had their own way,
and till France has "recovered" Egypt.

Mr. de Leon, then Consul-General for the
United States of America, wrote about the state of
the country in 1876, and said that " Egypt seems to
have been set apart by destiny as the battle-ground
of races, and so continues still."*

Since Mr. de Leon's day the changes which have
been wrought can scarcely be described in sober
language, the simple facts having the semblance of
romance. One of his countrymen, Mr. Edwin H.
Woodruff addressed a letter to the editor of *The
New York Nation*, which appeared in the number
for April 21, 1892, and in which his personal impressions of the present state of Egypt were recorded. I extract the following sentences to show
his views upon the problem which has been discussed in this chapter : " The reforms which
England has wrought in Egypt during the past
nine years are simply astounding. A looted
treasury, a disorganized and almost hopelessly
corrupt administration, a rebellious and cowardly
army, and a people crushed under unbearable taxa-

* "The Khedive's Egypt," p. 392.

tion, have in this short space of time, and in the face
of Oriental apathy and French obstruction, been
metamorphosed into order, plenty, and content.
This work of the English in Egypt is an achievement of which every Anglo-Saxon must be proud.
And yet there has been little romance in this restoration. It is chiefly a story of common-sense, honesty,
and straightforward hard work."

Does not the solution of the Egyptian problem
partly consist in continuing what has been begun?
The country has been wearied by the intrigues of
self-seeking competitors. Any sudden change would
now be mischievous. Interference from without is
to be deprecated above all things. There is no
danger of this if an intimation were made that it will
not be permitted. A little plain speaking may avert
many angry words and much hard fighting.   .

In future chapters I purpose setting forth in
detail the working of the administrative machinery
in Egypt. At present there is little friction or
waste of power, but can any expert deny that, if the
machinery were abruptly stopped or touched by un-
skilled hands, the result would not be serious
damage or an irremediable break-down? The presence of a British force warrants the hope that no
fanaticism at home or foreign intermeddling will
hinder the Egyptian problem from being gradually,
but surely, solved in practice. Should these troops
be untimely and inconsiderately withdrawn, chaos
might replace order in the Valley of the Nile; and
then the French would readily undertake the restoration of order and ensure its maintenance.

CHAPTER VIII.

MAKING BOTH ENDS MEET.

THE result of Sir John Bowring's investigations in
1837 and 1838 justified him in reporting to Lord
Palmerston that "Egypt has no national debt of
any sort. . . . No pecuniary charge upon time to
come has been left by the follies or necessities of
time gone by ; the generations are born released
from any claims emanating from preceding ones."
Judging from these words and comparing them
with those which have been written since they were
penned, it may be said without exaggeration that
Egypt has had a financial golden age. Her existing
condition is one of struggle and strife in certain
departments of finance. Egyptian rulers and administrators now consider themselves fortunate if
they can make their revenue balance the outlay while
doing justice to the country, and supremely blessed if
they can frame a Budget which shows a large surplus.

Some persons have argued that a huge national
debt is an incontestable public benefit. The citizens
of the United States of America were once able to
boast that their public debt was as gigantic as their
country, and they now boast, with the conviction of

exciting envy, that their public debt has been reduced with a rapidity which is unexampled in the
annals of finance. Everyone knows that the English
nation first borrowed money towards the close of
the seventeenth century, shortly after William III.
had become King by Act of Parliament. The sums
which were then obtained on the credit of the nation
were lent by those who gloried in belonging to it,
and the debt of the United Kingdom at the present
day, though very large, represents the sums which
have been voluntarily advanced by its patriotic citizens
when the country was considered to be in danger.

Till Said Pasha became Viceroy, the Egyptian
Government continued in the singular and happy
position of not owing anything. The engagements
which he had rashly contracted with relation to the
Suez Canal Company reduced him to as desperate
straits as Charles Surface. Having no portraits of
his ancestors to sell, he had to meet his obligations
by contracting a loan. Foreigners lent him what he
required, and did so upon terms which may fairly be
styled usurious. The Suez Canal, which is classed
among the triumphs of engineering, also holds a
high place in the annals of modern financing. It is
a work by which British commerce has benefited, by
which its shareholders have been enriched, and from
which Egypt has gained nothing as yet. In the
future, when the canal passes under the exclusive
control of Egypt, the monetary gain to the country
will be extraordinary ; but the present generation
has had to suffer in order that a future generation
may be unburdened with taxation.

Said Pasha took no thought for the future ; if he had done so he would not have signed the concession of the Suez Canal to Monsieur de Lesseps and his friends without having read it, and he would not have bequeathed to his successor a national debt of four millions sterling and floating liabilities of a still larger amount.   His successor, Ismail, the ex-Khedive, was not slow to copy his example in borrowing money at the expense of his subjects. He became ruler over Egypt in 1863 ; he was deposed by the Sultan of Turkey in 1879, and then the Egyptians were burdened with a debt of one hundred millions sterling.

The significance of the foregoing figures can be fully apprehended when a comparison is drawn between England and Egypt.   When the first Egyptian public loan was contracted, the revenue of the country was under five millions sterling; the revenue doubled before the final sum was borrowed by Ismail, yet half the revenue, being as much as it was when he became Viceroy, was required to pay the interest upon the public debt. When the revenue of England was five millions and the public debt fifty millions sterling, there was an outcry, of which Swift made himself the mouthpiece, that the country was irretrievably ruined.   In the short space of fifteen years the public debt of Egypt rose to an amount as great as that of England in fifty.   The creditors of England were her own sons ; the creditors of Egypt were foreigners.

While the money advanced by individual Englishmen to their country was not expended in re-

munerative undertakings, little had been squandered
on unpopular objects. The money lent to Egypt
was lavished as recklessly and foolishly as the portion of the Prodigal Son. When the day of reckoning
arrived, it was found that the creditors of Egypt,
whether Jews or Christians, could have given lessons
to Shylock concerning an infallible method for exacting the uttermost farthing.

The question has been repeatedly put, "Why
should many holders of Turkish Government bonds
have lost all their money while holders of Egyptian
bonds should have had the capital and interest
secured to them?"

No other answer can be given than that Turkey
is not Egypt, and that, while the European Powers
hesitate about meddling with Turkey lest she should
fall to pieces in their hands and a deadly quarrel
ensue about the fragments, they have considered
that Egypt might be taken in hand without detriment to any one of them, and with the probability
of money being extorted for the benefit of creditors.
Consequently, Egyptian bankruptcy has been averted,
while Turkish bankruptcy was tolerated. However
indefensible the original interference in Egyptian
affairs may be, the subsequent unforeseen and un-
intended advantages to the country have been great.
Egypt not only pays every creditor with admirable
punctuality, but does so at present without a cruel
strain upon the people. The country has been
partially regenerated as well as rendered solvent.

A circumstance commonly overlooked by those
who give a superficial glance at the matter is the

wide-reaching effect of the process which ended in putting Egypt upon her financial legs. The public debt, though crushing, was not the only great evil under which she groaned in agony. The Egyptians had been as great sufferers under Mehemet Ali, who never borrowed money, as they were under his grandson Ismail, who borrowed many millions. They were overtaxed when Sir John Bowring wrote the words to Lord Palmerston which are quoted at the beginning of this chapter; they are now less heavily burdened and harshly dealt with, notwithstanding that the country's indebtedness is nearly a hundred millions sterling.

The Fellaheen in the Valley of the Nile are sober and industrious; they have many virtues and but few vices, and when they are better educated they may become a model peasantry. It is improbable, however, that they will ever learn to pay taxes cheerfully.

There are countries in Europe, which are confessedly civilized, wherein an ignorant impatience of taxation is loudly expressed. It is not wonderful, then, that the Fellaheen should dislike a call from the tax-gatherer; but it is interesting to note that their natural reluctance in parting with money for a purpose which they were unable to comprehend was far stronger in bygone days.

Sir John Bowring gives examples of what occurred within his knowledge; similar cases cannot now occur. A public functionary told him of an instance where a Fellah was ordered to receive 100 lashes for non-payment of the land-tax, and who

declared, after they had been applied, that he had
no money. "Summoned again, he had 200 lashes
awarded ; and he still averred that he had no means
whatever of discharging the claims of the Government. He was sent for a third time, and 300 lashes
were inflicted ; but nothing could be obtained. A
fourth experiment was made, and 400 lashes were laid
on, when his extreme sufferings led him to promise
payment, and it was discovered that he had had the
money concealed about him from the first moment."*

Such a man as this and his comrades made it a
point of honour neither to serve in the army nor to
pay taxes, save under compulsion. Those who bore
torture without flinching, rather than hand over
money to the tax-gatherer, were styled heroes by
their friends and relatives. Formerly the Fellaheen
had this excuse for their obstinacy, that they were
dealt with unjustly, and taxed arbitrarily. One might
have to pay more than his share, and another less.
The tax-gatherers were tender towards those who
bribed them, and merciless towards those who did
not bribe. Mehemet Ali desired that all his subjects
should be righteously treated, but, like other auto-
crats, he was often badly served. His dependents
were petty tyrants, who copied and reproduced his
worst traits. The saying is attributed to him that
he had succeeded in bringing all brigands under
subjection to his will except the engineers and inspectors of irrigation. These oppressors of the
Fellaheen were as rapacious and cruel as the most
corrupt tax-gatherers.

* Report on Egypt, p. 47.

Such gross and disgraceful examples of mis-government belong to a past which is still recent, and which might be restored if the authority of Great Britain in the Valley of the Nile were not greater than that of any Egyptian ruler. The introduction of economy and method in the finances of Egypt has been followed by the prevalence of greater content and a better spirit throughout the country, and the Fellaheen, to whom the mere thought of taxation was hateful, now pay what is demanded of them without a preliminary flogging, and without murmuring more than taxpayers may fairly do by way of relief to their feelings. They now find for the first time in the long history of their sorely-tried country that the Government which imposes taxes also discharges duties. They receive a substantial return for their money. Their well-being is considered and advanced. Life and property are secure ; fields are irrigated in due season and without favouritism ; while saving is promoted by the knowledge that the possessor of money, honestly acquired, will be permitted to enjoy it in his own fashion. The interest on the public debt is regularly paid, without the country being absolutely impoverished.

Robbery in high places and low can no longer be practised by those who rule, and the equality of all taxpayers before him who is authorized to collect the taxes has led to an increase in the amount collected. The Budget has shown a surplus for several years, and the prospect of this surplus increasing appears to be bright. More satisfactory still is the fact that a substantial reduction in taxation has been made, and is but the prelude to further progress in this pleasant path.

I repeat that corruption of Government officials has been the chief difficulty with which the English administration of Egypt has had to contend. Where a bribe is taken, efficient service is seldom rendered. It may be true that in Turkey and Russia many servants of the Government must accept bribes in order to live, and it is quite certain that in Turkey and Russia the official who begins by accepting small bribes in order to get daily bread, ends by extorting large ones so as to enjoy luxuries.

Some of the bitterest complaints now expressed by Egyptians proceed from the mouths of Government clerks, who cannot understand why bribery should be discountenanced. Bribery under the guise of "backsheesh" was once as rampant in the military as in the civil service of the State, and its extirpation was one of the first duties of Sir Evelyn Wood, when Sirdar, or Commander-in-Chief of the Egyptian army. The following graphic account of the way in which Sir Evelyn Wood made his meaning clear is the best illustration which I can cite of the mode in which corruption was ended in the army. Eight years ago the Egyptian troops were paraded before the Sirdar. Having called upon a soldier named Ibrahim to step to the front, he said : " Soldiers, I am placed by his Highness the Khedive in command of this army. I intend that, except in matters of religion, it shall be conducted upon English principles. One English principle is that no man shall offer or accept backsheesh."

(Gasps of astonishment among the auditors at this simply revolutionary doctrine.) " Private Ibrahim, of X company, Y battalion, Z brigade, is it true that you paid an examining doctor £9 to be declared unfit ?"

The culprit murmured, " Yes."

" Is it true that you were, notwithstanding, con- scripted, and never received back your money ?"

Again an affirmative.

" Count over the money in that packet," throw- ing an envelope containing nine sovereigns at his feet.

There is much craning of necks among the soldiers. Ibrahim is evidently thought to be in luck ; the unhappy wretch himself hardly believes his good fortune ; but the money is picked up by a non-commissioned officer and counted, one, two, three, up to nine, into his hands, while his face gradually assumes a more cheerful aspect.

" Is that right ?" asks the Sirdar.

" Quite right," is reported.

" Then Ibrahim, private of the X company, Y battalion, Z brigade, is sentenced to twenty-one days' imprisonment for offering a backsheesh. For the future all such money will not be returned to the individual private, but will go to a common fund to be used as rewards."*

While bribery under every form and name has been prohibited by the existing administrators of Egypt, the term "backsheesh" cannot be said to have become unfamiliar. The first word an Egyptian child

* "Khedives and Pashas," pp. 253, 254.

learns is "backsheesh"; I have heard infants in arms
uttering it as loudly as their mothers. Edmond
About wrote some ingenious sentences to the effect
that asking for "backsheesh" was not begging.
The distinction which he draws is too fine for a
plain man's comprehension. Whatever may be the
character of the request, there is no doubt of the
fact that asking for "backsheesh" is a plague of
modern Egypt, and that taking it is one of its
curses. Since the British occupation, those in
authority have begun to set a good example to those
who are beneath them, and when the vile habit of
offering or accepting "backsheesh" shall have
entirely ceased in the military and civil service of
the Khedive, the time may not be far distant when
it will no longer be a custom of the country.

The Government departments in Egypt were un-
necessarily costly, as well as utterly inefficient, when
English administrators undertook their re-organiza-
tion. Every office was overmanned. While the
Dual Control lasted the scandal was at its height,
and Sir Donald Mackenzie Wallace enables us to
understand how badly served the country then was.
After the Dual Control ended, and when Great
Britain assumed the sole responsibility for the
administration of Egyptian affairs, it was found
necessary, on re-organizing the small department of
the Cadastral Survey, to "dismiss about eighty
officials who were utterly useless, and who were for
the most part foreigners."[*]

Writing some years later, Mr. Moberly Bell

* "Egypt and the Egyptian Question," p. 133.

quotes figures to show that the number of Government officials was nearly 30,000, whose salaries amounted to £1,550,000.

This implies that two per cent. of the male population were Government servants. In the United Kingdom the number is 1,000 less than in Egypt, though the population of the United Kingdom is five times greater. It may be stated, then, that the cost of administering Egypt a few years ago was 4s. 6d. per head, while in Great Britain in was 2s. 4d. Should a comparison be made with India, the difference would be more marked, as the cost there is 1s. 1d. only.*

Lord Dufferin reported to Earl Granville that if one-third of the natives in the Egyptian Civil Service " were dismissed to-morrow, the work of the ministries they encumber would be all the more efficiently performed." He was not blind to the scandal of some departments in which Europeans found places and salaries without doing anything in return to justify their employment. He expressly mentioned the Treasury of the Public Debt as a comparative sinecure which caused irritation in the public mind, and which does so still, though nine years have elapsed since he wrote. This department is simply an audit office, and a single auditor, assisted by a few clerks, could perform all the work. Yet there are six heads over this office, each representing a European Power, and each receiving £2,000 a year for his ornamental service. The staff costs £5,000 yearly, and Egypt, like another

* " From Pharaoh to Fellah," p. 96.

Sindbad, has to stagger under the burden of this
incubus. ·

Another instance of the impediments placed in
the way of the Egyptian Government relates to the
administration of the State domains. These domains
are hypothecated to the representatives of the
creditors who subscribed to the Rothschild loan.
They are managed by a commission of three, consisting of M. Bouteron, Mohammed Chékib, and
Mr. J. Gibson. It is generally believed that M.
Bouteron has his own way in the management, and
that neither his Egyptian nor his English colleague
thinks of thwarting him.   Anything more unbusiness-like than the management of the State domains
cannot be found outside of the island of Laputa.
The natural result is a yearly deficit which is veiled,
but not altered, by the phrase " insufficient revenue."

This corresponds to the phrase which some
debtors use when compelled to explain their
bankruptcy, " insufficient income."   The Egyptian
Treasury has to meet the deficit caused by the
unbusiness-like management of the State domains.
Another body, which is also international, but much
more practical, the Daira Sanieh, pays money into
the Treasury instead of taking it out.   The surplus
from the Daira this year is £38,000 ; while the
State domains show a deficit of nearly £140,000.

The difference of system in the two cases is the
cause of difference in the result. Upwards of 300,000
acres out of those under the care of the controllers of
the Daira are leased to tenants ; the controllers of
the State domains farm 70,000 acres, and the loss is

incurred by so doing. It may be asked, "Why does not the Egyptian Government interfere?" If the hands of the Government were not tied by irrational engagements, this scandal, like that relating to the Treasury of the Public Debt, would soon end. to the advantage of the country.

Complaints are frequently made in Cairo about the effects of the English methods which have been introduced into the Egyptian Civil Service. That service and the entire administration would be placed upon a more satisfactory footing if the innovations were greater and more thorough. All the idlers who have been dismissed from it are men having a grievance. In Egypt, as in France and the United States, an office under Government is sought with desperate eagerness and clutched with the tenacity of despair. The pay is small in Egypt, but the hours are short and the work is light, largely consisting in smoking cigarettes. A beginning has been made in reforming the Egyptian bureaucracy, but time and the exercise of a firm hand will be required to complete the task.

There is a prevailing desire among the intelligent class in the United Kingdom for Egypt being reformed and rendered self-sufficing and independent. To accomplish this object would be as noble and praiseworthy an achievement as any which Joseph performed for Pharaoh.

The reform can be effected, but the condition precedent is that the British occupation should remain undisturbed for several years. Evacuation may well follow the completion of the work, but reform cannot be effected simultaneously with evacuation. The improvements in the department of finance, as in other departments, have been wrought and are upheld because the presence of a British force in the Valley of the Nile insures the stability of existing Egyptian institutions. An Oriental country has never yet transformed itself; it may submit to change, but it does so owing to irresistible pressure from without. The danger in Egypt is that the marked advance which has been made, and which promises to be continuous, may be marred and permanently arrested by the injudicious withdrawal of the occupying force which has rendered it possible.

However gratifying it is to be told that progress has been made in rendering the government of Egypt at once purer and more efficient, it must be still more gratifying to have a voucher, and this I purpose supplying. Sir Evelyn Baring wrote ·as follows in his masterly report on the progress of reforms in Egypt, which was presented to Parliament in 1891 : " When I first came to Egypt, fourteen years ago, administrative corruption was almost universal. It would be no matter for surprise, and scarcely, indeed, a matter for just blame, that a large number of Egyptian officials were corrupt. . . . It is, I conceive, certain that administrative corruption has not altogether disappeared, but I have no doubt whatever that it has been greatly diminished. A trustworthy informant, who has exceptionally good opportunities for forming an opinion on the subject, writes to me : ' I think corruption is not one-fourth so great or extensive as formerly.'"

In the same report Sir Evelyn Baring stated that Europeans and natives had been placed on a footing of almost perfect equality as taxpayers in Egypt. The exception was that natives paid stamp duty, while Europeans were exempted from that impost. Since then the reign of privilege has been restored under pressure from France, and Europeans have again been freed from the obligation of paying a license-tax.

This is grossly unfair, and it is one of the many grievances which must be removed before Egypt can be contented. Why a Frenchman or an Italian, a Greek or an Englishman, should settle in Egypt, make a living by carrying on business there and go untaxed, is a question to which the only answer I have received is that, according to the capitulations, foreigners are exempted from taxation. If this be true, which I doubt, then the capitulations are anachronisms. It is as absurd to single out Europeans in Egypt for exceptional privileges as it would be to make them bear exceptional burdens.

The natives have a grievance of an agricultural kind which cannot easily be removed. They grumble because tobacco growing has been prohibited in the interest of the State. Imported tobacco is taxed to the extent of two shillings a pound, and the revenue benefits by smokers being compelled to contribute to the Exchequer. It may seem hard, no doubt, that a peasant must not grow tobacco though desiring to do so and looking forward to

being remunerated by the crop. In this case, however, the profit of the State is the supreme law. The
same reason has led to the same prohibition in the
United Kingdom. But the Egyptian Fellaheen
might find ample compensation in cultivating poppies.
Opium is as profitable as tobacco.

A certain number of Egyptians have a specific
and exceptional grievance as regards the way in
which taxes are levied. The most productive of
them all is the land-tax, which, as Sir John Bowring
pointed out, is the equivalent for rent. A dislike
to pay rent is as common as a dislike to pay taxes,
yet in all civilized countries both must be paid,
because they are the price of living in a well-
regulated community. Yet nowhere, save in the
Valley of the Nile and under the misgovernment
formerly prevailing, have farmers been forced to
pay rent for land which has disappeared, and to do
so under the penalty of being flogged to death.

In 1813, when Mehemet Ali ruled over Egypt,
a survey of the available land was made, and in
1867, when Ismail was Khedive, that survey was
used to classify land for the purpose of determining
the rate at which it should be taxed. It had been
forgotten or overlooked that some districts had
changed their aspect during the interval; that irrigation had rendered vast areas productive which
formerly were arid desert, and others, which once
blossomed like gardens, had become tracts of barren
sand. As a result, some possessors of fertile soil
paid nothing, while the unhappy owners of dry sand
were taxed as if they farmed rich ground.

The experienced and enlightened Englishmen who hold high office under the Khedive in the Department of Finance have set themselves to remedy this injustice as well as to lighten the pressure of taxation upon those who are the least able to bear it. While, then, the administration of Egyptian finances, as now conducted, assures the payment of all indebtedness, with the result of raising Egyptian bonds to the first place among investments, the material condition of the people at large has been marvellously improved. Sound finance and perfect justice have gone hand-in-hand since the British administration and occupation are converting Egypt into a State which may one day become a model among the minor States of the world.

The importance of the financial reforms which I have enumerated cannot be denied. No exception can be taken, I think, to the picture which I have given of their working. An unfriendly critic might remark, however: "Supposing all you say to be true, what reason is there for keeping soldiers in Egypt unless the annexation of the country should be intended? If the existing system be in as good order as you allege, why cannot it go on of its own accord?" Should the presence of a British force be an undoubted injury to Egypt, that force ought to be withdrawn. But to withdraw it and risk the collapse of what has been laboriously reared, and to do so for the purely sentimental reason that the French would then have less cause for jealousy of British influence, seems to me neither practical politics nor common-sense.

Before visiting Egypt and carefully examining on the spot the manner in which the administrative machine operates, I might have contended that enough had been done to help the country, and that it was better to conciliate France than to resuscitate its expiring credit and develop its natural resources.

I am now convinced, however, that our task is nobler and more necessary than I had supposed, and is not far removed from its beginning, though I am equally confident that, if its pursuit be continued in the prevailing spirit and with the same energy, the end will be glorious. As yet the administrative machine works through an artificial and extraneous impulse, the native motive power being insufficient to keep it in perfect order. Till European control, along with European methods of keeping accounts, came into play, there was utter confusion, as well as shameful corruption, in the Department of Finance. Order now prevails where muddle was the rule ; but the stricter system is not yet firmly rooted. The old plan has still many friends ; the innovations have as many enemies. Even in civilized countries vested prejudices die hard. They have countless lives in Egypt.

Much of the success which has attended the efforts of the Englishmen in the Khedive's service to place the finances on a rational basis has been due to the late Khedive's loyal support. He approved of whatever might benefit his people. He might have hindered progress out of pique or through ignorance. Happily for the country over which he conscientiously ruled, he displayed a single-

ness and honesty of purpose, combined with a rare
appreciation of what was best to do in given circumstances, which deserve remembrance and praise.

It is frequently asserted and generally believed
that the lavish borrowing of the ex-Khedive alone
brought Egypt to the verge of bankruptcy. The
truth is that Ismail's greatest blunder was to be
content with the terms upon which he obtained
money. He did not receive half of the millions
for which he pledged Egypt's credit. Baron de
Malortie has characterized his reign as one of
great projects, great results and large expenditure.
Though the expenditure was colossal, it would yet
have proved highly beneficial if it had been devoted
to fructifying objects, if public works, which increase
the general prosperity, had not been neglected for
others which cost vast sums and merely made a
great show. A judicious expenditure of public
money might have enabled the taxpayers to meet
the increased demands upon them, whereas much of
the money was squandered for the purposes of pleasure or the gratification of vanity, and the ex-Khedive
had to suffer the penalty of deposition for conduct
which was almost criminal.

A consequence of his maladministration of the
public funds was that various expedients have been
adopted to prevent the recurrence of such an evil.
During the time that the administrative machinery
was out of gear some plans were devised for putting
it in motion, and these have answered their purpose.
It now moves with less friction and more regularly
on the whole than before ; still, there are many parts

which stand in need of repair or renewal. Some
devices which were intended to aid its action have
proved to be hindrances. Several securities against
bad government are now obstacles to good government, and those who rabidly detest the British occupation are labouring to the utmost of their power in
maintaining these obstacles upright. What can be
more ridiculous than for the Egyptian Government
to have to obtain the consent of the Great Powers
before it can deal with a surplus? The creditors
are punctually paid, yet the superfluous and costly
members of the Treasury of the Public Debt insist
upon having two millions sterling under their control for a contingency which may never arise. It is
the interest and the desire of England that Egypt
should advance in the path of progress. The determination of some of the other Powers is to keep her
stationary.

Despite envenomed opposition, Egypt goes forward. Those who are grieved to witness many
shortcomings ought to be consoled with the proofs
of her financial stability. The Fellaheen are growing
richer. All true political economists are aware that
the increase in a country's imports demonstrates the
increased purchasing power of the people. In 1889
the value of the Egyptian imports was £6.748,000;
in 1890 it was £7,645,000; it exceeded £8,500,000
last year. What conclusively proves that the mass
of the people can now buy more is that the imports,
of which the proportionate increase is greatest, are
those which find a market among the multitude,
such as cotton goods, metallic articles, and coffee.

The administrators of the Egyptian finances have done more than make both ends meet, though they would have deserved high praise if they had done that alone.

The Budget shows a yearly surplus ; the people are no longer treated as mere tax-paying machines. The general well-being of the community is rising to a higher level. But one thing is needful in order that the distant future may be as much more glorious than the present, as the present is than the immediate past. This imperative requirement is the cessation of absurd demands on the part of irresponsible and sometimes ignorant politicians in Europe. It is highly discreditable that the Egyptian question should be an element in political struggles or inter-national rivalries, instead of being quietly left to the considerate care of men who have displayed alike their competence and their good-will in dealing with it. Those who have undertaken the work may repeat what the great Pharaoh, father of the Princess Meris who found Moses among the bulrushes, said to his God at Memphis : " We have cared for the land in order to create a new Egypt."

CHAPTER IX.

EGYPTIAN PUBLIC WORKS.

EGYPT is the home of gigantic public works. Some have made parts of the country among the most fertile on the earth's surface. Without them much of the rich red mud of the Nile, instead of fertilizing barren land, would pass away unutilized into the sea. These works vary in character as in object. While many of them contribute to human happiness, others are monuments of human vanity. Even those, however, which serve no useful end attract. attention and excite wonder. The spectator feels that there must have been giants in the days of their construction. The modern architect and engineer confess their inability to understand how the people of the country could have executed such imposing works with the crude appliances at their disposal. Visitors to Egypt are profoundly impressed with the rock temples of Abu Simbel and the grand Pyramids of Gizeh, but the Egyptians lay greater store upon the more prosaic undertakings which enable them to obtain several crops in the year, and make the desert yield cotton and sugar-cane, wheat and maize.

Among erections as grandiose as any contemplated by a Pharaoh, that which has been completed for damming the Nile at the apex of the Delta and providing water during the hot months of summer for irrigating a vast area which would otherwise pass out of cultivation is the greatest of its kind, and is the most fraught with benefit to that part of the country. The scientific men who accompanied Bonaparte suggested that the work should be undertaken, and Bonaparte sanctioned it. However, it was not till Mehemet Ali ruled over Egypt that the construction of the *barrage*, as it is commonly called, was begun.

M. Linant, a French engineer, prepared the plans. He estimated that the cost would be £1,550,000, and that, when finished, the *barrage* would enable 3,800,000 acres to be irrigated when the Nile was at its lowest. The story of what happened, after Mehemet Ali had ordered a beginning to be made, is succinctly told by Sir John Bowring. Preparations were instituted on an enormous scale for commencing what he styles "a stupendous undertaking, worthy the land of the Pyramids."

Two thousand acres of good land were encumbered with the quantities of stones which were collected. Twelve thousand workmen were engaged, and after an expenditure of £170,000 the works were stopped.*

Mr. de Leon gives particulars of what happened at a later period in connexion with an enterprise which Sir John Bowring considered to be "one of the

* Report on Egypt, p. 60.

greatest public works ever contemplated in Egypt."
He tells how the traveller who approached Cairo
by water from Alexandria used to be impressed by
the "sight of what seemed at once a turreted castle,
a bridge, and a breakwater across the stream. This
was the *barrage*, commenced by Mehemet Ali,
continued by Abbas fitfully, and abandoned by
Said." He adds that three millions sterling were
understood to have been expended before the incomplete *barrage* was left to become a ruin. Moreover, he states that "Said was so full of the idea
that he actually founded a city there, gave a three
days' *fête* on the spot, and struck off a silver medal
to commemorate it ; but the city stopped there, and
so did the works."

Mr. de Leon prints the following story which he
rightly calls "curious." It was told to him by one
of the French engineers employed on the *barrage*
by the Viceroy, Abbas Pasha. I shall quote the
story in order that it may have a still wider circulation : "Summoned by the Viceroy to one of his
desert palaces unexpectedly, the engineer repaired
with all speed to see him. He was at once greeted
with this suggestion : ' You are always troubling me
about your *barrage*,' said Abbas, ' and an idea has
struck me. Those great masses of stone, the Pyramids, are standing there useless. Why not take
the stone from them to do the work ? Is it not a
good idea ?'

"' Pull down the Pyramids !' stammered the
amazed engineer, aghast at the idea that his name
would go down to posterity in such a connexion.

"'Yes,' impatiently repeated Abbas. 'Why not? Are you silly enough to attach any reverence to those ugly, useless piles of stone? See if you cannot make use of them for the *barrage*. They have helped to build Cairo already.'

"The Frenchman made his salaâm and retired in despair. What was he to do? The obstinacy of Abbas was ever proof against argument, and he brooked no contradiction to his will, however extravagant the whim that prompted it. To refuse to carry out his orders would be equivalent to losing his place; to obey would, to his excited imagination, stamp his name with an immortality of infamy, as the destroyer of the Pyramids.

"Tossing restlessly on his sleepless bed all night, a bright idea flashed upon him. He would appeal to Abbas's avarice, to escape the desecration of the great historic monuments of Egypt. Taking a large sheet of paper, he covered it over with long rows of figures and calculations, and, armed with this, returned to the Viceroy the next day.

"'What is all this?' growled Abbas, glancing suspiciously at the sheet covered with what to him were cabalistic figures, and frowning darkly at the engineer. 'What rubbish is this you bring me?'

"'Highness,' was the reply, 'after receiving your orders to remove the stones from the Pyramids for the *barrage*, I deemed it my duty to make a rough calculation of the cost, and here it is.'

"'Well, well,' said Abbas impatiently, 'what do I know about your hieroglyphics? Tell me, what will it cost?'

" The engineer immediately named an enormous
sum for the cost of taking down and transporting
the stones ; and after some severe cross-questioning
from the Viceroy, who seemed suspicious of his
good faith, finally persuaded him to abandon the
design of pulling down the Pyramids ; sooner than
aid in doing which, he swore to me, he would have
resigned and left the service."*

The story as told by Mr. de Leon is correct in
all particulars with the exception of that relating to
the cost of the work executed, which did not exceed
£1,800,000, though these figures are large enough
when it is considered that they represent an outlay
which was wholly useless for many years. I shall
continue the story with facts collected on the spot,
and with the aid of an unpublished account of the
completed work from the pen of him to whom the
chief merit is due, Colonel Sir Colin Scott Moncrieff,
R.E., who for several years was Under-Secretary of
State in the Department of Egyptian Public Works.

Let me first explain further, on Sir Colin's authority, what the *barrage* is. It consists of a dam
formed of two bridges thrown across the Rosetta and
Damietta branches of the Nile, where they bifurcate
at the apex of the Delta. Gates, which can be moved
up and down, are fitted into the arches of the bridges.
When the gates are lowered the water in the river
is diverted from its bed into three canals, which
supply water for the irrigation of Lower Egypt.
There are sixty-one arches of 5 yards span in the
bridge over the Rosetta branch, and seventy-one over

* " The Khedive's Egypt," pp. 263-265.

the Damietta branch, the length of the two bridges
being 1,095 yards. The *barrage* was considered
serviceable in 1861 at a cost, as Sir Colin Scott
Moncrieff states, "of £1,800.000, besides the unpaid
labour of uncounted annual *corvés*, and whole battalions of soldiers." Yet the work was but partially
executed, extending to the Rosetta branch only,
where gates were fitted into the spaces between the
arches, the Damietta branch being left incomplete,
with the view, possibly, of seeing how far the Rosetta
branch would subserve its purpose. When the latter
branch was first tested, ominous fissures appeared
in the structure; some time later the whole
threatened to collapse, and in 1867 the attempt
to make use of it was abandoned. It had been
calculated that, when the intercepting gates were
lowered. the level of the river would be raised to
the height of 14 feet 9 inches. When the experiment was made with the finished part of the
barrage, the highest level of the water behind it
was not greater than 5 feet 9 inches.

The ex-Khedive Ismail recognised the great
advantage which the *barrage* would prove for the
Egyptian Delta if it could be rendered efficient, and
he applied to Sir John Fowler, an engineer whose
capacity is beyond cavil, for a technical opinion on
the matter. Sir John's decision was that, in order
to render the work efficient, £1,200,000 would have
to be judiciously expended.

Such was the state of things in 1883, when
Colonel Sir Colin Scott Moncrieff, whose success in
hydraulic engineering in India had been remarkable,

visited Egypt and was consulted by the Khedive as
to the condition and possible utility of the *barrage*.
Both foreign and English engineers advised Sir Colin
to leave the *barrage* to its fate.   They felt confident
that it would commemorate a magnificent failure.

The Minister of Public Works had decided that
it was hopeless ever to expect that the *barrage* could
subserve the purpose for which it was designed,
and, as the adjacent land would remain waste unless
water were provided, he had contracted with a
private company to irrigate the Western Delta
through the medium of water pumped from the river.
The payment agreed upon was to be £50,000 a
year, and the condition was imposed that the contract should last till 1915.   Sir Colin's advice was
asked as to whether it might not be wise to extend
this system of supplying water to the whole of Lower
Egypt at a first cost of £700,000 and an annual
payment of £248,550.

Sir Colin asked for time to consider the scheme,
and he resolved to examine the ruined *barrage* before
pronouncing a decision.   He made the examination
in concert with Mr. Willcocks, an engineer of marked
ability, who had acquired great experience in India.
What they both ascertained by careful examination
may be best put in Sir Colin's own words: " The
work had been so long neglected that timbers were
rotten, iron was rusted, there were no appliances or
tools, and attached to it there was a large establishment of superannuated and incompetent men who
for years had been doing little besides drawing their
pay."

The whole had been badly built ; the arches of the Rosetta branch were cracked from side to side, and the condition of the portion under water might be inferred from that of the visible structure. To all appearance there was ample justification for the advice to let the *barrage*, like many another thing in Egypt, go on its destined road to ruin. However, Mr. Willcocks determined, with Sir Colin's sanction, to make an attempt to save it from the destruction which seemed inevitable.

Plans were drawn up ; workmen were employed to carry them out, and money to the extent of £25,611 was expended, with the result that, in the spring of 1884, the surface of the water, when the Nile was at its lowest, attained an elevation of 7 feet 2 inches ; the canals were flushed, the irrigation was improved. The yield of cotton that year was the largest on record, and the General Produce Association of Alexandria publicly thanked the two English engineers for the remarkable and beneficial feat which they had performed.

The task of patching the unsound *barrage* was continued in 1885, and again the result was seen in improved irrigation. It was then resolved to continue the operations of repair and completion in a thoroughgoing fashion. Sir Evelyn Baring's urgent requests for financial aid were favourably entertained by the Great Powers, who permitted a loan of a million sterling to be issued in 1885 for irrigation works. Sir Colin Scott Moncrieff required efficient helpers as well as funds, and he found them among his old Indian comrades in the persons of Lieutenant-Colonel Western, R.E., who was appointed director-general of the new works, and Mr. A. G. W. Reid, who had been engaged upon the Punjaub canals, and who was now put in charge of the operations at the *barrage*.

Year after year the engineers continued their labours in the teeth of difficulties which would have daunted less energetic and determined spirits. The working season was short. While the *barrage* was repairing it was always in use, and this, as Sir Colin puts it, is equivalent to "mending a watch and never stopping the works." Still, there was un-interrupted progress, and in 1890 the task was accomplished. Great in itself, the triumph is the greater when it is considered that men of high scientific attainments had pronounced the restoration and finishing of the *barrage* impossible except at an outlay of £1,200,000. The sum expended when the end was reached was £405,170. If the cost of the temporary measures in 1884 and 1885, and some extras to give a finish to the whole are reckoned, the total does not exceed £464,000.

What has been the gain to Lower Egypt from this expenditure? The exports of cotton since the *barrage* was made to fulfil its purpose have been so much in excess of the preceding years that the annual return in money is equal to £834,732. Other crops have given a largely increased yield, and the prospects for the future are even brighter. This has been effected by raising the level of the water, at low Nile, 9 feet 10 inches. Sir Colin Scott Moncrieff purposes raising it to the height of

13 feet, and this means an enormously augmented supply to the irrigating canals, and the power of bringing under cultivation many thousands of acres which are now barren.

The canals, which had become useless, were cleared of impediments and rendered available for irrigation and traffic, and a new one, the Tewfikieh Canal, was constructed between 1887 and 1889 at a cost of £372,900, and formally opened by the Khedive on January 11, 1890. An undertaking quite as difficult and useful as any of those which I have enumerated was the regulation or training of the Nile at the part where the *barrage* is erected. If the river had been suffered to follow its own erratic course, the line of railway, which had been cut in three places during the floods, would have been swept away altogether, while the left flank of the Rosetta *barrage* would have been turned, and that part of the *barrage* would have been left high and dry. This catastrophe was averted by building massive stone groynes in the water, anchoring trees, and gradually diverting the current into its present bed. As a result of what has been accomplished, spurs where the water was forty feet deep are now four hundred yards inland, and surrounded with crops. When Sir Colin Scott Moncrieff sketched the history of the *barrage* he had to apportion praise to his principal associates, and he generously as well as truthfully remarked : " The credit of restoring the *barrage* belongs in the first place to Mr. William Willcocks, who showed the greatest courage and ability in dealing with a work known by

us all to be unsound and universally condemned."
He wrote, too, in high and well-deserved praise of
Colonel Western, whose health broke down, and
who was obliged on that account to leave the
Egyptian service; and of Mr. Reid, who returned
to India bearing well-earned laurels after five years
of very hard duty in Egypt.

Next in importance to the completion of the
barrage is its maintenance in a state of efficiency.
The prophets of evil, many of whom speak French,
have predicted its early collapse. I do not wrong
them, I think, if I say that they would have been
gratified if the work had never been completed.
That English engineers should have performed an
achievement which is admitted to be one of the
greatest in the modern history of Egyptian enter-
prises, and in a field of labour where French
engineers had suffered defeat, is galling to the pride
of the critics and opponents of English supremacy.

A year after Sir Colin Scott Moncrieff wrote the
document from which I have extracted many details,
he wrote another, wherein he could affirm that the
results of sufficient experience had confirmed his
most sanguine anticipations. It may now be maintained, without fear of any contradiction which has
facts for a basis, that the whole summer supply of the
lower Nile is intercepted at will by the controllers of
the *barrage*, and is diverted into several canals, none
of the fertilizing water flowing uselessly into the
Mediterranean. This means that engineering skill
has brought the Nile in Lower Egypt under subjection
to the service of man. It may be noted, to prevent

misapprehension, that the *barrage* has not yet had the effect of greatly adding to the cultivable area of the Delta ; but it has had the almost equal advantage of enabling the owners of land which formerly yielded one crop only to take two from it within the year. While the husbandman has benefited in the first instance, the traders have been benefited in as great measure in the second. The navigable canals are now as well able to subserve their purpose as those which supply water for irrigation. Vessels laden with merchandise can sail or steam from Cairo to Alexandria and from Cairo to Damietta at all times in the year.

Too much water, even in Egypt, is as great a calamity as in other countries. The absence of any water-way may end in the most fertile tract returning to the desert. An inundation will render it the despair of the husbandman. In olden days nations fought for what they styled the balance of power. Nature is always fighting for it. When Nature is beaten there may be peace, but there is certainly a solitude. The large areas in the Delta which were unproductive marshes almost equalled in extent those which were arid desert, and the problem of draining the marsh has involved nearly as much skill as that of watering the sandy wastes. Sir Colin Scott Moncrieff, and those working under him, deserve as much credit for their system of drainage as for their perseverance in making the *barrage* a success. In Lower Egypt and the Fayoum large tracts now yield good crops which, till recently, were salt marshes. Land which

is not a marsh may become water-logged, and, unless
the superabundant water be removed, no remunerative crops can be obtained from it.   Drainage, then,
is the concomitant of irrigation.   Last year the sum
expended in draining the fields of Lower Egypt was
£140,000.   The drains through the fields there now
extend to the length of 1,500 miles.

Two years ago Egypt might have been characterized as an extraordinary land through which one
of the great rivers of the world ran and in which
there were no roads.   It was then impossible for a
cart laden with agricultural produce to go from one
centre of population in the Delta to another.   Many
of the canals were not navigable, being exclusively
adapted for irrigation.   Nearly everything had to be
carried on the backs of camels.   Now the camel,
which is at home in the desert, is unfitted as a beast
of burden in the Delta, where the ground is soft and
slippery.   The inhabitants raise no objection when
called upon to pay rates for the purpose of making
roads, and a network of roads is gradually covering the Delta, to the great profit and unalloyed
satisfaction of all the dwellers in it.

A public work quite as noteworthy and beneficial
as this *barrage* remains to be constructed in Upper
Egypt.   There is a period of the year during which
the Nile is too high, and another during which it is
too low.   The *barrage*, as I have already explained,
is an artificial means for intercepting the current
when it is at its lowest point, and, by hindering its
flow, raising its level till the current flows into canals
on either side.   Another one of a different character,

but adapted for the same end, would intercept and store up the excess of water when the river is in flood. The rich red water of the Nile is a fertilizer as well as an irrigant ; it adds elements of the most productive character to ground which was unfruitful, while bringing existing soil into a condition for yielding its increase. At present the cultivated area of Egypt extends over 5,000,000 acres. If the prolific mud of the Nile which is held in suspension were carried by the water over ground which now forms a part of the desert, the cultivable area of the country would be doubled, and the prosperity of Egypt would again become equal to what it was in that remote past of which the extant accounts appear fabulous.

Should this be accomplished in the Delta the result would be owing to what had been brought about in Upper Egypt; indeed, the Valley of the Nile, from Wâdy Halfa to the Mediterranean, would then outstrip any part of the earth's surface in repay·ing the toil of the husbandman. The problem to be solved is not difficult, provided money be forth·coming ; the object in view would justify almost any outlay. Suppose the land in Upper Egypt and Nubia to be subjected to constant irrigation, the crops would be doubled, and perhaps trebled, each year. It is but necessary to mention this to enable anyone to realize the importance of the contemplated undertaking. In a report to his Excellency Mustapha Pasha Fehmy, President of the Council of Ministers, which Sir Colin Scott Moncrieff presented last year, it was stated that Sefi or perennial irrigation may be extended to the whole Nile Valley at an outlay of £8,000,000. However, as the government of Egypt is primarily conducted in the interests of bond-holders, any great scheme which would benefit the people must be put aside if its execution should involve a large expenditure. I repeat that, if but half the public money wasted by Ismail when he was Khedive had been judiciously expended in remunerative public works, the flourishing state of Egypt would have been the admiration of the world.

Though the English engineers in the service of the Khedive cannot do all the good they desire to accomplish, yet they are anxious to perform as much as they can, and, with that object in view, they have made elaborate plans for turning the Nile to the best account, at the lowest possible outlay, throughout a thousand miles of its devious course in an incomparable valley. It must be borne in mind that the year in Egypt has three seasons only : summer, flood, and winter. The last of the three is the one which strangers know the best and enjoy the most ; but millions of Egyptians have to live and labour in the country during the whole of them, and their lives, unlike those of winter visitors, are passed in constant toil. From the 1st of April to the end of July summer reigns ; the Nile is in flood from the beginning of August to the end of November ; and winter, or the temperate and pleasant season, begins in December and ends with March. The summer crops are cotton, rice, and sugar-cane ; the flood crop is maize ; while the winter crops are wheat, beans, barley, and clover. As Mr. Willcocks points out in the report to which I have already referred : " The winter and flood crops provide food for men and cattle, while the summer crop contributes to the capital of the country."

In olden days, and for centuries during which Egypt was the granary of Europe, no special trouble had to be taken to secure large crops of wheat, barley, and beans. It was sufficient if the fields were under water when the Nile was high, from August to December, for the land to repay him who sowed the seed when the flood subsided. He could count upon reaping a harvest at the end of April. But maize and rice would not germinate and fructify unless the land were specially irrigated ; while cotton and sugar-cane required irrigation also, and at the time when the Nile had fallen to the lowest point.

When the river does not rise high enough in Upper Egypt much of the land becomes *sharaki*, that is, incapable of bearing crops through lack of water. In exceptional years the loss to the exchequer from this cause has exceeded a million sterling, while the loss in average years is as much as £88,000. If the exchequer be such a loser, what must be the fate of the tiller of the soil ? Sir Colin Scott Moncrieff never ceased during his tenure of office to devise methods and execute works which shall protect both against such a calamity.

Lieutenant-Colonel Ross, to whom the duty had been entrusted of removing this hindrance to general prosperity, has proved to the satisfaction of Sir Colin Scott Moncrieff that, by a judicious system of canals, sluices, siphons, water-escapes, and weirs, even when the Nile has not risen to an average height, the whole valley through which it flows may receive a due share of rich mud-charged water. Provision is to be made for the distribution of the water, which is a point of the utmost importance, because, as Colonel Ross has pointed out, " where red water has been brought straight into a corner which has not enjoyed it, the yield is increased by upwards of 500 lb. of grain per acre, or, say, 8 bushels."

The works in progress throughout Upper Egypt, which will probably be completed next year, consist of many small canals, watercourses, and dams, remote from the river in several cases, and designed to give those who have been neglected heretofore the same advantages as their more favoured fellows have enjoyed. The total cost is estimated at £600,000, and Sir Colin Scott Moncrieff anticipates that when these works are completed, " the lands of Upper Egypt will yield their full crop, however defective may be the Nile flood."

The scheme on a grander scale for utilizing the Nile than any yet executed, which is now in contemplation, is mentioned in the two last reports on Egypt which have been presented to Parliament. It implies damming up the river several hundred miles above Cairo, in order that all the surplus water in it shall be turned to profitable account.

Mr. Willcocks, whose services in putting the *barrage* into a condition for answering its purpose, have already been set forth, was commissioned to examine and report upon the require-

ments of the upper Valley of the Nile, and to
suggest how they should be met. In his report
he states that, if summer irrigation were provided, Southern Egypt would return an annual increase of £4,170,000, whereof the Treasury would
receive £610,000. If the benefits of irrigation, other
than that which is due to high flood or laborious
pumping when the Nile is low, were extended to
Nubia, the cultivable area there would no longer
be represented by a fringe along the banks of the
river. The date-palms, which now number thousands, would then number millions, and the additional yield would be £800,000. Mr. Willcocks
considers that Nubia would have a great future if
this were done. He admits, however, that there
would be years of distress while the irrigation works
were constructing, though he considers that the compensation would be " years of prosperity and plenty
such as that miserable country has never known."

To effect these results the construction of another
barrage, or dam, across the Nile is indispensable.
Where to place it is a problem only equalled in
difficulty by the other problem of how to construct
it. I need not enter upon a critical examination of
the several projects. Suffice it to say that the site
which Mr. Willcocks originally deemed the best is
at Syene or Assouan, immediately above the first
cataract. One drawback was that if it were chosen
and the work executed, then the Temple of Philæ
would be submerged for several months out of the
twelve. The civilized world would resent the desecration of such a historic monument as this temple. Mr.

Willcocks takes a more prosaic view, and proposes to raise money for the work by selling the temple in detail to European museums. Half the value of the temple is in its site. I understand that this plan has been modified so as to avert the flooding of the beautiful temple. Another project is to erect a huge dam above Wâdy Halfa and below Sarras. It is held that a site superior to any other is at Dal, about seventy miles beyond the provisional frontier. If this prove to be as suitable as has been represented, then it ought to be chosen, even if doing so necessitated the resumption and extension of authority over the Soudan by the Egyptian Government.

Any account of the public works which have been executed or projected in Egypt since British influence was supreme would be incomplete which did not contain a reference to Mr. Cope Whitehouse and his labours. He is an American gentleman who, when studying the authors of antiquity, was inspired with the ambition to re-discover the ancient Lake Moeris, and who visited Egypt in order to ascertain how far his speculations could be verified by careful researches on the spot. His prolonged investigations confirmed him in the belief that he had made a great hit which might give him fame and the Egyptians food. Sir Evelyn Baring has frequently referred to Mr. Cope Whitehouse's discovery in official reports, and has intimated that his proposals merit careful attention. The plan which he desires to carry into effect consists in diverting the Nile, when at its highest level, into a natural depression in the desert, and forming a reservoir covering

25 square miles, from which many thousands of acres might be irrigated and rendered productive. He maintains that if his project were carried out, a new province would be formed in the Delta, and nearly half as much again be added to the cultivable area of Egypt at the outlay of a million sterling.

No reader of the documents in which Mr. Cope Whitehouse sets forth his views can fail to be struck with his ingenuity and earnestness. He is an American philanthropist of a rare type. I have been told that his project would have a still greater value in practice if combined with a comprehensive scheme which should include a reservoir at Wâdy Halfa or Dal and a *barrage* at Assouan. I pronounce no opinion as to this, preferring to remain neutral while the professors of the art of irrigation fight their own battles, which they will assuredly do with adequate pugnacity. When the projected engineering works are executed, the future of Egypt will be brilliant. Several years must elapse before they can be completed, and their execution would be postponed indefinitely if the existing condition of Egypt should be altered. At every turn of the story which I have to tell of the progress which has been made since the British occupation of Egypt began, I am obliged to repeat that external interference would mar her advance in prosperity and wealth. The facts which I have cited are authentic, being drawn in every case from official sources. It may be alleged, however, that personal and patriotic feeling may have had an undue influence over me in marshalling them, and may have led to my using them in such a way as to make a foregone conclusion plausible. If such a suspicion should prevail, I hope to remove it by citing the testimony of an observer, of whose personal acquaintance I cannot boast, and whose opinions I quoted towards the close of the Seventh chapter because they had the character of perfect impartiality. Till I read in *The New York Nation* the conclusions at which Mr. Woodruff had arrived, I was unaware that an American investigator was studying the nature and results of the British occupation of Egypt at the same time as myself.

Instead of giving any of these conclusions in a condensed form, I shall transcribe a significant passage from Mr. Woodruff's communication to *The New York Nation :* " A few instances of the economies effected by the English engineers may not be uninteresting. In 1885 at a cost of £5,000 for cutting a main drainage channel between the canals Tanah and Gabadah, 30,000 acres, water-logged and worthless from salt infiltrations, were reclaimed. In 1886 a new head channel was given to the Kurtamia Canal at a cost once for all of less than £2,000, thus saving an annual outlay of £1,500 for silt-clearance. The Samana Canal had been neglected for twenty years, and all the lower portion of the tract it should have supplied with water had been thrown out of cultivation, and was inhabited by a few Bedouins ; but a judicious expenditure of £3,000 on the canal brought back into cultivation 50,000 acres, and the deserted villages are all re-built. To clear the Sahel Canal of silt each year used to require 13,000 men working for forty days ;

but by a junction canal and a siphon, the canal now clears itself, or, in other words, by an expenditure once for all of £5,400, an annual saving of £7,000 has been effected. . . .

"A word must be said as to the character of these engineers who have been foremost in the redemption of Egypt. They have had to contend with vested abuses on every side, learn the spoken Arabic of the common people, and overcome religious prejudices and superstitions, which, as Balzac says, are the most indestructible form of human thought. While the French engineers always stayed in Cairo, each of the present irrigation inspectors travels over his district again and again, often on foot, suffering many hardships, and seeking the shelter of the humblest mud-huts, lest, by accepting the entertainment of the wealthy proprietors, he be suspected by the poorer natives of having been bribed. In Ismail's time the canals were first tapped for the estates of the Khedive, then for the Pashas and village Sheikhs, and last of all for the poorest natives, but now all are served alike. In times of scanty supply, the water is given in rotation to the land without reference to the owner.

"In former days a poor man was completely at the mercy of his rich neighbour and of the corrupt native inspector, who, unless bribed, would not open a sluice at the critical time for the crops. Now the poor no longer have to bribe for water; they have confidence in the English inspectors, and have learned that petitions will be listened to and wrongs redressed. The actual head executive officer of

public works is Sir Colin Scott Moncrieff; the
chief of irrigation works is Colonel J. E. Ross, who
knows every canal thoroughly, and something of
nearly every landowner in Egypt.   Of course these
public improvements are not a record of monotonous
successes.   There have been mistakes and failures,
but the errors were almost worth committing for the
sake of the candour, no less refreshing than astonishing, with which they are admitted in the official
reports.   Here is a sentence from Moncrieff's report
for 1886 : ' The dredging contracts have been altogether badly drawn up. a circumstance I regret
all the more that I am directly responsible for
them.' "*

I mean to add, after giving a few words of
explanation, the remarks made by Mr. Woodruff
on the abolition of the *corvée*, or the substitution of
paid for enforced and unremunerated labour.   Nubar
Pasha and Riaz Pasha, who are two of the ablest .
Egyptian statesmen, were in favour of abolishing
it, and contributed towards doing so.   But the
opposition was very strong even in official circles,
while French influence was used to hinder such a
great measure of justice and humanity as the substitution of voluntary and paid labour for that which was
compulsory, unpaid, and grinding.   However, the
change has been made, and the wilfully blind alone
deny its wisdom.   After describing the nature of the
corvée, Mr. Woodruff proceeds to say : " The English
set about to abolish this system, and to substitute

* *The New York Nation* for the 21st April, 1892, pp. 298, 299.

paid contract labour, but were met with a prophecy that wages would not bring the labourers, and only force could drive the Fellaheen to clear the canals. Nevertheless, the gradual suppression of the *corvée* was undertaken. In 1883, the amount of this forced, unpaid labour was equal to 202,650 men working for 100 days; in five years it had been reduced to 58,788 men for 100 days; and in December, 1889, the *corvée* was totally abolished, for the first time, probably, in all the thousands of years of Egyptian history."*

One thing which had been lacking for the due protection and proper use of the canals and watercourses was supplied in April, 1890, when the Egyptian Canal Act came into operation. In India, Italy, and other countries where irrigation is practised on a large scale, legislation provides for the many questions which may arise. The subject had been discussed for three years before the Khedive signed the Act which I have just mentioned. It has been found most serviceable in averting as well as in settling disputes. Its usefulness would be greater if it were universally enforced. Foreigners resident in Egypt refuse to be bound by it. Some who desire that Egypt should be exclusively governed by Egyptians speak and write on the supposition that such a result would immediately follow the evacuation of the country by the British troops. Many thousand foreigners would remain in the country, each of whom would contend that he was

---

* *The New York Nation*, April 21, 1892, p 299.

independent of the law of the land. An anomaly such as this would not be tolerated in any other country, and the influence of England will not have been exerted in adequate fashion unless, as I hold and now reiterate, the fair treatment of Egyptians by all foreigners be insisted upon as emphatically as the fair treatment of all foreigners by Egyptians.

CHAPTER X.

EDUCATING THE EGYPTIANS.

THE wisdom of the Egyptians has become a puzzle and a tradition. Young men do not leave Europe to acquire it, while many young Egyptians visit Europe in order to be enriched with its mental treasures. In modern as in ancient days, Egyptian children are taught to write and read; but teaching in the mosque schools terminates in the majority of cases when the art of forming Arabic letters has been mastered, and the memory has been stored with several chapters from the Koran. Those who can fluently repeat these chapters in after-life may become the wonder, and gain the confidence, of their fellows. Arabi Pasha rose to be Dictator of Egypt because he could string together verses from the Koran on the spur of the moment, and would continue reciting them till his listeners had been convinced or wearied by his incoherent eloquence.

In a worthier spirit, but in as arbitrary a fashion as Cæsar Augustus decreed that all the world should be taxed, did Mehemet Ali decree that all Egypt should be educated according to European methods. He nominated a council to carry out his wishes.

He was convinced that his efforts would lead to the regeneration of Egypt. Prince Pückler-Muskau records that he once said to him : "Some day my grandchildren will reap what I have sown. You know Egypt has once been the first country of the globe, and a shining example to all others. Now Europe has taken its place. In time, Egypt may possibly become again the seat of civilization."*

It was easier for Mehemet Ali to desire and decree that boys should be taught than to collect them together in schools. He instituted a conscription for school-boys as he had done for soldiers, and those whom their parents refused to part with were taken by force, and conducted in chains to their lessons. Fifty primary schools were established, in which the pupils were to number 5,500. All the pupils were boarded and clothed at the expense of the State, and they were allotted a sum monthly for pocket-money. These inducements may appear great enough to overcome any parental scruples, yet they were not sufficient to allay the fear of Egyptian fathers and mothers, which was not baseless, that, after their children had been taught in the schools, they would be retained in the Viceroy's service as soldiers.

It is to Mehemet Ali's credit that, while resolving the children of his subjects should be educated, he did not remain ignorant of the elements of education himself. He was forty-five before he could read and write ; but at an age when learning to do either

* "Aus Mehemet Ali's Reich," p. 189.

is a harassing labour he set himself to the task, and mastered the rudiments of instruction.

The progress in education, which began under Mehemet Ali and continued during the short reign of his son Ibrahim, was arrested by Abbas Pasha, the nephew of Ibrahim and his successor in the Viceroyalty. He was not a man of genius, yet he was inspired with an original idea. In consequence of it he ordered a general examination of the teachers, and their elder pupils in the schools of Cairo, to be held in his presence. The teachers, as well as the pupils, answered the questions which were put to them so badly that Abbas pronounced public education to be worthless, and commanded all the schools to be closed. During his Viceroyalty no other training establishment was permitted save the Mafrouza, in which young men were trained to enter the army as officers.

The national schools remained closed during the Viceroyalty of Said, his successor. Koenig Bey, who retained much influence over the Viceroy after ceasing to be his tutor, once appealed to him to re-establish the national schools. The Viceroy declined to grant the request, adding : " Why open the eyes of the people ? They will only be more difficult to rule " !

When Said was succeeded in 1863 by his nephew Ismail Pasha, the system of national schools intro-duced by Mehemet Ali was restored and extended. The teaching was chiefly in French, and many of the teachers were Frenchmen. In Mehemet Ali's day the best-educated Egyptians had been trained

in France.   He sent numbers of young men to France
at his own expense, and maintained them there till
they had passed through the curriculum of the
schools.   One hundred of these youths were
receiving instruction at Paris in 1834.   He hoped
that on their return they would impart their
knowledge to their fellow-countrymen.   When forty
of those whom Mehemet Ali had sent to France in
1826 returned to Cairo, he gave a private audience
to each, and handed a work in French to him, dealing with the subject which he had specially studied,
and commanded him to translate it into Turkish.
All these young men were shut up in the citadel
till their tasks were performed.   Their translations
were printed at the office which Mehemet Ali had
erected in Boulac, and distributed among the teachers
and pupils in the schools.*

When the national schools had been re-organized
by Dor Bey, a Swiss whom Ismail commissioned to
do so. they were soon crowded with willing pupils.
The views of the Fellaheen regarding the education
of their children had undergone a complete change.
The schools were no longer filled by means of the
conscription, and the spectacle ot mothers weeping
and lamenting over their boys being led away to be
educated was a thing of the past ; neither was it
easy to believe that it had ever existed.   As those
who distinguished themselves at school might rise to
high office in the Government, both parents and
children now regarded learning as most desirable.

* "L'Instruction Publique en Egypte," par Jacoub Artin
Pasha, pp. 72, 73.

The schools in which pupils were boarded, educated, and supplied with pocket-money became
overcrowded, and many had to be refused admission.

When Tewfik succeeded his father as Khedive,
the educational system was remodelled. The
State could not then afford to support many
boarding-schools in which no fees were paid, and
where the pupils received pocket-money monthly.
Parents were called upon to meet the cost of their
children's education. The charge made for boarders
ranged from £14 to £20, and for day-pupils from
£6 to £18. Bursaries or scholarships were instituted, and the pupil who obtained one was educated
for nothing. If absolute poverty could be pleaded,
the doors of the school were thrown open gratuit-
ously to a limited number of pupils.

The Minister of Public Instruction stated in his
report for 1886 to the Khedive that many parents
resented paying for the training of their children,
because they had themselves been educated free of
cost in the days of Mehemet Ali. Egyptian
children learn more than lessons at school. The
lives which they lead there are entirely different
from those in their native villages, or even in their
parents' houses in the older part of Cairo. They
become cleanly in their habits to an extent unknown before, and they partly do so owing to the
example of their teachers. Moreover, they have
the advantage of drinking filtered water, and of
learning that it is wholesome. The report mentioned above contains a paragraph to the effect that

the health of the pupils improves when the Nile
water which they drink has been filtered ; but they
are slow to recognise this, the popular belief being
that filthy water is preferable.

The system of exacting fees and making
gratuitous education the exception, which, as I have
said, encountered much opposition, gradually became
rooted in the minds of the parents, and was recognised by them as equitable. In 1881 the sum received
for fees was £2,323 ; in 1886 it had increased to
£8,794.   The report for 1889 shows the amount for
the year to have been £12,745.   Last year the
amount in round numbers was £20,000.   These
figures have an eloquence which would be marred
by comment.

It is not intended that the national schools
should be wholly supported by fees ; but it is considered fitting that the pupils who attend them, and
who, in addition to instruction, receive their mid-day
meals, should contribute towards the expense. The
actual expenditure must be met by a Government
grant. and the story as regards this grant is far
less creditable and instructive than that relating to
the payments made by the pupils. I may here
note that, when Tewfik became Khedive, remodel-
ling the public schools was one of the objects
dearest to his heart, and he gladly assented to
any suggestion from his Ministers which was designed to extend education and to increase the
efficiency of the existing system. The sum allocated
to these schools, with his entire approval, amounted
to £103,000 in 1883.

In that year the claims preferred by the Egyptian bondholders or their agents obtained precedence over those of the Egyptian children, and the sum of £35,000 was taken from the service of the schools and devoted to paying the exorbitant interest on the public debt. If anyone should suppose that the reduced grant was adequate, let it be compared with that which is not considered excessive in other countries. The population of Scotland is about half that of Egypt. In Scotland the Imperial grant for educational purposes is £700,000, the sum actually expended being much larger, the addition being derived from the produce of the local rates. Yet those who thought they were treating Egypt fairly considered £68,888 a year to be sufficient for the Department of Education. It may be alleged that it was no business of the bondholders or their representatives to inquire how the money was raised for the payment of the coupons, and I readily admit that evidence is lacking of any anxiety as to the existing or future well-being of Egypt having been shown by the bondholders, whose representatives compelled the Egyptian Government to find money in satisfaction of their demands. Following the evil precedent which was then set, the Department of Finance has continued to be as niggardly as it dared in meeting the just demands of the Department of Education. The sum provided for the expenditure of that department was £80,000 in 1890, £88,500 in 1891, and £91,000 in 1892. Nearly ten years have elapsed since the grant was £103,000. During the interval, the contributions on

the part of parents in the form of school fees have
risen from £3,000 to £20,000. This sum is paid
into the Treasury. If the proportion of fees now
paid be deducted from the sum now granted, it will
be seen that the contribution on the part of the
Government is £32,000 less than it was ten years ago.

Foreign interference with the disposal of the
annual surplus is partly the cause of this lament-
able result. Nevertheless, the present advisers of
the Khedive are chiefly responsible for the manner
in which public education is starved, and they deserve
some of the blame cast upon their predecessors for
thinking exclusively of the bondholders when the
sum required for the service of the public schools
was ruthlessly cut down.

Though responsible, the Khedive's present
advisers are not without excuse. They are unduly
hampered by arrangements which were made and are
maintained in the interest of bondholders who may
think that they serve Egypt by accepting Egyptian
money. It is quite possible, without impairing the
efficiency of the preposterous department which is
entitled the Treasury of the Public Debt, to save
£10,000, and the addition of such an amount to the
Budget of the Department of Public Education
would be an inestimable boon to the younger
generation of Egyptians. But the holders of sine-
cures in the Treasury of the Public Debt would
make a great outcry, and the representatives of the
Great Powers would refuse to help Egypt in econo-
mizing her expenses, if this rational proposal were
formally made. That splendid but unhappy country

has been crippled by those who formerly led her into extravagance, while those who would now guide her in the right path find their task almost insuperable.

I have mentioned the Treasury of the Public Debt as a department in which saving could be effected, and it is but one out of several which might be named. However, in that department, as in the others, the voice of France would be heard objecting to whatever Great Britain might propose, and the voice of Russia would chime with that of France. Indeed, discussion is wholly superfluous when the result is known beforehand, and the voting in the Treasury of the Public Debt is always four to two when the representative of England proposes anything. Should France or Russia make a proposal, the matter is discussed on its merits.

Meantime the Department of Public Education must do the best it can with the scanty means at its disposal, and what has been performed seems of good augury for what may yet be accomplished.

While the public schools in Egypt are adapted for communicating a sound and useful course of instruction, the Government considers it useful that selected pupils should have the further benefit of supplementary training in a foreign country. Most of these pupils proceed to France, as was the rule for their fathers to do in the days of Mehemet Ali. But a certain proportion may be sent to England, Germany, or Italy, should the parents desire it, or should the pupils themselves display special aptitudes for something that is best taught in one of the last-named countries.

In 1887, fifty young Egyptians were acquiring
knowledge in France. Half the number had all
expenses paid by their Government; the others
were maintained at the cost of their parents under
the supervision of the head of the Egyptian Scholastic Mission. The pupils who were subsidized by
the Government had to send monthly letters to the
Minister of Education in Egypt, containing an
account of their progress and experiences. In the
Minister's report for 1887 he informed the Khedive
that the pupils in France had visited Dieppe in
August of the preceding year during their holidays,
and enjoyed sea-bathing. Next year they visited
England, spent a few days in London, during which
they saw the sights, and then they went to Brighton,
where they passed their time in studying Arabic
and English, in taking walks, playing at games, and
bathing in the sea. This excursion is said to have
been both salutary and informing, and to have made
an excellent impression upon the pupils' minds. It
is pleasing to find it added that they returned to
France full of vigour and health, being well fitted to
resume their studies, and being charmed with the
novelties which they had beheld.

The business-like tone now prevailing in the Department of Education was strikingly displayed in
1889, when the character of the scholastic missions in
Europe was entirely altered. Seeing the readiness of
the heads of families to send their sons to Europe, the
Minister of Education rightly determined that, while
it was proper to encourage this spirit and to arrange
for the supervision of the young men during their

sojourn there, the Government should be absolved
from making sacrifices for their maintenance abroad.
Young. Egyptians now proceed to Europe at the
expense of their parents, and the Minister of Education cites cases of brothers in Egypt having paid
for the education of their brothers in Europe. This
is highly laudable, and it is a form of fraternal help
which would elicit special praise from Dr. Smiles.

From Mehemet Ali's time till now the favourite
European place of resort for young Egyptians has
been France. The existence of latent or overt
French sympathies among educated Egyptians is
not due to the mythical services of France to
their country, but to a liking for France which
has been naturally engendered by sojourning there
when young men. Tigrane ˋPasha, the present
Minister of Foreign Affairs, and one of the ablest of
Egyptian statesmen, owes his French ideas to his
education in France. He speaks French quite as
fluently and correctly as the tongue of the country
in which he was born, and of which he is a brilliant
representative, and far better than that of his
mother, who was an Englishwoman.

It is to be regretted that education is more expen-
sive in England than in France. If the cost of it were
not greater in England many more young Egyptians
might prefer it to France as a country in which to
complete their education. Several have made the
experiment, and they have had good cause to feel satisfied with the result. Five pupils were sent to England in 1887. Four of them devoted themselves to
the practical study of engineering and telegraphy, and

they returned home qualified to teach others what they had learned or else to act as engineers and telegraphists. The fifth went to Cambridge, where he studied law. The Minister of Public Education made special mention in his annual report to the Khedive of the valuable and unremitting services rendered by Messrs. Thomas Cook and Son to the young Egyptians who had been sent to England.

In 1889 three students of the Khedivial Training School for Teachers were sent to England to continue their studies at the training college which was then in the Borough Road, and is now at Isleworth. They were treated with marked favour, and they showed that they deserved it by distinguishing themselves when in the college, and by returning to Egypt with certificates of the highest class.

Germany has attracted a few Egyptian students, and Italy has done so also; but the majority of those who wish to be trained or to complete their training in foreign parts select France or England.

Before passing on to describe some of the other schools which deserve notice, I may state that a national school has been opened for the education of young girls, and that seventy pupils were attending it according to the last report of the Minister of Public Education. I have visited many of the schools for boys, but I can write about this one at second-hand only, and in doing so I cordially re-echo the hope of the Minister of Public Education, that it will become the starting-point of a system which may have far-reaching results.

The greatest innovation in the Egyptian national

schools is but a year old; it is due to the practical
spirit of Mr. Douglas Dunlop, their Inspector-
General. Jacoub Artin Pasha, the Under-Secretary
of State for Education, cordially encouraged it. This
consists in making out-door games a part of the
pupils' instruction at a time when the latter are
not engaged in the appointed curriculum. For an
Egyptian lad to play, or to see others playing,
football or cricket was an unknown sensation till
Mr. Douglas Dunlop afforded the opportunity, and
then it became a fresh pleasure. The result has
been gratifying. Lads who were regarded as too
listless to engage in physical exercise have developed
a marked liking for the games which are the delight
of schoolboys in America and throughout the British
Empire. Matches are played between selected
representatives of different schools in or near Cairo,
and those who take part in them cannot complain
that their comrades do not follow the games with
personal interest. Till Mr. Douglas Dunlop had
the courage and foresight to try the experiment, no
one had supposed that Egyptian boys resembled
those of other nations, and that they were as ready
to engage in muscular exercises as any healthy boys
in civilized countries. That their physique will
benefit by these games cannot be doubted by those
who know them. It has been their misfortune
hitherto to be treated as if the cultivation of their
intellects was the sole end of their existence.

This new departure, as the Americans would
phrase it, has been witnessed with disapprobation
by atrabilious critics. The most vehement con-

demnation of the new system has come from the
French teachers in the national schools.

Whether they consider cricket or football the
more objectionable cannot now be determined, my
own impression being that they detest both in equal
measure.   They have this justification for their attitude, that each game is purely English and is
unfamiliar to them.   The English teachers, on the
other hand, join their pupils in the playground amid
the undisguised contempt of their French colleagues.
Readers of French newspapers published in Cairo
are taught to laugh or sneer at the English teachers
in the national schools for introducing English
games, and for actually demeaning themselves by
taking part in them.

It would be a gross exaggeration to say that the
English and French teachers in the Egyptian schools
form a happy family.   If they display few outward
marks of antagonism, this may be due to good-.
breeding.   Their aversion for each other, though
most unfortunate, is not unnatural.   The instruction of the young is their primary duty ; but it is
impossible for them to forget that the glorification
of their respective countries is expected of them by
their countrymen.

Several illustrations of this attitude might be given,
and some would appear as ludicrous and discreditable
as the following.   A year ago prizes were offered by
the French and English residents in Cairo to the
pupils in the national schools who displayed the
greatest aptitude in the languages of France and
England.   The ceremony of presenting the prizes

was rendered as impressive as possible, the leading members of both colonies being present, and healthy emulation was promoted among the pupils. To the annoyance of the French, the increase in competitors for prizes was greater on the part of the pupils who had elected to learn English than on that of those who studied the language and literature of France. A year before these prizes had been offered by the English colony, the number of pupils who had voluntarily chosen to learn English was 66, whereas the number rose to 1,312 in the year that the prizes were instituted. The proficiency displayed was quite as remarkable as the augmentation. As many as 541 gained 50 per cent., and 533 gained 75 per cent., of the maximum marks.

This result excited much bad feeling in the French colony, and Jacoub Artin Pasha was overwhelmed with remonstrances. It being obviously improper for him to favour the French at the expense of the English, or the English at the expense of the French, he has suppressed prize-giving on both sides in the hope of ending recrimination. The real sufferers are the Egyptian schoolboys.

This case exhibits the greatness of the tension in the relations of the English and French in Egypt. Its actual effect will be trifling. A language lives and grows, not because prizes are given for its cultivation, but because it has become a necessity in the intercourse of the human race. A correspondent of *The Athenæum*, commenting on the occurrence of which I have just given particulars, remarks : " Apparently this puts both languages on an equality,

but in reality French will be restored to its old state
of preference, as its students will have the advantage
in the greater premiums of public employments."*

This is plausible, but it is not convincing.
Several of the worst rulers over Egypt spoke
French as if it were their mother-tongue ; several of
the ablest administrators of the present day speak
and write it as if they were native-born Frenchmen.
Some of the official reports appear in French, but a
larger number appear in English.   As a spoken language French has countless merits, and as a written
language it has incomparable beauties.   Those who
know it best admire it the most.   It is no exaggeration to say, however, as Macaulay did in the first
chapter of his *History of England*, that the
English tongue is " less musical indeed than the
language of the South ; but in force, in richness, in
aptitude for all the highest purposes of the poet, the
philosopher, and the orator, it is inferior to the tongue
of Greece alone."

The tongue of modern Greece is often heard in
Egypt, but those who speak it find that they must
speak English also if they would prosper in business.
I was impressed with what a Greek shopkeeper in
Cairo told me as the result of his personal experience.
He left his native land fifteen years ago, and after
many struggles he succeeded in establishing a shop
for the supply of the articles most in demand by
visitors.   In his earlier years he had to learn French
because the majority of his customers spoke it ; in
his later years he has had to acquire a knowledge of

* *The Athenæum*, May 28, 1892, p. 698.

colloquial English, because for one customer who now speaks French nine speak English.

Messrs. Thomas Cook and Son have done more to extend the use of the English language throughout Egypt than could be effected by the award of hundreds of prizes to as many proficient pupils. They employ thousands of Egyptians who must know English ; their Nile fleet carries many thousands of tourists every year who cannot have dealings with the natives unless English be spoken, and these influences, until arrested by some measure which would be equivalent to a revolution, must operate to render the English speech predominant among the foreign tongues which are spoken throughout the Valley of the Nile. The national schools, which are kept in a state of high efficiency owing to the unwearied and intelligent exertions of Jacoub Artin Pasha and of Mr. Douglas Dunlop, cannot fail to aid materially in civilizing the country. The next generation will live in a transformed Egypt.

A work might be written on the Egyptian schools. Within the limits of a chapter I can but give particulars of a general kind, nor can I do much more than enumerate the schools which best deserve notice. Besides the national schools there are several Government colleges, in which medicine, law, languages, and engineering are taught. One of the latest is the Tewfikieh College of Agriculture. Though but two years old, it has already shown that it fitly supplies a want in the land. To improve Egyptian agriculture is to render Egypt an incalculable service. The prosperity of the country

depends upon its harvests, and the methods of preparing and reaping the crops of grasses and cereals
in common use have not been improved since the
days of Moses.   On the contrary, the implements of
husbandry have deteriorated ; the ploughs which are
represented on the walls of the tomb of King Ti,
who lived five thousand years ago, being superior in
some respects, while resembling them on the whole,
to those which are employed at the present day.

The soil of Egypt stands in as great need of intelligent cultivation as the minds of the young Egyptians.   This was recognised by the late Khedive,
and it was at his special request that the Agricultural
College was established, the sum of £4,000 being
set apart for the purpose.   Suitable premises were
found in the outbuildings of the Gizeh Palace, the
palace itself having been converted into a museum
for the accommodation of the antiquities which were
imperfectly housed at Boulac.   There were hundreds
of applicants for admission when the college was
opened, in November, 1890, fifty-nine being selected
out of the number, the majority having completed a
four years' course in the national secondary schools.
The charge for board and education was originally
fixed at £12, and it was afterwards raised to £25.
Out of the fifty-nine youths who were students the
first year, no less than fifty returned in the second
to continue their training.

These students are the sons of landowners ; the
parents of six possess as many as 1,000 acres each,
while none possesses less than 100.   The subjects
taught them are twelve in number, embracing all the

branches of theoretical and practical farming, with the adjunct of veterinary hygiene. A farm of 300 acres which has been attached to the college is used for experimental purposes. Much of the prosperity of Egypt in the future depends upon the result of scientific investigations. The crops of cotton and sugar-cane which are now taken off the land exhaust it to a much greater degree than the crops of grain or grass which were reaped in the days of the Pharaohs, when the fertility of the soil was fabulous.

Unless fertilizers are found which shall counteract the drain upon parts of the land, the returns will fall to an unremunerative point. Mr. Williamson Wallace, the efficient and popular director of the college, and the staff of professors under him, are eager in ascertaining how to treat the land everywhere to the greatest advantage, and in communicating their experience to the pupils.

The experiment of founding this college has been successful, and the value of the instruction given is thoroughly appreciated. It is proposed to add another and a lower class, recruited from the primary schools, in which the pupils may be trained to become farm-bailiffs or stewards, or skilled agricultural labourers. In all countries where tilling the soil is the chief industry, an intelligent and instructed farm-servant is a treasure, and such a man would have a value in Egypt far exceeding what he might possess elsewhere.

No Egyptian Government institution is more practical in its methods, or has been more fruitful in results, than the *École des Arts et Métiers;* that is, the School of Arts and Handicrafts. This school was founded by Mehemet Ali, suppressed by Abbas, and reorganized after its re-opening under Ismail. The pupils who pass through a five years' course leave the school well qualified to earn their bread in any part of the world where competent wood-engravers, house-decoraters and painters, brass-founders and copper-smiths, iron-founders and tele-graphists, cabinet-makers and carpenters, painters and lithographers, are in demand.

The school accommodates 300 pupils, the majority of whom are boarders, and nearly every pupil pays for his treatment and training. They are not admitted without a certificate showing that they have passed through a primary school, and they must not be younger than twelve or older than fifteen. They cannot remain after the age of twenty. Each day they spend three hours in the schoolroom and seven in the workroom. Mottoes in Arabic, like the following, cover the walls : " The knowledge of a handicraft is an inexhaustible treasure." The pupils are taught music by way of relaxation, while an amateur fire brigade affords them instruction which is at once practical and recreative. I was much impressed with the general air of neatness everywhere, and with the comfortable character of the dormitories.

The lad who leaves his native village for this school learns for the first time to sleep in a bed instead of on the floor, to be cleanly in his ways according to European ideas, and to sit at table and eat his food in the European fashion. After five years have been spent under these conditions, the customs of his native village assume a different aspect in his eyes. He has unlearned primitive and rude manners while acquiring a handicraft.

Those who have passed through the course of the school with credit are presented with a diploma, and a certain number of those holding diplomas find immediate employment in the railway-machine shops belonging to the Government. A gratuity of £10 wherewith to buy tools is awarded to the most deserving pupil on leaving the school. The teaching in it appears to produce results rapidly. As many as thirty pupils left it in the course of a few months to fill situations which were offered to them, though they had not been pupils for a longer term than from a year and a half to two years. Sometimes, also, the pupils earn as much during their holidays as will keep them for the rest of the year ; in short, the benefits of the school are appreciated because they are real. A further proof of this fact is that applications have been made by the inhabitants of other towns throughout Egypt for the establishment in them of a school of arts and handicrafts resembling that at Boulac. A beginning was made a year ago to meet the wishes of the applicants by the foundation of a division in the school at Mansourah on the lines of the one at which I have described.

While all the schools and colleges under the control of the Government have made a progress during the last few years which is most gratifying, the work yet to be done towards educating the people is immeasurable. If Jacoub Artin Pasha and Mr. Douglas Dunlop had but adequate means at their disposal for giving effect to their ideas, the educational system of Egypt would soon be as comprehensive and praiseworthy as that of Germany or Great Britain, of France or America. Happily, the advance which has been made is so marked that retrogression is not to be feared in normal circumstances. Those who have gone forward to a certain point become ashamed to go back. The poorer Egyptians have learnt for the first time in their long and chequered history to value the education of the young, and they would now object, as they never could have dreamt of doing before, if the existing school system were not upheld and extended.

There is a university in Cairo which was founded in 975, where 9,000 students learn that the sun revolves round the earth, and other matters equally useful and correct. While those who pass through the Government schools and colleges never study · at the university of El Azhar, its graduates often attend these schools and colleges in order to recast and complete their education. Children are admitted to El Azhar. The majority of the students leave it at the ages of twelve or fourteen imbued with texts of the Koran, and able to repeat the Muslim catechism. At that university the world is still in the fourteenth century, and there, as in other universities during that century, theology is the chief study. Theologians are unprofitable servants in Egypt to-day. Artin Pasha justly remarks that a young man may consider he is sure of happiness in a future life by mastering the Koran, yet in order to live on earth he ought to become acquainted with the arts and sciences which successive Viceroys have introduced into Egypt.* The day may not be distant when a university shall be founded in Cairo which will be as worthy of the nineteenth century as El Azhar is of the tenth.

Even when the ignorant and prejudiced Abbas was Viceroy, some schools were kept open in Egypt at the expense of foreigners, and they were con-temptuously tolerated by him. Their primary object was the diffusion of certain forms of Christianity, and most of them contributed more towards in-stilling dogma than towards adapting the youth-ful mind to reason and judge for itself. Never-theless, the work was not barren in commendable results. It still continues, but some of the mission schools find it harder every day to compete with the national schools. The members of the many foreign colonies settled in Egypt naturally desire that their little ones should be taught in a school representing their own nationality. Hence, the existence of such foreign schools is not imperilled by competition on the part of those which are sup-ported by the Government.

In a history of education in Egypt an account of each foreign school would have to be given ; but in a sketch of the educational facilities which are now afforded, the salient features can alone be de-picted. Among such scholastic establishments, the most conspicuous and noteworthy are those belong-ing to the American Mission, which dates from the

* "L'Instruction Publique en Egypte," p. 110.

year 1854. The work of the American missionaries is chiefly supported by members of the Presbyterian Church in America. Their achievements are as impressive as they are creditable. They are due to the practical business sense of the Americans, as much as to their self-denying spirit and untiring zeal. Americans rightly recognise that a missionary or teacher is powerless for good unless he be a master of the language of the country in which he sojourns, and those who are commissioned to do duty in church or school in Egypt are obliged to qualify themselves for the task by acquiring Arabic.

I visited many of the American schools in the Nile Valley, and I frequently met an official in a Government post-office who had been educated in one of them. If the preachers and teachers are expected to converse fluently in Arabic, it is with the view of being better capable of imparting a knowledge of English. The children who pass through the American schools are proficient in the foreign language which is daily becoming essential to an Egyptian. The schools in connexion with the American missionaries number 108; the pupils number nearly 7,000. Among the pupils about 1,000 are the children of Muslim parents. It is an additional proof of the good sense of the Americans that no undue proselytizing is attempted in the case of Muslim children, the missionaries wisely holding that, if these children are rightly educated, the religious problem will solve itself. Much of the work of these missionaries lies among the Copts, who, though Christians in name, do not often differ for the better from Muslims in fact.

In conversation with the Rev. Dr. Watson in Cairo, who has had thirty years' personal experience of Egypt, with the Rev. J. R. Alexander, who has had an experience of fifteen years, and who presides over the admirably-conducted training college at Assiout, and with the Rev. C. Murch at Luxor, who has been ten years in the country, I learned many facts about the land and its people which no reading could give me, and which I might not have ascertained after residing there as long as any of these gentlemen. They are familiar with the workings of the native mind ; besides, they understand the wants and aspirations of the natives, and they can speak of the existing condition of things in the Valley of the Nile with a knowledge which is unrivalled and with an impartiality which is absolute.

In the opinion of those whom I have named, and many of their colleagues whom I also met, the improvements effected in Egypt during the last ten years are incalculable in value as well as extent. They believe that the country is not only prospering materially, but is better capable than it has ever been in living memory to receive the seeds of civilization. They hold that it is a mistake to believe that the evil spirit of fanaticism is wholly extinct, and they consider that, if the opportunity were afforded, a rising of the worst elements in the country might furnish a parallel to the excesses which have made the memory of Arabi Pasha detested by all humane men. In their judgment

the prospects of continued progress are most cheer-
ing, provided no radical change be made. They
hold, as all unbiassed and independent observers
must do also, that, when the native Egyptian has
had fair play and time in which to develop his
aptitudes under congenial conditions, the government of the Valley of the Nile by the dwellers in
it will be perfectly feasible. They expressed the
hope to me that the British occupation would continue meanwhile, and such an opinion from men of
their nationality and stamp has an importance which
cannot be controverted. They speak as men having
authority. They are entirely divorced from Egyptian
politics, and devoid of any other aim than promoting
the welfare of the interesting people among whom
they toil with apostolic zeal.

It is probable that, as a consequence of the
labours of these Americans to educate the Egyptians,
coupled with efforts of the Government to improve·
and increase the number of the schools, the independence of Egypt may cease hereafter to be merely
an aspiration. Moreover, British interference has
tended, and may still further contribute, to render
that country self-sufficing and fitted to play its own
part on the world's stage.

One of the few rational speeches made by Arabi
Pasha was delivered at Zag-a-Zig in advocacy of
a free school there. He told his hearers that,
before any native of Egypt came into contact with
Europeans, " he was content to ride on a donkey, to
wear a blue gown, and to drink water, whereas now
he must drive in a carriage, wear a Stambouli coat,

and drink champagne. Europeans were in advance of us. But why? Is it because they are stronger, better, or more enduring than we are? No; it is only because they are better taught. Let us, then, be educated, and the boasted supremacy of the Christians will disappear."*

The Christian nation whose influence now preponderates in Egypt can desire nothing more sincerely than that her mission should be brought to an honourable close by the Egyptians attaining a European and American standard in education, and becoming capable of conducting their own affairs in their own fashion.

"The Egyptian Campaigns," by Charles Royle, vol. i., p. 32.

CHAPTER XI.

EGYPTIAN COURTS OF JUSTICE.

LORD DUFFERIN wrote in 1883 that "the chief requirement of Egypt is Justice." He informed Lord Granville that he hoped, before leaving the country, to see it "endowed with a justice that shall be pure, cheap, simple, and rapid." He had good reason for desiring such a consummation, as at that time upwards of two thousand persons were awaiting trial, many of whom had been several years in prison, while six thousand civil suits were pending before the dilatory provincial courts.

The want of a rational system of law impartially administered had been a grievance of the Egyptians long before Lord Dufferin prepared his memorable report. The arbitrary will of a single man, cruelly put in practice, had usurped the place of justice between man and man. However, there had been an improvement several years before his arrival, and cases of a revolting character had become rarer. Few rulers after Mehemet Ali dared to act as Belzoni records that Mehemet's son Ibrahim did while Governor of Upper Egypt. When an unfortunate culprit was brought before Ibrahim, he asked a few questions, and then sent him to the Cadi, "this being the signal for taking the culprit to a particular cannon, to the mouth of which he was tied ; it was then fired off, loaded with a ball, so that the body was scattered about in pieces at a considerable distance. In the case of two Arabs who had killed a soldier, not without provocation, this Pasha had them fastened to a pole, like two rabbits on a spit, and roasted alive at a slow fire."*

Atrocious punishments like the foregoing were not regarded with as great horror by the Egyptians of a former generation as they would excite if per-petrated now. Even before Ibrahim succeeded his father the administration of justice had become milder, though not 'less summary. Sir John Bowring reported to Lord Palmerston that, "upon the whole, the common interests are tolerably well provided for," and he gives instances within his own know-ledge in support of this statement. When he was at Alexandria a European complained to the Governor of a robbery from his lodgings, and the Governor said that, as one man only could have committed it, and he was in prison, he did not believe the story. On inquiry it was found that the man had escaped from prison two days before. A search being made, he was apprehended and taken before the Governor, who exclaimed on seeing the man, "You committed this robbery !" The robber, fearing lest damnatory evidence might be forth-coming, and hoping to obtain mercy by confession, acknowledged that he was guilty. Thereupon the

* "Discoveries in Egypt and Nubia," vol. i., p. 49.

Governor simply remarked, " I have pardoned you four times before, it was all in vain, so go and be hanged." Sir John Bowring adds, " He went out and was immediately executed."

When at Cairo and conversing with the Governor, who was administering justice according to his lights, Sir John learnt from him the particulars of another case in which a noted robber displayed as philosophic a contempt for death as Socrates. This man had been frequently arrested and punished. Having committed burglary on a large scale, " he was again taken, and brought to the citadel.

" ' Now, what is the use of my perpetually punishing you ?' said the Governor to the robber. ' You always begin again ; you always get into some new scrapes. I must be more severe.'

" ' You are right,' said the robber ; 'it is no use to go on punishing me, I shall go on as before. With the blessing of Allah let me be hanged.'

" ' Inshallah, if God will,' replied the Governor, and the man was walked away, and submitted without a murmur to be hanged at the city gate."*

In his *Autobiographical Recollections* Sir John gives an instance of what happened to himself, and it may be gathered from it that the Oriental methods of doing justice are sometimes very comprehensive. He had visited the Pyramids of Gizeh, and, as he writes, " in one of the dark chambers I was robbed of the purse which I carried concealed in my sash. We had been followed by a crowd of Arab boys, and on my telling Selim Bey of the

* Report on Egypt, pp. 122, 123.

robbery he offered to hang them all on the spot so as to make certain of having punished the thief."

A scene at which Sir John Bowring was present is very curious, and the account of it cannot be made more attractive than in his own words ; it recalls, as he remarks, one of the most impressive events recorded in the New Testament.

" A man was brought before the tribunal in Cairo, being accused of burglary. There was an immense clamour in the court, and wild cries of ' Let him be hanged ! let him be hanged !' and the judge instantly condemned him, and ordered him to be conveyed to the gates of the city, to be suspended there. The judge inquired of me how such a criminal would be dealt with in England, to which I answered that he would probably be transported to a distant colony.

" ' And at what cost ?' asked he.

" I mentioned some amount that appeared monstrous to his imagination.

" ' And what, in your country, is the cost of a rope ?'

" ' A few paras ' (pence), I answered.

" ' Then I think,' said he, ' you must be great fools.' "*

From the days of Mehemet Ali down to those of Ismail there was no substantial improvement in Egyptian courts of law. Fewer gross scandals were made public, but instances of oppression and cruelty, in the abused name of justice, were then common.

* "Autobiographical Recollections of Sir John Bowring," pp. 187, 188.

The first Khedive was himself an offender ; but his
worst actions, as in the case of Ismail Sadyk Pasha's
removal, were veiled from the public gaze.   In the
absence of judges who were trained to discharge
clearly-defined duties, and of courts having a well-
defined jurisdiction, the simulacrum of law was administered at haphazard, excepting when the suitors
were rich or powerful.   The judge commonly sided
with him who had the longest purse and held the
highest rank.   Indeed, the judge was then as great
a terror to the innocent as to the evildoer.   I have
conversed with those who remember the days in which
justice was a mockery, and I have read what others
have put on record, but I know few things which
are more instructive than some passages from Baron
de Malortie's unpublished diary, written in 1881 and
1882.   They convey a vivid picture of the national
courts of justice in Egypt before their reform was
undertaken by English jurists in the service of his
Highness the Khedive.   One of the most influential
men in the country told Baron de Malortie that the
" Mudir is supreme, and, as there is no appeal, people
are afraid of bringing grievances before him.   Out
of fifty cases of murder and theft, not three are
brought to light, for as it is the custom to bring the
witnesses also in chains, and to handle them very
roughly, people are not particularly anxious to appear. It is most difficult to get an Arab to denounce
another Arab ;   they seldom   peach ;   torture   is
abolished by law, yet by *nefas* still constantly applied : bastinado and thumbscrew are pet stimulants
for opening the mouth of the Fellah.

"Only the other day one of Count della Sala's servants was horribly tortured, simply because he was suspected of knowing the whereabouts of an escaped female slave; and here I may mention that when a female slave escapes and gets her card of liberty she is immediately accused of theft by her late master in order to bring her to justice and get her tried. In this case the slave had belonged to the brother of the police doctor, and Count della Sala, the head of the anti-slavery department, after giving her a card of liberty, sent her to the house of one of his married servants to be taken care of; the next day he heard that his servant had been arrested and subjected to the thumbscrew—I have seen the mutilated fingers myself—and it required Count della Sala's official influence to get both his servant and the slave released, though he expressed to me a doubt whether he should be able to obtain the dismissal of the doctor and the magistrate.

"As to the bastinado, it is of daily occurrence. A short time ago a murderer was brought before the Mudir of X with fourteen witnesses in chains; not one of them would speak. The Mudir, sitting on his divan and smoking cigarettes, called on one of the witnesses. He advanced and crouched down on the floor. Nodding kindly, the Mudir said:

"'Now, friend, tell me all.'

"The witness swore the most sacred oaths that he had not seen anything.

"'Come, come, I know you were present; tell me all, my son.'

" Again the witness denied more solemnly than ever any knowledge of the case.

" The Mudir frowned. ' Nonsense ; speak out, you son of a donkey !'

" Third and still more vehement denial. The Mudir, turning smilingly to an official, muttered the magic word, ' Courbash.' The witness screamed, howled, implored, and swore he would tell every-thing. So down they settled once more. The Mudir called him again ' My friend and my son,' and the fellow swore again that all he could say was, he knew nothing ; and so they went on for more than an hour, until the bastinado finally opened the lips of the recalcitrant witness. He was only the first of the fourteen, and you may imagine, added my Pasha, the time wasted by our system of paternal cross-examination."*

The greatest vice of the system was the absence of judicial rules impartially applied by independent men in all cases. Those who acted as judges were the slaves of those in authority over them, while they could be bought by him who would pay their price. Sir D. Mackenzie Wallace gives an instance within his own knowledge of how the sub-Governor of a district acted in obedience to orders from Cairo, those who were aggrieved by his conduct being without hope of legal redress. At the time of the occurrence Arabi Pasha was in power. He wished for a supply of grain, and he ordered that grain should be collected. In one district the sub-

---

* " Egypt : Native Rulers and Foreign Interference," from the author's diary, pp. 86-88.

Governor had to apply the bastinado to the village Sheikhs before they furnished the grain which the sub-Governor forwarded to Cairo as a patriotic gift. When the Khedive was restored to his previous position of authority, the loyal sub-Governor caused the same village Sheikhs to be flogged again for having encouraged the insurrection through the medium of patriotic gifts.*

Mr. Moberly Bell, writing several years later, and doing so with an unrivalled knowledge of the country and people, said : " Except as regards Englishmen, there is no punishment for crime in Egypt. Natives, whether innocent or guilty, are punished and acquitted according to the price which it is convenient to pay for either condemnation or acquittal."

The foregoing passage was penned after the International Tribunals had been established. They were the first courts of justice in Egypt which could be trusted to decide a case on its merits alone. Yet their jurisdiction is confined to civil causes and to those in which a native and a European are at variance. If a foreigner commit murder he must be judged by his Consul, and this form of consular protection is, as Mr. Moberly Bell tersely remarks, "synonymous with free-trade in crime."

Long before any change was made in the administration of justice the need for it was admitted. Even Ismail, who had no scruple as to the means employed in getting rid of those who were obnoxious to him, professed anxiety for the establishment of law courts on the European model. He thought,

* "The Egyptian Question," p. 107.

probably, that they would gratify his subjects, make a pleasing impression upon foreigners, and not hamper him in the slightest degree. He may also have hoped, as his astute adviser, Nubar Pasha, undoubtedly did, that when such courts were established the rights which foreigners in Egypt professed to have acquired under the Capitulations might be extinguished. In reality these rights were usurpations, but they had so long been tacitly acknowledged by the rulers of Egypt that foreigners might plead prescription in their favour.

Nubar Pasha was Minister for Foreign Affairs in 1867, when he drew up a scheme of international courts to which natives and foreigners should be subject. The French Ministry of the day withheld the assent of France. Lord Stanley, now the Earl of Derby, assented to it on behalf of England. Two years later the opposition of France was withdrawn, and delegates were appointed to represent Great Britain, Prussia, France, Austria-Hungary, Russia and Italy, on a Commission which met in Cairo under the presidency of Nubar Pasha, to consider the scheme which he had framed, and to agree, if possible, upon one that should be acceptable to the great European Powers.

Some progress had been made towards arriving at a common understanding when the Franco-German war silenced, amid the clash of arms, these proposals for legal reform. Before the Commission could be reconstituted and resume its labours, the Sultan of Turkey intimated his disapproval of what had been done or contemplated, assigning as a reason that permission to engage in such proceedings had not been asked by the Khedive. Both Great Britain and Russia sided with Egypt on this occasion, and the Sultan, yielding to pressure from their representatives, withdrew his objection.

After protracted negotiation, and after many changes had been effected in Nubar Pasha's first scheme, a general agreement would have been arrived at if France had not refused to be a party to it. This occurred in 1875, and then the Egyptian Government boldly intimated that should France persist, the Tidjaret courts would be closed, and French citizens in Egypt would find themselves deprived of legal redress for their wrongs. The threat sufficed, and the French Assembly passed a measure giving the sanction of France to the Egyptian International Tribunals. On New Year's Day, 1876, the first of these courts was opened in Alexandria. The date is also memorable in the annals of Egypt for the substitution of the Gregorian for the Coptic calendar.

There are four of these tribunals, one of First Instance sitting in Cairo, one in Alexandria, and one in Mansourah, while Alexandria is the seat of the Appellate Court. The design of their founder has not been fulfilled. Foreigners who assume that they are entitled to certain privileges under the Capitulations still assert them, and their claims are not rejected by the Egyptian Government. Seventeen Consuls contend that they have exclusive jurisdiction in criminal cases over the members of their respective nationalities, the result being, as I have intimated already, that when a foreigner, who is not a British subject, commits murder in Egypt, he virtually does so with impunity. Highly-paid judges, who are Belgians or Frenchmen, Americans or Italians, with some native colleagues who understand little of what goes on in their presence, listen to a French, an Italian, or a Greek counsel arguing a cause before the International Tribunal in which a few pounds are at stake between a European and an Egyptian. There is a great expenditure of judicial force and time, while the gain to justice is not a compensation for all the trouble that has been taken. If the International Tribunals had been comprehensive in their jurisdiction, they might have fulfilled all that was expected of them. As it is, they deserve the merely negative praise of doing little harm.

In the native courts the official language is Arabic. In the international courts, on the other hand, Arabic is but one of three tongues in which counsel may address the court, the other two being · French and Italian. The president of the court speaks French, whatever be his nationality, and the judgments are delivered in the French tongue as well as in the French method.

A small minority of the judges understand Arabic, and plaintiffs or defendants who understand nothing else must have their depositions interpreted for the information of the judges who are not conversant with the language of the country. This is but one of the many anomalies connected with the International Tribunals, and it is not the most absurd. The judges wear a broad sash made of parti-coloured ribbon, which passes from the right shoulder across the breast to beneath the left arm, a metal ornament depending from the lower end. This gives them the look of Foresters out for a holiday. Counsel appear in the robes and bands and caps which are worn in the courts of France or Italy. Those who practise must have been formally admitted to the bar of these tribunals. I could not learn that any Englishman had practised before them ; the counsel whom I heard in court were Frenchmen, Italians, and Greeks. The French counsel endeavour to introduce precedents from courts of justice in France, and the judges have much difficulty both in laying down and applying principles which are not borrowed from the jurisprudence of other countries. Indeed, these International Tribunals are hybrids, and they are destined, I hope, to be superseded by courts of a less heterogeneous character.

There is a comic side to the tribunals which Mr. Moberly Bell was swift to note when they were first established, and this he made one of their judges set forth in the following terms : " It requires the united intelligence of five nations to try every petty case. You see, the balance of power might be disturbed if an Englishman or Frenchman alone were to decide a question of five pounds between Ali Mahomet and Spiro Dimitri. So the other Great Powers must be represented too ; and Greece, because Spiro is a Greek, and Egypt, because Ali is an Egyptian ; and if Greece, why not Holland and Denmark ? And then consider the important interests of the United States !"*

* " From Pharaoh to Fellah," p. 25.

The statesmen and patriots of Egypt do not appreciate the comedy played by these International Tribunals. They unduly burden the country to a degree quite as heavily and as indefensible as the Treasury of the Public Debt. Seventeen foreign judges were appointed at the outset, England, France, Austria, Italy, Germany, Russia, Denmark, and the United States of America nominating one each, while Belgium, Sweden and Greece nominated two each, and Holland was permitted to nominate three. Ten of the judges were Egyptians. The European judges were rewarded for consenting to serve by being paid twice as much as their native colleagues, the salary of the former being £1,600, and of the latter £800.*

If these International Tribunals had taken the place of the seventeen consular courts, their existence might have become a benefit to the country; as it is, they are an extra expense without compensating profit. It is unlikely that these courts will continue to exist after the other institutions of Egypt attain the degree of perfection whereof they are capable. The country is learning to walk alone far more quickly than had been anticipated, and it would make still faster progress if the Great Powers and several of the minor ones did not combine and continue to keep it in leading-strings.

Four years after International Tribunals had been created, it was resolved to reform the native courts of justice. In 1883 Fakhry Pasha wrote to Lord Dufferin saying that a Commission having that

* "Egypt under Ismail," p. 182.

object in view was appointed in 1880; that its labours had been frustrated by events over which the members of it had no control, and that a second Commission had then formulated a scheme for the improvement of the law and its administration. The new code and the new form of procedure had been sanctioned by Sir Benson Maxwell, a jurist of large experience in India, who had been appointed to the responsible office of Attorney-General in Egypt.

The condition of Egypt in 1883, as regards the general administration of justice, is thus depicted by Lord Dufferin : " At this moment there is no real justice in this country. What passes under that name is a mockery both as regards the tribunals themselves and the *corpus juris* they pretend to administer. . . . None of the occupants of the Bench in any of the native courts has had a legal training, having been promiscuously selected from the general public without reference either to character or qualifications ; and there are no real laws in existence to guide their proceedings. At one time the French codes are invoked ; at another the regulations formerly in force before the old mixed tribunals ; and at another the precepts of the Mohammedan religion."

Though the design of the new code was to render the criminal law clear and just, yet the good intentions of its framers produced unforeseen mischief. A great difficulty had to be surmounted in criminal practice. Justice had been administered as if the accused must be guilty, and it went hard with any prisoner who could not bribe his judge.

Even when the prisoners were guilty of murder and the judge did his duty, it was often impossible to obtain a conviction. Mohammedan law required that two witnesses should testify to having seen the crime committed by the accused, or that he should confess his guilt, and unless either event occurred his life could not be taken. The witnesses who should refuse to give evidence were tortured till they told what they knew, or what was demanded of them.

In the absence of two witnesses, the prisoner was tortured till he admitted that he was a murderer. It was quite possible that the avowals wrung under torture were untrue, and it was also possible that evidence given by malicious witnesses might be wholly false. Provision was made in the new code for counteracting any such miscarriage of justice as might arise in the case just put ; but its framers were so afraid of being severe upon a criminal that they made his conviction almost impossible. Recent legislation has remedied this defect, and the spectacle of the perpetrators of notorious crimes, walking about their villages without anyone daring to lay hands on them, has now become impossible.

A code of law is not necessarily a panacea for all the judicial ills which may afflict humanity. A man may be ignorant of law, and yet he may give satisfaction as a judge. Such was the good fortune of Admiral Sir Basil Keith when he was Governor and Chief Justice of Jamaica. He understood seamanship, but he was ignorant of law, and he hesitated to accept an office for which he considered himself unfitted. He applied for advice to Lord Mansfield,

who was a friend of his family. His lordship's
reply was: " Basil, you have excellent common-
sense ; always decide according to that, and nine
times out of ten you will be right. But mind, never
give a reason for your decision ; that will infallibly
be wrong."

Now, the native judges who had to interpret the
new Egyptian code had the double disqualification of
not understanding its provisions, and of not deciding
fairly, according to excellent common-sense. They
had no training as lawyers, and they had no scruples
as men. They administered justice in view of the
longest purse, till the English occupation was followed
by changes in the administration of justice as well as
in other departments of the Government.

Even in 1884, when the native courts were recon-
structed, no general improvement was immediately
perceptible. The new courts which were expected
to exhibit an advance upon the old were established
throughout Lower Egypt only, the rest of the country
continuing to be burdened and harassed by corrupt
and ignorant judges.

Corruption often took the form of a refusal to
render a decision till the judge had received what he
considered to be an adequate payment. Those who
were poor had to submit to wrong rather than apply
for a judicial decision. It was accounted foolish
for a Fellah to go to law with a Pasha, and if two
Fellaheen were in litigation, the one who had a Pasha
as his friend was certain of success. This sad state
of things blighted life in Upper Egypt after the
dwellers in the Delta could go into court without

fear, and without having to rely upon bribes or the
support of a protector to win the favour of a judge.

The first change consisted in the establishment
of five Courts of First Instance in Lower Egypt, and
of a Court of Appeal sitting in Cairo. Never before
in the annals of the country had native judges been
paid such high salaries. The President of the
Court of Appeal received £1,200 a year; the Vice-
President £900; the other members of the court
receiving £720 each, and the assistant judges £540.
I do not give these figures with the expectation that
they will impress the minds of European readers.
Egyptians think them large, and they admit that the
judge who receives the smallest salary which has
been named can live in comfort and maintain a
family. The salaries previously paid did not exceed
in most cases £120 a year. Under-officials in any
Government department, who are underpaid, must
be angels of light if they preserve their integrity
unsullied. It may be doubted whether any angels
might not forfeit their characters if they had to provide themselves with food, clothing, and lodging on
grossly inadequate salaries.

No stronger testimony needs be given concerning
the popularity of the remodelled courts of law than
the application of the inhabitants of Upper Egypt
to have them introduced there after they had been
established in the Delta. It was as natural in the
circumstances that such a request should have been
made as it was proper that it should have been
granted. The new courts differed as greatly for the
better from the old, as the Nile in flood differs from

the Nile when it is scarcely navigable. A Nile that does not rise to a certain level means famine throughout the land. Courts of justice that do not rise to a certain standard entail wide-spread discontent; the old courts fell below the standard; the new attained it.

Corruption gradually ceased under the new system; while neither the prisoners nor their witnesses were publicly tortured at the bidding of the judge. A Pasha could not divert the course of justice. Equality before the law became the rule. Such was the condition of the reorganized courts at their best; yet every court did not deserve encomiums from the Minister of Justice. The inherited methods of procedure could not be exchanged in a day for others which were more logical and more humane. Judges of unquestioned capacity could not be created by decree. Torture was sometimes inflicted privately, despite express prohibitions; bribes were frequently taken, though they had been stigmatized as illegal. A trained and competent staff of judges is one of the highest, as it is one of the latest, products of civilization; and the Valley of the Nile, though prolific in food for man, does not yet produce jurists in abundance.

Egypt is a land which is as fertile in surprises as in food. Ten years ago the skilled observer would have pronounced it bankrupt; now its credit is higher than that of many European countries which boast of pre-eminence in Christianity and civilization. Two years ago the new judicial system appeared to be on the verge of collapse; now it is a model for lands which have enjoyed advantages during centuries such as modern Egypt has not known before. The great engineering feats which I have described in the Ninth chapter, and the noteworthy advances which I have recorded in the Tenth as to how the Egyptians are being educated, are now matched, if not surpassed, by the practical and splendid results which have been achieved in the department of justice since Mr. Scott became judicial adviser to his Highness the Khedive. Mr. Justice Scott had been previously one of the judges in the International Tribunals ; afterwards he was appointed to a judgeship in Bombay, and he returned to Egypt in 1890 with personal experience which profited him in the duties he was then called upon to discharge, these being to examine and report upon the native courts. Both experience and tact, combined with legal knowledge and freedom from legal prejudices, had to be displayed by him. In order that he might have the power of giving effect to the recommendations in his report, he was appointed judicial adviser to his Highness the Khedive in 1891, with the right of a seat at the Council of Ministers. Mr. Justice Scott found many native courts established throughout Egypt. In Upper and Lower Egypt there were twenty-three courts of summary jurisdiction. In addition, there were eight Courts of First Instance ; the cities in which they sat being Cairo, Alexandria, Bensha, Tantah, Zag-a-Zig, Beni-Souef, Assiout, and Keneh. A Supreme Court of Appeal sat in Cairo.

The Public Prosecutor's department was organized on the system which prevails in France and Scotland. The staff was large, consisting of ninety-five members and three heads of departments. Five branches of it were assigned to Upper and Lower Egypt. The Attorney-General presided over the whole, and an Advocate-General was under him. The salaries of the judges were liberal, without being excessive, ranging from £1,200 a year, which the President of the Court of Appeal received, down to £300, which was that of supplementary judges of the lowest class. The Attorney-General's salary was £1,560. Out of the twenty-six judges composing the Court of Appeal at present, seven are Europeans and four of them are English. Three Europeans are members of the Court of First Instance. These figures make it apparent that the native courts are formed chiefly of Egyptians.

It has not been easy, however, to find competent judges for the native courts. Before Mr. Justice Scott carried out his reforms, there was a drain upon judicial strength without suitors receiving due consideration. He took great pains, in the first place, to select and nominate suitable and trustworthy judges. Those who were notoriously unfit were removed, and their places were filled with men whose characters were unstained, and who had received a legal training. All these changes were effected in concert with the Minister of Justice. Summing up what he had accomplished in two years, Mr. Justice Scott states in his last report that thirty-three changes in the judicial staff have been made ; and that " the new judges, almost without an exception, hold a legal diploma, a very few having been admitted exceptionally on account of special capacity, in spite of their possessing no diploma."

In the second place, he set himself to stop the waste of judicial strength. He found that the most petty case, whether civil or criminal, was tried by a court in which three judges sat, one doing the work, and the other two looking on. He resolved to increase the number of courts, without adding to the judicial bench, and he accomplished this by appointing a single judge to preside over each court. He also conferred upon the provincial Courts of First Instance the power of hearing appeals when the amount in dispute was limited. Fellaheen who lived at Assouan, which is nearly six hundred miles from Cairo, could scarcely be expected to make the journey between the two places when a few pounds were at stake, and they had deemed it a grievance that the Court of Appeal was so far away.

The experiment of courts presided over by a single judge, which was first tried in Upper Egypt, was not popular at the outset. Suitors had grown familiar with three judges listening to their plaints, and they did not consider that one man could be as incorrupt and impartial as three. They ought to have remembered that in days which were not remote the courts composed of three or four judges made justice a mockery, prolonging the proceedings, unless they were bribed, and even refusing to deliver judgment, after the cause had been heard, till they had been bribed again.

On the other hand, some of the suitors appreciated the rapidity with which cases were tried and appeals were heard. Formerly, a case would be spun out for three or four years, which was heard and determined in the new courts within as many months or days. Moreover, the single judges were sent at stated intervals to the villages and towns where their services were required, and thus spared suitors from having to make a journey to their courts. This innovation gave great satisfaction. The best proof that public sentiment favoured the change was the fact that, several months after it had been effected, the inhabitants of Lower Egypt prayed that the system of courts with single judges might be extended to their part of the country, while a like petition was afterwards made by the citizens of Suakim.

The punishment inflicted in criminal cases had been vindictive rather than exemplary. Mr. Justice Scott rightly determined that the sentences should be apportioned to the offences. Till he did so, a simple robbery was punished with a minimum of five and a maximum of fifteen years' hard labour ; after he had made the change, the maximum penalty was three years' imprisonment.

When the new courts had been in operation a year, Mr. Justice Scott could write of them as follows with perfect truth : " These summary tribunals have been introduced very gradually throughout the country, but they are now thirty-three in number. The result is excellent. On all sides the people express their satisfaction. The law has been brought within reach of every subject of the Khedive, and the justice administered is both expeditious and good."

It would have been foolish and vain to expect that these courts, if left entirely to themselves, could act immediately without a trace of friction, or without a sign of failing. The machinery of a great ocean steamer is never expected to work without strain or fault during the first few voyages. After it has been thoroughly tested, and strengthened where a flaw is perceived, then it may be relied upon to continue in a trustworthy state. The time may come when the native courts of justice in Egypt will require no supervision, and will take a pride in upholding the traditions which they shall have inherited; but for the present they require careful watching, and for this Mr. Justice Scott has made ingenious and practical provision.

It was of primary importance that a judge who sat alone in a distant part of the country should be encouraged and complimented if he showed himself equal to his task, and criticised and cautioned if he failed to do his duty. With a view of ensuring efficient and recognised service on the part of the judges, a Supervisory Committee has been appointed, of which Mr. Justice Scott is the head, and upon which M. Moriondo and M. Grelle serve as members, Hassan Bey Ussein and Ali Bey Fakhri being attached to it as inspectors, and Osman Bey Mortada, who is a well-trained and most intelligent advocate, acting as secretary.

The functions of the members of this Committee cannot be better described than in Mr. Justice Scott's own words: " 1. They inspect all tribunals in turn, going into the provinces one week in every four. 2. Specimen *dossiers* [or briefs] chosen at random in every tribunal are sent to them weekly, which they examine and report upon to the Committee. 3. They receive periodical returns from all tribunals as regards the business done, and they report upon them to the Committee. 4. The Judicial Adviser, with an inspector, makes periodical visits to the tribunals, so as to see the work of each tribunal at least once a year."

Owing to the existence of this Committee, the judges have acted under a greater sense of responsibility. They are aware that if they shirked their duty the suitors would make complaint, and that if they performed it slovenly the Committee would advise them to mend their ways. The knowledge that they are subjected to strict professional supervision has proved a stimulus to exertion in the right path. On the whole, the new native courts did exceedingly well last year. The figures given in the last report of the inspectors are as gratifying as they are instructive : " Out of every 100 civil judgments, an average of 67 was accepted without appeal ; and of the 33 appeals, 29 were confirmed. Out of every 100 *délits* [misdemeanours], an average of 79 was accepted without appeal ; and of the 29 appeals, 11 were confirmed. Out of every 100 judgments in crime, an average of 40 was accepted without appeal ; and of the 60 appeals, 31 were confirmed, 20 were modified, and 9 reversed." Comments might explain without increasing the significance of these figures, and if it had been predicted ten years ago that such results could be obtained, the faith which implicitly accepted the statement would have been akin to that which removes mountains.

It is with a feeling of satisfaction as well as pride that I make a last quotation from the sober and measured, yet most creditable as well as conclusive, report of Mr. Justice Scott :

" I have confined myself to the broad lines of progress. The improvement is great. The law is clear, and may be known to all. The tribunals are free from arrears. Their agency is spread throughout the country. Government itself is liable to be sued for any abuse of power. The courts are no longer used as engines of private malice. The dread of arbitrary intervention is passing away. The poorest peasant feels that his rights and liberties are safe-guarded."*

I read this report after I had begun to write the present chapter. Though the notes which I made on the spot agree with all the statements in it, yet I have thought it better to quote from an official document than to print what I had written.

The general conclusions which Mr. Justice Scott has stated in the foregoing terms are wanting in one thing which his modesty would not allow him to add. It is chiefly due to his own exertions that the existing condition of the courts of justice is so gratifying. Since he has held the office of Judicial Adviser to the Khedive the change for the better in Egyptian law courts is marvellous. The judges have been animated to do their duty expeditiously, as well as conscientiously, while suitors no longer shun the courts on the ground that the delays are

* *The Times*, June 4, 1892, p. 6.

intolerable. A few examples will demonstrate the correctness of this statement.

The native courts were established in 1884; the number of cases heard and judgments rendered in that year was 22,695. In 1889, the year before Mr. Justice Scott's arrival, the number was 57,214. A year after he had stirred up the judges to greater activity, the figures rose to 75,894. The difference in the number of cases, between the first year the native courts were established and the first after they were reorganized, is 53,199. A few other figures will exhibit why more business could be transacted within the same period, and show that the waste of time had been grievous and disgraceful.

I turn to three criminal cases which came before the courts at Beni-Souef, Assiout, and Keneh in 1884, 1888, and 1889, and I find that, as regards the first, the prisoner was acquitted after his case had been under consideration for five years, seven months, and seven days; as regards the second, that it was before the court one year, nine months, and four days; and that the third lasted six months. Three cases of a similar character were tried at the same places in 1891, the first being determined in nine days from the date of the occurrence, the second in eight days, and the third in fifteen. I have collected statistics which would fill a page, and tell the same tale; yet those which I have given ought to suffice.

I visited some of the courts in Upper Egypt and the Courts of Appeal in Cairo, and I was struck with the business-like way in which the work was done in them all. No president of a European tribunal could display greater tenderness towards those brought before him than the President of the Court of Appeal in civil cases did while I was present. A family of villagers had succeeded in an action, and the defendant appealed. They had twice come before the court, and each time the defendant's counsel applied for a fortnight's postponement. This application was made for the third time, and the head of the family said a few words to the effect that staying in Cairo was costly, and that, having spent his money, he could not employ counsel. After a very brief consultation with his two colleagues, the President appointed one of the counsel in court to act for the family, and he ordered that their evidence should be taken on commission in their village. They seemed much gratified with this, and the wife first expressed a few words of thanks, and then went on most volubly to give her version of the case, till the usher was obliged to enjoin silence.

I witnessed a scene of a different kind in the Court of Criminal Appeal. In this court seven judges sit; in the court for minor appeals the number is three, and in that for more important cases it is five. The appellants in this case were nineteen men, being the principal members of two bands which had committed several robberies and many murders in Upper Egypt.

Four out of the number had been sentenced to death; the sentence upon the others was penal servitude for life. The proceedings were conducted on

the French model. The official who in England
and Ireland would be the Attorney- or Solicitor-
General, and in Scotland the Lord-Advocate or
Solicitor-General, was here the chief of the Public
Prosecutor's department, and he sat at the end of the
bench of judges. In the United Kingdom his place
would be among the counsel in front of the bench.
The difference is trifling, but not unimportant.

The particulars of the case were given by the
Public Prosecutor in a clear and detailed speech.
A minute narrative of the facts made it evident
that several persons had been murdered, that all
of the band in court had been active or passive
agents, and that the prisoners, of whose guilt
there was no question, ought to suffer death.
His speech was closely followed by each of the
prisoners, the ringleader, who was a Bedouin, being
particularly attentive. Two counsel appeared for
the appellants. One of them was the leader of the
Cairo Bar, a distinguished graduate of El Azhar
University, and reputed to be the greatest Egyptian
orator of his day. He evidently knew that he had
a hopeless task to perform. He spoke briefly and
to the point in Arabic of the purest kind. What he
aimed at was impressing upon the court that a
mistake might have been made, and that those of
his clients who had been condemned to death were
possibly no more culpable than the others whose
lives had been spared. While he spoke, the
Bedouin chief turned round and looked at him with
undissembled admiration, and, unless the expression
of his features was deceptive, he appeared to think

that he might be innocent after all. If it had not
been that the language spoken was Arabic, I should
have thought that Sad Zagboul Bey was Sir Charles
Russell slightly disguised. The resemblance between the manner of the two men was extraordinary;
not less striking was the similarity in manner and look
between the counsel who followed on the same side
and Sir Edward Clarke. This counsel was more
emphatic and rhetorical than his leader; his language
was less scholarly, and he did not produce as great
an impression upon the court. The unexpected
result of the appeal was that the court quashed the
death sentences, and pronounced penal servitude for
life upon the whole band.

The members of this Court of Appeal hold their
offices for life, or during good behaviour, while
those of the courts below may be removed without
notice or compensation till they have served for ten
years. The Committee of Supervision does not
concern itself with the Appellate Courts. This is
unfortunate, because the Court of Criminal Appeal
has manifested great weakness and dread of responsibility, often quashing the sentences of the courts
below, even when they were proper and just, and
had been deliberately arrived at. A strong judge
who knows the law and administers it without hesitation commands the respect of suitors and is
dreaded by wrong-doers, while a well-constituted
Court of Appeal respects and confirms his decisions.
In fact, appeals from him are rare, when it is found
that they are useless. But a capricious Court of
Appeal is a great misfortune, and its baneful

influence extends to sapping the self-respect of judges in the courts below. I insist upon this point, because it is the one failing in the native Egyptian judicial system. Till the Court of Criminal Appeal eschews false sentiment and does its duty, the country will be inadequately governed.

The International Tribunals and the native courts of justice are not the only courts which deserve notice, though their modern and unfamiliar character may cause them to stand in need of explanation. Yet the oldest court in the land, which is the Mehkemet Chareih, over which the Grand Cadi presides, likewise deserves a few words of description. Foreigners have no personal concern with it. The testimony of a Christian would be rejected if tendered. Those who sue for justice before the Grand Cadi are genuine Egyptians, and many of the suitors are women. The English court of justice most closely resembling it is the Court of Probate and Divorce.

The building in which the Grand Cadi sits is old, and is situated in one of the oldest parts of Cairo. The corridors and ante-rooms are crowded with men, women and children. Peripatetic vendors of edibles appear at mid-day with cooked food and round, flat loaves, and the suitors and the spectators take their dinners on the steps leading up to the court, or on the first landing-place.

Round a room leading out from that landing-place the scribes are seated writing out the judgments, which they hand to the suitors, the Grand Cadi or his deputy not delivering judgment in person.

I was honoured with an introduction to the Grand Cadi. He invited me to sit on the divan beside him, and there, in the intervals of conversation, I drank the inevitable cup of coffee and smoked the inevitable cigarette. He professed to be gratified that a member of the English Bar should have paid him a visit; I returned the compliment by saying, as I could truthfully do, that I had heard much in praise of his erudition from his countrymen, and that mine desired nothing more ardently than that he should administer impartial justice. He smiled, and assured me that to do so was the desire of his heart. I parted from him with a compliment in as Eastern a strain as I could devise; he replied with good wishes for my health and prosperity, and I left him feeling pleased that I had enjoyed an interview with the representative of an old faith and an equally old law, while he may have felt pleased that his reception of me was over. So long as the court presided over by the Grand Cadi continues to be one of the principal courts in Cairo, civilization in the Valley of the Nile will not make as rapid a progress as would otherwise be possible.

The present Khedive and his predecessor have shown anxiety that justice should be done to all their subjects. They have not sat in the judgment-seat as the Pharaohs did; but their names will be resplendent in the future, if the impartial historian shall write about their conduct as rulers in terms as flattering as those employed by Herodotus concerning the judicial conduct of Menkaura, the son of Cheops, who built the third pyramid at Gizeh in the year 3633 B.C: "His justice in the decision of causes was beyond that of all the former kings. The Egyptians praise him in this respect more highly than any of their other monarchs, declaring that he not only gave his judgments with fairness, but also, when anyone was dissatisfied with his sentence, made compensation to him out of his own purse, and thus pacified his anger."

Enough has been written in this chapter to show that an advance has been made towards civilizing the Egyptians. The progress has been faster than the most sanguine could have expected. The generation which is now at school in Cairo will scarcely credit, on attaining manhood, that Egyptian justice was once a mockery, and that the judicial bench was filled with men whose ignorance of law was a by-word, whose venality was a reproach and who prostituted their office without shame. That generation will have grown up while the law had been purely and competently administered, and will find it hard to believe that there ever was a time when such abuses were rampant as those which shall have been recorded in history. If the improvements in education are preserved, and the reorganized courts of justice maintained in their present state of efficiency, a new Egypt will serve as a model among Muslim countries, and afford delight to all who are best acquainted with the Valley of the Nile, and have sympathetically watched the development of its population.

CHAPTER XII.

PUBLIC OPINION IN EGYPT.

Is the modern and reconstituted Egypt which I have depicted in the preceding chapters, the Egypt which thousands of visitors from all parts of the globe behold with amazement mingled with gratification, a pure figment of my own imagination? Has the presence of British administrators and troops been a curse to the Valley of the Nile? Were the Egyptians happier when brutally flogged till they paid taxes which were unjustly levied, and when they were compelled to labour for others without remuneration? Are the finances in hopeless confusion? Can it be true that the improvements in irrigation are shams? Is it the fact that the young Egyptians are worse educated than their most ignorant parents, and that the new courts of justice are flagrant impostures?

Answers to these questions, and the explanation of any difficulties which they may suggest, ought to be found in the well-reasoned remarks of competent journalistic organs of public opinion. It is maintained by the people of any country which has ceased to be barbarous, that the journalists and reviewers with whose services they are favoured both express what is generally thought and contribute to ensure right thinking. Hence it was a pleasure, as well as a duty on my part, to seek for confirmation or correction, in the Egyptian public press, of the observations which I had made, and of the opinions which I had registered. I was delighted to find that Egypt has reached the enviable stage in a nation's career when it can boast of supporting several daily newspapers, many weekly journals, and some monthly magazines. I turned to them with the same interest that the traveller through an unfamiliar region turns to his compass to learn how the land lies.

Egyptian newspapers are among the most recent growths in the country. They are but a little older than the schools, the public works, and the existing courts of justice, yet they are still very juvenile, and some exhibit the worst faults of youth. Fifty years ago an official journal appeared in Egypt, at irregular intervals, when a Government decree had to be promulgated. It was printed in Arabic and Turkish. A competitor in French was styled the *Moniteur Egyptien*, and appeared in Alexandria between August, 1833, and March, 1834, at the cost of the Government. At present forty-six daily and weekly newspapers, one fortnightly and one monthly magazine are published in Egypt.

In Cairo the journals printed in a European tongue number eleven, and those in Arabic number seventeen. Three Arabic and eleven European journals appear in Alexandria, while Port Said has one in Greek, one in Italian, and two in French.

The *Bosphore Egyptien*, a French paper appearing in Cairo, is fourteen years old ; the *Egyptian Gazette*, which is printed in English and French, and published in Alexandria, is in its eleventh year. *L'Imparziale*, an Italian newspaper, is the youngest, the first number having been published in Cairo on the 1st of March, 1892.

The questions with which this chapter opens were suggested after a diligent perusal, during several months, of the French newspapers appearing in Port Said, Alexandria, and Cairo. I had read others in Italian and Greek and English, but I did not find in any of them the slightest reason for distrusting and reviewing my own impressions. Both the Greek and the Italian newspapers give more attention to commercial than to political matters, and their supreme desire appears to be that quietude should prevail in Egypt. According to them, the form of rule is comparatively unimportant. Many Greeks and Italians reside in Egypt to make money as rapidly as they can, and honestly if possible. Unless they are misunderstood and belied, their conduct would sometimes furnish texts for moral sermons.

Neither the large Greek colony nor the large Italian colony in the Nile Valley professes any dissatisfaction with the Egyptian Government of the day. Few, if any members of either, systematically libel the English, who keep the peace in Egypt and help to protect the Government from external interference.

In the *Bosphore Egyptien* for the 21st of January, 1892, there is the following reply to my question, whether the presence of English administrators and troops has been a curse to the Valley of the Nile ? " We see but a single category of individuals in Egypt that can hope to fish in troubled waters ; it comprises exclusively these pseudo-saviours who are crushing Egypt as they have crushed India ; these insatiable Budget-suckers who have gladly left their foggy country to recruit their stomachs and their purses at the expense of the Egyptian tax-payers ; in a word, they are the English who pre-sume upon the internal state of Europe to prolong their civil and military occupation, despite their ' solemn engagements.' "

What England has performed in Egypt appears to be of no permanent character, if beneficial, and of no lasting mischief, if injurious, provided the *Bos-phore* for the 4th of January, 1892, be correct in saying, " Might may be right for a time ; absolute egotism may triumph ; but neither might nor egotism strikes deep roots. Everything which England has established in Egypt, whether as regards the administration, the army, or the police, is founded upon sand."

When the *Bosphore* is most rabid in its language it is weakest in its logic. The following passage is strong even to fury ; it appeared on the 8th of January, 1892 : "Will the English occupation end, or will it be perpetuated ? We cannot tell, but it appears to us that the longer it is protracted the more disastrous will the consequent experience be-come for a nation which chiefly exists on remnants of the glory which was gained in days that are past and gone. The Colossus still imposes upon spec-

16

tators, though it is strangely shrunken, and one
would fain learn what extraordinary aberration makes
its 'statesmen' induce neighbouring nations to take
its exact measure."

Next day the same journal contained this passage, which does not appear to harmonize with the
foregoing : " The Khedivial authority which passes
into the hands of Prince Abbas is firmly established;
the security of the frontiers is absolute ; the finances
are flourishing, and the Egyptian people, including
the inhabitants of the lost provinces, are longing for repose, work, and peace. Hence, evacuation is more imperative than previously, and the country's moral and
material revival can alone be effected at that price."

I asked in the first paragraph of this chapter
whether the finances are in hopeless confusion, having
read in the *Bosphore* that the accounts of the War
Office are not audited to its satisfaction, and having
read in that journal and its French contemporary,
the *Sphinx*, that the surpluses of the successive
Budgets are fictitious, and that the deficits are systematically underestimated. Competent and responsible authorities have assured me that the pressure of
taxation would be reduced if it were not that French
opposition hinders the Minister of Finance from
dealing with the greater part of his nett revenue.
With this fact impressed on my mind, I read with
bewilderment in the *Bosphore* for the 14th of December, 1891, that " All the nations of Europe have
experienced and cursed the fiscal exactions which
characterized ancient Rome, while in Egypt, at the
present day, similar exactions impress an indelible

stamp upon the acts which the all-powerful English perform or suggest. The Treasury agents 'devour hamlets, cities, and entire countries,' and fill the huge strong boxes of the Treasury of the Public Debt; such are the men who cast to the lawyers— these other ravening dogs—the unhappy and insol- vent landowner, and who, with crooked fingers, tear the fruits of their toil from the working class." If I had read this passage in Europe I should have com- miserated the Egyptians; having read it in Cairo, I pitied the mental condition of the writer.

It might be thought that the public works in Egypt could be criticised without prejudice or heat, that engineering might be considered as being out- side of the political field. Anyone who has eyes can see these public works; anyone who has the faculty of calculation can estimate their value. It might be considered that they are substantial benefits con- ferred by Great Britain upon Egypt. The editor of the *Sphinx* is not as other men. He sees what suits him, and he draws the inferences which tally with his foregone conclusions. This is evident in the article which appeared on December 23, 1891 : " The period, which has been inauspicious for Egypt and the Egyptians for commerce and European interests in general during which the '*English* intrusion' has reigned supreme on the banks of the Nile, will be signalized by an exaggeration of the number, the diversity and chiefly the cost, of the public works which have been begun, com- pleted, or left in course of construction by the 'able Englishmen' who have forced their services upon the Ministry of Public Works. . . . Henceforth it is indisputable that large amounts of capital have been sunk in barren and abortive undertakings, such as the *barrage* of the Nile, the canal which was cut and filled up, bridges which were erected and demolished, canals which sterilized from the starting-point the soil that they traversed and flooded that wherein they ended."

The number of the *Sphinx* for February 7, 1892, contains an article which is entitled a manifesto from the natives of Egypt, in which it is affirmed that the accession of Abbas Hilmy, the reigning Khedive, ought to close the era of Egypt's gratitude to Great Britain. Four days later the view is expressed in the same journal that not the English troops only, but also the English officers in the Khedive's service, should speedily quit the country. The French press in Egypt deserves the credit of being as outspoken as it is unfair and inaccurate. The object aimed at is openly avowed, and the mere close of the armed occupation would not satisfy the French colony in the Nile Valley. The end in view is the expulsion from the country of every British subject holding office under the Khedive, and, so long as the occupation lasts, this fraternal design cannot be accomplished.

No distinction is made in these newspapers between any of the foreign advisers of the Khedive whose nationality is British. They are all hateful in the eyes of French journalists. I had thought that the most carping and censorious French critics would have admitted that Mr. Justice Scott had carefully considered their susceptibilities in retaining the forms of French procedure, despite his natural preference for the more familiar and excellent procedure in the courts of justice wherein he had been trained. He took the feelings of Frenchmen in Egypt into account, with the result of being attacked and slandered by French journalists. When illness overtook him. and his life was in jeopardy, the malignant attacks upon him were redoubled. A Frenchman in Europe plumes himself upon his good manners; in Egypt he often seems to compete for notoriety as a boor. After Mr. Justice Scott was able to leave the sick-bed upon which he had languished during several weeks, the *Sphinx* for the 12th of February, 1892, contained the following paragraph: "Mr. Scott, the Judicial Adviser, has gone to Upper Egypt to recover from his late illness, which had confined him to bed for three weeks. The Judicial Adviser will be three weeks absent from Cairo, which is exactly as long as his illness. Well! to speak frankly, the officials of the Ministry of Justice will not think his absence too long. Quite the reverse. They will enjoy three weeks of tranquillity. Would that it might last for ever!"

One of the best Egyptian newspapers in French is the *Phare d'Alexandrie*. Its conductor is a Greek. He is not subsidized by France, and, though he sides with the French in their most outrageous charges and demands, he generally does so as if he were ashamed of himself. Whenever the editor of this journal writes in an ungracious tone about England, he is eulogized by his French colleagues in Egypt.

The editor of the *Sphinx* praised him highly in the
number for the 7th of February, 1892.   The article
in the *Phare d'Alexandrie*, to which this honour
was accorded, intimated that England ought to quit
Egypt in order that France and Russia might
exercise their legitimate influence.   I wish that the
" legitimate influence " of France and Russia had
been defined.   The phrase is vague and obscure.
It may be that England has no right to occupy
Egypt, but how can France and Russia have any
claim to meddle in Egyptian affairs so long as
French and Russian bondholders receive full interest
on their investments ?   Supposing Portugal to make
default, would that be a justification for any foreign
Power occupying Lisbon ?   Unhappily, however,
Egypt has been treated as a toy with which the
foreign Powers might play, and because England
was left as the last player, some of the Powers feel
aggrieved that they are not now in England's place.

After reading the principal newspapers published
in Egypt during many months, and forming the
impression which I have set forth in the foregoing
paragraphs, I met with a French book which I perused
with extreme interest.   Its title is *John Bull sur le
Nil*, and the writer, whose pseudonym is Frédolin,
makes John Bull appear very ridiculous.   M.
Frédolin is perfectly honest, and he makes a parade
of his hatred of England and the English.   He is
an open foe who wields a facile and pointed pen.
If those of his countrymen who are journalists in
Egypt could write half as well as he, their articles
would be doubly more effective.   He spent eight

months in the country before writing his book, and then his greatest regret appears to have been the discreditable character of the French newspaper press in Egypt. Knowing the papers intimately, he says : " I cannot forget that a truly French organ is wanted whose conductors shall conscientiously study facts, take to heart the requirements of the natives, strive to bring about urgent reforms, and never forget that the name of France should be everywhere synonymous with progress and justice. Then such an affair as that of the *Bosphore* would never occur —a disastrous affair in the estimation of everyone whose heart is truly patriotic." This related to the part played by that journal in favour of Arabi Pasha. Another, which occurred recently, may prove a salutary lesson to the conductors of the *Bosphore*. No consular protection could avert an action for shameful libel brought against them by Dr. Milton in the Cairo International Tribunal. A decision was given in his favour of £1,000 damages with costs, and an order was added for its publication in the *Bosphore* and two other journals.

Egyptian public opinion is not faithfully mirrored in *Al Ahram*, an Arabic newspaper published in Alexandria, which exhibits unstinted admiration for Turkey and France. The Sultan of Turkey has conferred a decoration upon its editor. The respect of the conductors of *Al Ahram* for the Gazi, Mouktar Pasha, who is the resident and unwelcome Turkish Commissioner, is scarcely less profound than that for France and her people. In the number of *Al Ahram* for the 24th of December, 1891, it is said that France does her duty in opposing the British in Egypt on all occasions. In the number of the same journal for the 6th of February, 1892, the statement occurs that English functionaries ought not to fill important offices in the Government ; it is added that in Ismail's time competent Muslims were at his side, and that the late Khedive was hindered from calling the best men to his councils, while the hope is expressed that his Highness Abbas Hilmy may be more fortunate. Nothing about *Al Ahram* has impressed me more than the fidelity with which the prejudices of the most prejudiced Frenchmen are flattered in its leading articles. *Al Ahram* may be written by men who possess authority as well as special information, yet it does scant service to the party and the cause which are under its protection.

In all countries which are blessed with a powerful newspaper press, there are certain journals about which everyone is curious to learn full particulars. If I were writing a history of the Egyptian press, I should feel it a duty to mention and characterize each of the newspapers published in the country. My present purpose is limited in scope. I shall have attained it if I convey a fair notion of the representative Egyptian journals and magazines.

The two daily newspapers in Arabic, which are both remarkable and instructive, are *Al Ahram*, of Alexandria, to which I have already referred, and *Al Mokattam*, of Cairo, of which I now intend to give an account. The conductors of the chief Arabic journal in Cairo cannot boast, as their comrades in Alexandria may possibly do, that the Sultan of Turkey has conferred decorations upon them, and that a foreign power affords them support and accords them its protection.

Till the founding of *Al Mokattam*, in March, 1889, no native newspaper in Egypt was free from European influence. Most of the Arabic papers took their news and their cue from French contemporaries. Their conductors wished to be on the winning side, and the likelihood of France regaining her supremacy had not then ceased to be entertained. The founders of *Al Mokattam* are highly educated Syrians who have made their homes in Cairo. One of them, Dr. Nimr, produced a most favourable impression on the English public, through an interview with a representative of the *Pall Mall Gazette*, when he was in London a year ago. A few sentences which then appeared may be reproduced now. When asked what the Egyptian view of the British occupation was, he replied that the majority have ceased to notice it, and have settled down to business, not anticipating any radical change for some time to come. Some of them, he added, expect that the French would occupy Egypt if the British force were withdrawn, and "all certainly believe that France would try to restore her interest in Egypt by every possible means without regard to Egyptian interests. A great argument in your favour, by the way, is that your interests and the interests of Egypt go together; and this is one of the reasons why you have gained confidence in that country."*

* *Pall Mall Gazette*, October 14, 1891, p. 1.

The daily circulation of *Al Mokattam* is 2,500, which is very large for Egypt.   It has the extensive staff of forty correspondents between Alexandria and Wady Halfa, and the news printed in its columns can be relied upon.   It has resident correspondents in Damascus, Beyrout, and Constantinople, and it is the only Arabic newspaper which has special correspondents in London, Paris, and New York. When Father Ohrwalder and two nuns escaped from captivity at Omdurman, which has become the capital of the Soudan, a correspondent of *Al Mokattam* met them after they had entered Egypt and penned a vivid and deeply interesting narrative of their adventures, the accounts in all the other papers being far less graphic and detailed.   Each number contains many extracts from English, Italian, French, German, and American newspapers ; Reuter's telegrams are printed in its columns, while a daily statement of commercial affairs at Alexandria is sent by telegraph.

The founders of *Al Mokattam* had an uphill struggle at the outset.   They were informed that they must fail if they did not obtain help from France in return for upholding French pretensions. Other Arabic papers, they were told, had been kept alive in this way, while they were assured that an independent native paper could not exist.   It was known that the English Consul-General would not subsidize any newspaper, the English belief being that a journal becomes so much waste-paper the moment that it is the paid organ of any Government.

It is obvious from the success of *Al Mokattam* that a large party in Egypt desires to learn facts, and is accessible to argument. The French press in Egypt has done almost irreparable mischief. It is fortunate for the perpetuation of the good understanding which happily prevails between France and England that the newspapers published in Egypt are seldom read by Englishmen. If their misstatements were familiar to many English readers, the bitterness which would ensue might baffle diplomatic skill to remove. The leading journals of France are as temperately written and as deserving of admiration as any in the world. Many papers which see the light and live for a brief space in Paris are disgraces to journalism, and some French papers in Egypt closely resemble the least reputable Boulevard organs. The mission of a newspaper, if it have one, is to supply facts and to obtain a large circulation. To convey instruction does not appear to be the aim of the conductors of Egyptian journals in the French tongue. Fortunately their readers are few.

The object of *Al Mokattam*, in contradistinction to that which is apparently pursued by other Egyptian newspapers, is to give authentic information to the public and to comment upon the news of the day without extravagance of feeling or language, and with a single-minded desire to exhibit the advantages which might accrue to Egypt from pursuing a patriotic policy. A few extracts will display its manner and tone. On the 16th of December, 1891, it wrote: " France has promised to evacuate Tunis, just as England has done as regards Egypt. Yet what a difference is there between the good faith of these promises! England has continued to renew hers, and we have every reason to hope that she will keep them. Has France always kept hers? England has never broken her engagements. Has France invariably kept hers in mind? She has buried them in oblivion." On the 10th of January, 1892, this journal contained the following avowal: " We are charged with following an English policy. We challenge anyone to prove that our policy has not been that of our Government. We could frequently have cited our late sovereign as the authority for our statements." The *Bosphore* briefly and grossly commented on this statement by saying to the conductors of *Al Mokattam* : " You lie ; and you are calumniating the memory of Khedive Tewfik." This is neither in good taste nor convincing. In the number for the 15th of January, 1892, *Al Mokattam* stated that the problem which seems insoluble is how the Valley of the Nile can remain free should the English troops be at once withdrawn from it. In the interests of the country the evacuation should be postponed. Egypt has no complaint to make concerning it : " Neither ought Egypt to be disquieted if the occupation should be prolonged ; the sojourn of the English force in Egypt, or its cessation, wholly depends upon the Egyptians. It is for them to demonstrate that they can dispense with European support." Reverting to the same topic on the 9th of February, 1892, *Al Mokattam* explained and discussed the modern Colonial policy of England, and then said : " After obtaining possession of the Ionian Islands in 1809, she gave them up in 1863 at the request of the people, who desired that they should be united to Greece. She acquired the island of Heligoland in 1807, and restored it last year to Germany. . . . It is incorrect to say that France pursues a policy in Egypt which is of advantage to the country. The aim of the French is to promote the interests of foreigners, and she will not suffer the savings effected in Egypt to be employed for the advantage of Egyptians. . . . We do not defend English interests, but those of Egyptians. Let France cease her obstructive policy, and everything will go on swimmingly."

Another native paper, the *Nil*, had written in the same strain three days before, saying that the sympathy of France for Egypt would be more marked if she withdrew her opposition to the disposal of surplus revenue for the benefit of the country.

These extracts from the Egyptian native press may be concluded with two more from the French, which, if not pleasant reading, are fraught with instruction. The *Bosphore* began the new year by making a *canard* the subject of a leader, the *canard* being that a project was in contemplation for placing Egypt under the protectorate of England. The *Bosphore* felt certain that, if this happened without a protest, then annexation would follow. The article continued in the following terms : " While awaiting annexation or evacuation, the English will painfully resume the course of their ' reforms.' We say ' painfully,' because they cannot deceive themselves any longer

as to the sterility of their efforts.   They may occupy
the posts from which they have expelled the non-
English soldiers ; create new duties for the benefit
of the new recruits in the civilian army of occupation ; but the pretended reforming mission with
which they say they are charged, and of which the
field grows wider after each request for an explanation from the Suzerain, will not make further progress ; the equilibrium of the Budget will always
be based on the excessive burden which presses
upon the 5,000,000 Fellaheen and the 100,000
European colonists ; native justice directed by the
blind will continue to grope in the dark ; public
security will continue an empty phrase, and arrangements for sanitation and the public health will continue myths, because the necessity for throwing dust
in the creditors' eyes by showing a surplus when the
Budget is published renders the Administration
powerless to accord to these public works the nerve
of everything, and that is money.   Public education,
upon which the English did not dare to lay their
hands till now, is about to be 'Anglicized'; school-
masters who are out of situations in the United
Kingdom are at last seating themselves at the
banqueting table alongside their friends, the engineers, and it is possible that, despite the inevitable lowering of the educational standard, the
Egyptians may succeed, under the care of fourth-
rate masters, in speaking English, or at least in
being able to read the prose of the ' *Official Journal*
of the Egyptian Government '; but what the English
will never do is to teach the Egyptians to love the

invader, who does not even give himself the trouble
of dissembling his settled purpose of absorbing the
country, and who has not managed to obtain pardon
for his hateful interference by raising agriculture to
a higher level, by encouraging commerce, and by
protecting industry."

The foregoing diatribe is not wanting in viru-
lence; it would be still more powerful if it were based
upon facts. Egypt as it is to-day cannot be understood unless the facts are ascertained, and the French
press in Egypt, which is ably seconded by some
Parisian newspapers, either withholds facts or mis-
represents them.

If the wickedness of the English in Egypt be
really as great as their incompetence, which the
article I have just quoted from was written to demonstrate, why should the same journal accuse England
a month later of not investing enough money in
the country? In the *Bosphore* for the 4th of
February, 1892, it is said : " Despite constant appeals which commerce and industry have made for
help from British gold, not a farthing has been
invested in Egypt." This is not correct, as more than
one English company can exclaim with sorrow ; but
why should British gold be poured into the country
unless there be absolute security that the money
will not be confiscated ? If the intended annexation
of Egypt by England were not a craze which has
turned many French heads, and if France would rely
upon the pledges given, then the stream of British
gold would flow Nilewards, while the interest on
the public debt could be reduced and the market

price of the bonds would rise rapidly.   The French
public press in Egypt may be slanderous with impunity, but it ought at least to be logical.

I should have greater respect for the French
newspapers in Egypt if I knew less about them.
I cannot trust them implicitly ; and I doubt whether
any of them really reflects intelligent public opinion.
I have read so many things in them which I know
to be false that I accept every statement with great
hesitation.   I have seen the genesis of a newspaper
myth under the Egyptian sun, and the story may be
a useful warning to those who too readily consider as
gospel whatever they see in a newspaper.   Shortly
after the accession of the reigning Khedive, a paragraph appeared in a French journal published in
Cairo, to the effect that his Highness had shown
great coldness to Sir Frederick Grenfell, who was
then the Sirdar, and to Sir Evelyn Baring, the
British representative, and that he insisted upon
certain odious formalities being observed when
either desired an audience.   The statement was a
pure fiction.   It was reprinted in a Paris newspaper,
and translated by the esteemed and zealous correspondent of the *Daily News*.   It was retranslated
into French, and printed in the *Sphinx* for the
12th of February, 1892, with the comment : " This
language of the London newspaper confirms what
we had announced."   Thus it is that contemporary
history is written in Cairo by French journalists !

I have stated that, in addition to many newspapers of varied value, Egypt can boast of a
fortnightly and a monthly magazine.   The fort-

nightly magazine is published in Alexandria, and it is the organ of the Athenæum there. The contents are chiefly papers which have been read before the members of the Athenæum, and they are printed in Italian, French and English.

A national magazine, printed in Arabic, is *Al Mukataf.* Its editors are Y. Effendi Sarruf and T. Effendi Nimr, who also edit *Al Mokattam.* This magazine was an entire novelty when it appeared. No periodical of a purely scientific, literary and industrial nature had previously appeared in Arabic. The magazine has been a prosperous venture. It is entering on its seventeenth year. At the start the circulation was 500 copies, and the pages numbered twenty-four. The pages now number seventy-two, and nearly 3,000 copies are circulated. I do not know many more striking contrasts than that between the first number and the last which I have seen. The contents of the first are : The Moon ; the Microscope ; Arabian Astronomers ; Rain ; the Hymieritic Language ; Glass-making ; Turkey-red ; Notes ; Questions and Answers. The last number has a long list of contents which I give in full, as I think it serviceable to show what educated Arabians read at present : 1. Biographical Sketch of the late Khedive ; 2. Abbas Pasha II., the Khedive of Egypt ; 3. The Bacillus of Influenza ; 4. The Emerald Mountain ; 5. The Diminution of Drunkenness in Norway ; 6. The Dust in the Air ; 7. Experiences among Animals ; 8. Truth and Falsehood in Mesmerism ; 9. The Progress of Science in 1891 ; 10. Mersina ;

11. A Historical Research Concerning the Town of Aidab; 12. Our Agricultural Department; 13. Correspondence, filling eight pages, in which Syrians and Egyptians discuss literary questions; 14. Notes on Engineering and Industry; 15. Mathematics, in which problems are given in Conic Sections; 16. Reviews of New Publications in Arabic; 17. Questions and Answers, of which the former number twenty-three, one being from Prince Ridakaby, of Mirza, in Russia, desiring particulars about the Nature and Composition of Meteorites. Another is dated from Korosko, in Nubia, concerning pearls and the mode of obtaining them, while a third is from Beyrout, in Syria, and relates to the clarification of oil. They are all practical. The 18th and concluding article is on New Discoveries and Inventions.

A magazine with such a table of contents is of immense help in instilling into the Arabian mind the wisdom of the European. Most of the articles are translations from French, English and American works, the original articles being few in number. The readers of this magazine are being educated unconsciously. They imbibe new ideas when passing the time. They acquire facts which are novel, and they become as well acquainted with the names and achievements of European and American men of science and letters as they are with their neighbours next door. The conductors of this magazine deserve to be congratulated on its success.

The Egyptian Government cherishes old-fashioned ideas about the newspaper press. These ideas were imported from France. A special department has been formed in Cairo to muzzle journalists. Its office is on the ground-floor of the palace, built by the Moufettish, in which the Ministry of Finance is installed. Baron de Malortie presides over it. A more amiable man than he could not be entrusted with a more uncongenial duty. Though a Hanoverian by birth, he is an Englishman from choice, and he is the last man in Egypt who would put a bearing-rein on the press. He has little power for good. The native journals, which are comparatively harmless, and seldom commit a greater error than gravely disseminating as truth the fiction of some French newspaper, are entirely subject to his control ; while many of the journals printed in a foreign tongue may calumniate the Government without interference from him. The foreigners who conduct the obnoxious and untruthful prints are under the protection of their consuls. No one would be damnified if the Press Bureau were abolished. The remarkable talents of its accomplished chief could be turned to better account in another branch of the Administration.

As an assiduous reader of Egyptian newspapers during several months, I expected to have learnt much from them. What I did learn was that very few of them represent public opinion. The majority delight in squabbles as aimless and silly as those which agitate the inhabitants of a shanty city in Western America. Their mendacity is phenomenal. Ananias and Sapphira must have left a family which has increased and multiplied, and supplied editors to several Egyptian newspapers.

I repeat that *Al Mokattam* is one of the trustworthy journals, and that its columns contain a
reflex of educated native opinion. Yet the Fellaheen, who rarely read newspapers, entertain views
which are seldom set forth in the public press. I
expected to find them grateful for the even-handed
justice which is meted out, and, in particular, that
they would appreciate the abolition of the forced
labour regulations under which they had to leave
their fields and families and work for others without
pay. I suggested that they must benefit by the
impartiality, as well as completeness, with which
their lands are now irrigated, and also by the equity
and despatch with which justice is administered.
The children of the Fellaheen, who are now being
educated, will value these things more than their
parents appear to do. Some of the parents would
not object to the bad old times returning. I thought
that I should not hear any objection raised when I
inquired, "Are not the taxes equally distributed now,
and levied with scrupulous fairness?" The answer
was in the affirmative; but it was given with qualifications which I shall state in my own words: "Formerly the tax-gatherer was exacting and cruel; he
might compel some Fellaheen to pay twice, and he
would torture the recalcitrant till they handed over
the sums which he demanded. However, a certain
number escaped paying anything. They might
bribe the tax-gatherer, or they might not succumb
to torture. Those who succeeded in going scot-free
were accounted heroes by their neighbours. They
were envied as those are who draw large prizes in a

lottery. Now the line is drawn, and no movement
to the one side or the other is possible. Escape or
delay cannot occur. The tax-gatherer appears at
the appointed time ; he demands the proper amount;
he cannot be bribed by those who wish to escape
from paying the whole sum ; and he dares not flog
them till they produce the money. His remedy
against them is in a civil court, and the court is
always on his side, enforcing its decrees at the
expense of the debtor, who must either part with
his money, to which he clings as tenaciously as any
drowning man can cling to a straw, or else submit
to the sale of his property."

What has just been stated is familiar to those
who have had experience of tax-collecting in India.
In British India the natives are not the victims of
extortion, neither can they expect abatement ; they
must pay at the appointed date, or else they will
suffer the consequences of refusal or neglect. In
the native states there is great laxity in enforcing
still heavier demands, some being forced to pay who
might reasonably be spared, while others who can
easily pay find means of escape. Indeed, a semi-
civilized people, whether in Egypt or India, is quite
reconciled to semi-civilized methods.

The diffusion of a sound education is the
one thing needful. When the inhabitants of the
Nile Valley shall have risen higher in the educational scale, they will be thankful for the fair treatment which prevails. As soon as they attain to a
higher level of culture, the newspaper press will
influence their minds for the better, as surely as

the high Nile fructifies their land. Their almost
inarticulate voices will then give forth notes of warning or praise ; they will proclaim what they desire,
and they will express their satisfaction when their
wishes are gratified. There is much guess-work at
present as to the feelings of the people. They may
be credited with opinions which they do not entertain, and their actual opinions may remain unknown.

The newspaper press is still an exotic in Egypt.
It is becoming acclimatized ; yet, as a whole, it
cannot be accepted as an authentic representative of
public opinion throughout the land. Any newspaper which sets forth the conclusions of a clique
can never be a national organ ; hence the French
newspapers in Egypt have no more title to be
accepted as reproducing the aspirations of Egyptians
than they have to be cited as reproducing the aspirations of the Esquimaux. The Italian, Greek, and
English journals are in the same category. So far
as the native journals do not make a point of disseminating English, French, Italian, or Greek ideas,
they are representative organs of an undeveloped,
but not inoperative, public opinion. I have given
reasons for making a special exception in favour of
Al Mokattam, and, whenever Egypt shall have
many newspapers of the same stamp and quality,
Egyptian public opinion will then take tangible
shape, and become an organized power.

CHAPTER XIII.

ON THE SOUTHERN FRONTIER.

EGYPT means the Nile to a large number of
persons. They speak of spending a winter on the
Nile; they seldom speak of wintering in Egypt.
They associate nearly all that is pleasant and
wonderful with the river, and, if they ever think of
the land, they do so in connexion with the monuments upon it.

The Nile exercises a magical influence. The
existence of the fascination is unquestionable; and,
though it may be criticised or condemned, it cannot
easily be resisted. Nature has made provision
for a trip on the river being most easily taken
at a season of the year when it is most enjoyable.
During the scorching heat of summer the river can
scarcely be navigated. Towards the autumn the
banks are overflown in parts, while, during the
winter months, there is enough water for navigation
and enough heat for comfort.

Those who desire to see and understand Egypt
must make use of the Nile. It is easy to traverse
France and Germany, Austria and Hungary, the
United States and Canada without sailing upon the

Seine and the Rhine, the Danube and the Missis-
sippi, the Hudson and the St. Lawrence; but the
Nile provides the only continuous passage between
Alexandria on the Mediterranean and Wâdy Halfa
on the confines of Nubia. This water-way continues as far as the Equator; but, for reasons to
which I shall not refer at present, it is closed
alike against the Egyptian trader and the English
traveller. I have shown in the Ninth chapter how
the rich red water of the Nile is the life-blood of the
land, and how the increased prosperity of Egypt can
be best brought about when areas which are now
parched and barren shall be adequately irrigated.
If it were not for the river the whole country would
be a desert. This may seem an irrational commonplace, but the readers of Volney's works must be
aware that it might once have been a terrible fact.
A project far more audacious than that of piercing
the Isthmus of Suez fermented in the mind of
Albuquerque, the great Portuguese explorer and
conqueror. His purpose consisted in cutting a
passage for the Nile through the mountains of
Abyssinia and diverting its course into the Red
Sea. He contemplated and desired the entire ruin
of Egypt. The success of his infamous project
would have achieved it, and he might have gloried
in the fiendish result.

Happily for the valley through which the Nile
flowed in the days of Albuquerque, it flows and swells
there still, and fertilizes the adjacent soil. The great
river is now, as it was in his time and for countless
centuries before him, the silent pathway upon which

the trader can carry his wares to customers, and the peasant can carry the produce of his fields to market. At some parts of its course the surface is thickly covered with boats, in which tourists would not trust themselves, but which are picturesque features in the landscape, many of them resembling the craft with the shoulder of mutton sail in which Robinson Crusoe and his boy Xury escaped from Morocco. At longer intervals the Dahabeyah, which is peculiar to the Nile, sweeps along when the wind is fair, flying the flag of the country to which its occupants belong, the Union Jack and the Stars and Stripes being the flags most frequently displayed. Steamers often glide along at a fair speed, upwards and downwards, however the wind may blow, and most of them fly the ensign of Messrs. Thomas Cook and Son. This firm is well known and popular all over the globe, but nowhere is its presence more conspicuous and welcome than on the tawny bosom of old Father Nile.

To have rendered the land of Egypt, and the Nile in particular, easily accessible to the traveller is one of the services for which that firm, and especially its responsible head, Mr. John Mason Cook, have earned the thanks of those who travel by land or water through the modern kingdom of the old Pharaohs. They have a hard task in satisfying tourists. The more that is done for their comfort the more exacting do they become, and fault-finders, even when few in number, are generally blatant in speech. Travellers in olden days told stories to enliven the journey. The modern tourist is more ready to grumble than to make himself agreeable, and he fancies that he becomes a personage of note by indiscriminate complaining.

Whoever desires to ascertain how inconsiderate men and women can be, let him take a trip on a Nile steamer and listen to the empty and childish objections which the more vulgar passengers are certain to make. This matter concerns the Messrs. Cook, and they doubtless regard it as one of the penalties of their position. A far more important one deserves mention because it concerns the Egyptians.

In bygone days the villagers along the Nile were in dismay when a boat was moored near their dwellings and a demand made for supplies. The steward landed and the Sheikh met him and learned his requirements. After a little delay the articles were produced, and they were paid for according to an arbitrary scale which the steward had prepared. The sum of money due to the villagers was handed to their Sheikh, who put into his pocket what he considered a proper percentage, and gave the remainder to those who had furnished the articles. This system satisfied the village Sheikhs, but it did not commend itself to the villagers. Nowadays all the provisions are paid for directly to those who supply them, and the sum thus circulated by Mr. J. M. Cook and his agents among the Fellaheen has tended to render them prosperous. If the tourist traffic on the Nile were to cease, and it will certainly fall off when British influence or example wanes, the lot of the toiling villagers along the river's banks from Cairo to Wâdy Halfa will again be as hard as it was in the bygone days of abject poverty and intolerable oppression.

But there is another side to the picture. I have dwelt upon the over-exacting character of tourists without defining it. Of course it will readily be understood that the commonest and most ludicrous grievances relate to the food and accommodation which are provided. In ninety-nine cases out of a hundred there is not an iota of justification for these complaints. Yet those who admit that they are excellently treated, and as luxuriously catered for as they could be in their homes, may still groan over a fancied breach of agreement between them and the Messrs. Cook.

These persons make a trip on the Nile, not to learn anything about the condition of the country or the people, but to see ancient ruins. If the ruins do not come up to their expectation they consider themselves defrauded, and if a day passes without a ruin being visible, they consider it a day wasted. A sort of ruin-mania is one of the maladies to which American and European voyagers on the Nile are subject. It was manifested even in the days before the name of Mr. J. M. Cook, which is now a power in Egypt, had become familiar there. Miss Harriet Martineau, who had as strong and well-balanced a mind as any of her sex, avows that temple-hunting grew upon her till it became a pleasure, and that she felt "real grief" when it came to an end. She adds : " We found, even before we left Nubia, that we were hardly satisfied to sit down to breakfast without having explored a temple."*

* " Eastern Life : Present and Past," vol. i., p. 209.

I did not journey to the second cataract with the object of exploring temples, though I readily admit that such an amusement, when kept within reasonable bounds, is harmless and unobjectionable. I was more interested in the lot of the people who are now living than in the ruins left by an extinct race. The ordinary traveller much prefers to talk about the Egypt of the past, because he can pick up plenty of inaccurate information about it at second-hand, whereas, neither his guide-book nor his dragoman communicate to him many authentic details about the Egypt in which he is a sojourner.

Yet it sometimes happens that a party of tourists on the Nile may derive great benefit from an acquaintance with the memorials of antiquity on or near its banks. Such a party ascended the river in the spring of 1892 as far as the first cataract. Most of its members were native Egyptians who knew little of their own country outside of Cairo. They were teachers and selected pupils in the Government schools, numbering fifty in all, the head of the party being Mr. Douglas Dunlop, Inspector - General of Education. The trip was commemorative as well as educational.

Mr. J. M. Cook, at whose expense it was made, put the steamer *Prince Abbas* at the exclusive disposal of the party, with all the accessories which are provided for an excursion of the first class. The objects were celebrating the accession of the present Khedive, and acquiring a knowledge of the country. A few words which Mr. J. M. Cook addressed to the party which had accepted his

generous and timely hospitality merit preservation :
" I remember that in several conversations, our
departed friend the late Khedive Tewfik, Pasha,
explained to me his regret that so many of the
young men in Cairo, who have the means, never
think of leaving the city in order to see the
antiquities of Egypt ; and on making inquiries of
well-to-do and well-educated natives, I have found
that hardly any of them have visited Upper Egypt,
with the exception of Government officials who
have chanced to be sent up the river on duty. . . .
But if Egypt is ever to be governed and controlled
by her own children, every one of you should see
all the famous places in the land, and strive to
understand its history and special requirements in
the far past as well as in more recent times ; it is
in this way that you may become able to deal
intelligently with important problems in its commerce and administration. These views, coupled
with the fact that I know how deep and enlightened
is the interest shown by his Highness the Khedive
Abbas Hilmy in all that concerns public instruction,
make me feel sure that I could find no more fitting
way to celebrate the accession of his Highness than
by offering you this voyage to Assouan."

All voyagers up the Nile become familiar with
one or two places at which a stoppage of some
length is always made, and of these the first is
Assiout, which is 250 miles from Cairo by water, and
is connected with it by rail. A steamer takes three
or four days to make the trip, which can be accomplished by rail in ten hours. Those who are in a

hurry prefer the railway ; while those who can spare the time, and cannot live happily in an atmosphere of sand, choose the steamboat. Assiout has a population of 40,000 inhabitants ; it is modernized in many respects, and it is prosperous.

The bazaars, however, are the chief attraction for tourists, and they contain as much rubbish, picturesquely displayed, as any others in Egypt. I was pleased to find in this city private schools for boys and girls which a munificent Copt had founded and endowed. They have not been long in existence, and they are probably one of the fruits due to the impetus which has been given to education since the British occupation. Here, too, is the training college of the American missionaries which I mentioned in the Tenth chapter.*

The buildings forming the college are large, well-planned, and they stand in an open space. Three hundred pupils are educated here, of whom one-third are girls, the school for the latter being a separate structure not far removed from that in which boys are taught. The education imparted is of as high a standard as that in the Government schools. Not the least useful part of the training consists in the improved material conditions under which the pupils, many of whom are boarders also, live while under this roof. They learn habits of life which are a gain second only to the knowledge which they acquire.

A difficulty has arisen which cannot easily be removed. Bishop Colenso, as is well known, found

* See p. 203.

that a Zulu had puzzled him. The youths who pass through the training college at Assiout, and who do not wish to become clergymen, find it easy to pass the examinations qualifying them for employment in the Civil Service. Indeed, if all of them became clergymen the supply would soon far exceed the demand. As members of the Civil Service, they have to work on Sundays, and they are taught to regard this as wicked. Friday is the Muslim's Sunday. The Government cannot be expected to alter existing regulations concerning the days upon which the public offices are closed. As it is, the post and telegraph offices are open on Friday, while the railways run on that day. The temptations to prefer the career of a Civil Servant in Egypt to that of a missionary clergyman are almost irresistible in the eyes of most natives. The salary is larger, the labour is less, and the chances of promotion are greater. I have merely stated the problem without venturing upon a discussion or offering a solution.

Luxor is 200 miles by water above Assiout, and is a halting-place for all tourists. Some depart as soon as they have visited the tombs of the kings, the remains of hundred-gated Thebes, and the grand ruins of Karnak. Many stay for weeks or months, comfortable hotels being one attraction, and an incomparable climate, for those who are strong, being another. Enough has been written about Luxor as a health-resort to satisfy the curiosity of the public, and the late Lady Duff Gordon depicted the charms of the place in a manner which defies rivalry.

If she could revisit Luxor, her surprise would be as great as that of any tourist who sees it for the first time. The house wherein she dwelt, which had been erected among the ruins of the temple, has disappeared ; while the huge pillars and slabs of stone, being the imposing remains of the temple, are cleared of the rubbish which then almost concealed them. A large hotel behind where she lived, and two others lower down on the river's bank, afford comforts to the sojourner such as were unknown in Luxor when she was a resident. That she was prepared for the opening of a hotel, is shown by a letter written on the 28th of August, 1867, in which she says, "There is a pretty white house behind mine at Luxor. The owner, a Copt, is going to open a hotel there. I dare say it will answer very well."* While these things would excite in her mind a sort of bewildered pleasure, another novelty would assuredly elicit warm praise. As nothing is to be found about it in guide-books, I shall give a detailed description of the Luxor Hospital for the ailing natives of Upper Egypt.

Mr. J. M. Cook originated the hospital, and supplied the largest part of the funds required for buying the ground on which the building stands and erecting it. Mr. Brunner, M.P., and others who had visited Luxor, contributed what was wanting. The hospital is situated behind the Luxor Hotel, the structure forming a hollow square, with a garden in the interior. Roses flourish in the garden, and shoots of eucalyptus trees are the

* "Last Letters from Egypt," p. 155.

beginnings of what will become a pleasure to the eye and a preventive of fever. The hospital was opened by the late Khedive in February, 1891, when Mr. J. 'M. Cook made a free gift of it to the inhabitants of the district, promising to con-tribute to its support, and hoping to induce charitable persons to aid him. The Khedive, speaking in English, declared his gratification at being asked to dedicate the Luxor Hospital to the poorer inhabi-tants of Upper Egypt, and he added :

" If the imposing remains of Luxor and Karnak testify to the might and power of those who erected these majestic temples, the humble edifice you have raised to charity shall make people think of the goodness of your heart ; and the gratitude of those who shall be healed in it of their diseases and maladies shall bear witness to it before the Lord of heaven and earth. Let His mercy be spread over all of us ! According to your desire, I declare this hospital open to the poor sick of this district."

Khedive Tewfik displayed great coolness when Alexandria was being bombarded, and when the rebellious soldiers were intent upon killing him ; he displayed both courage and humanity when he hastened to Cairo where the cholera was raging, and visited the hospitals which were crowded with patients, whom he cheered with his voice and presence. Hence, in opening this hospital at Luxor, he was performing a congenial duty. If wanting in some of the sterner qualities which make a ruler feared, he had a large share of the kindlier sym-pathies which render a man beloved, and the people

18

of Egypt will be devoid of the nobler virtues if they should fail to cherish and revere his memory.

The Luxor Hospital has proved of great service to suffering humanity in Upper Egypt. Patients flock thither from 266 villages between Assiout and Assouan, a distance of 330 miles. Dr. Zeidan is in charge of it. A Syrian by birth, he pursued his medical studies and took his degree in London. He appears to be fully equal to the responsible position which he holds. I obtained some statistics from him which will interest others as they did me. The number of out-patients during the first year that the doors of the hospital were thrown open was 6,001. The largest number of out-patients in any one month was 1,390, the smallest 266, the month of March showing the maximum attendance, and the month of July the minimum. The wards, which can accommodate 40 in-patients, are airy enough, as the windows and doors can be kept open any day in the year. It is owing, probably, to the abundance of air and sunlight that patients make good recoveries after undergoing serious surgical operations.

Some of the operations which Dr. Zeidan has successfully performed would be termed heroic by the members of his profession, and they appear wonderful to a layman. He has removed a stone weighing two ounces and a half, by means of supra-pubic lithotomy, from a man of eighty-two, who was discharged perfectly cured several days afterwards. Another man of sixty-two recovered after a tumour weighing upwards of seventeen pounds had been removed from his thigh. Many other cases of a minor, yet important, kind are on his list of cures. The patients under his care whom he had alleviated, but failed to restore to health, were the victims of consumption, which is as incurable among the natives of Upper Egypt as it is among people living in less balmy climes. The hospital staff is not large, consisting of Dr. Zeidan and two native assistants, a porter and a cook. Mr. J. M. Cook has rendered inestimable service by organizing travel in the Nile Valley ; yet nothing does him greater credit as an English philanthropist, or deserves to be longer remembered in his honour among Egyptians, than the establishment of this free hospital at Luxor.

Though many of those who pass the winter at Luxor are invalids, yet the three hotels there contain a considerable proportion of visitors whose object is enjoyment, and who have a sufficient stock of health for the purpose. The out-door amusements are few in number, unless making excursions can be reckoned among them. There is good duck-shooting in the winter, and quail-shooting in the spring, within an easy distance. The villagers, as well as the visitors, derive pleasure from the meetings of the Sporting Club, which take place in a large field near the Luxor Hotel. The excitement among the hundreds of native spectators is as great at such a meeting as it is among the competitors for prizes. There is plenty of variety in the sports, as the following extracts from the printed programme of a meeting, at which I was present, will show :

1. Donkey race for donkey-boys without saddle or bridle.
2. Camel race.

3. Ladies' donkey-race, the winning donkey at previous meetings
to start five yards behind the others.
4. Three-legged race for boys.
5. Horse race.
6. Ladies and gentlemen's race.
7. Buffalo race.
8. Wrestling on donkeys for boys.
9. The tug of war.

At Assouan, which is 133 miles from Luxor, the
first cataract is seen, and Upper Egypt ends. To
ascend or descend this cataract is the ambition of
many a tourist, who would boast less of the feat
which he has performed if the word "rapid" were
substituted for "cataract." The rapids of the St.
John River, where it flows into the Bay of Fundy,
and those of Lake Superior, where it flows into St.
Mary's River, are quite as wonderful as the cataracts
of the Nile, though they are less talked about, and
do not excite extravagant expectations. From the
first to the second cataract, the Nile passes through
Nubia, which is now called the Frontier Province.
It is governed by Wodehouse Pasha, one of the
English officers in the service of his Highness the
Khedive, who has done admirable work. Both the
civil and the military administration are in his
hands, and he is the head of the Chief Court of
Justice. Crime is rare within his jurisdiction, and
the people over whom he exercises authority regard
him with respect and confidence. Another Englishman, Beck Bey, is the capable and courteous super-
intendent of the railway running from Assouan to
Shellal, which lies above the cataract, facing the
island of Philæ, and is the starting-place for the

small steamers, propelled by wheels at the stern, which navigate the Upper Nile.

Writers about the Nile have failed to make the contrast generally understood which exists between the land and scenery above the first cataract and that below it. The people who dwell south of the cataract are of a different race and speech from those to the north; they dress differently, and irrigate their fields in another manner.

Throughout Nubia, water is almost invariably raised from the river by a Sakia, or bucket-pump, which is actuated by a horizontal wheel turned by a bullock; while in Egypt proper the Shadoof, or long pole with a bucket attached to one end, working on a joint in the middle, and drawn up by the opposite end after the bucket is filled with water, is the machine which is most commonly used. The scenery differs also. It is much rarer for a cloud to veil the deep blue sky, and it is rarer still for rain to fall. At sunrise and sunset the effects on the horizon are fine in Egypt, while they are magical in Nubia. I never witnessed anything to equal them in marvellous tint and grandeur, save in the extreme north of Canada, when the aurora borealis fills the heavens by night with hues as brilliant as those of the rainbow. The aurora borealis appears in perfect beauty at long intervals, while the after-glow in Nubia is a nightly spectacle which always attracts and is always different. The scenery along the Nile's bank in Nubia is as varied and picturesque, though without the same rich vegetation, as that between Bingen and Cologne on the banks of the

Rhine ; while the scenery in Egypt proper is as tame and unimpressive as that between Cologne and Arnheim.

While the ruined edifices are fewer in number in Nubia than in Egypt, some of the most striking among the relics of antiquity are to be seen here, chief among them being the temples and statues at Aboo Simbel on the west bank of the Nile. The architects of ancient Egypt were more capable of impressing than of pleasing those who gazed upon their handiwork. Art, in the modern sense of the word, is often lacking, while grace of outline and aspect is very rare. But the colossal statues of Rameses II., which have been hewn out of the living rock at Aboo Simbel, are among the most artistic and graceful works which the human hand has ever fashioned. It is possible to reproduce the great pyramid, or one of the obelisks which many admire ; but I doubt whether there is a living man who could mould a colossal figure which should rival one of those hewn out of the rock on the hillside in commemoration of Rameses II.

Any statue or temple, whether ruined or not, excites interest among thousands who visit Egypt in order to view such things. A battle-field in Belgium or Lorraine has as great attraction for tourists on the Continent of Europe. Now Toski, which is not far from Aboo Simbel, receives scant notice, though it was the scene of the fight consequent upon the last great effort of the present Mahdi to invade Egypt. His army numbered 3,300 fighting men. The force on the Egyptian side, under the direction of Wodehouse Pasha in the first instance, and afterwards of the Sirdar, Sir Frederick Grenfell, when he reached the scene of action, was 1,450. Of this force the majority were Soudanese ; so that the fight was one between the Soudanese who submitted to the Mahdi, and the Soudanese who preferred to live under the Khedive. The decisive combat, as witnessed by Mr. Kidd, from whom I received the following particulars, began on the morning of the 3rd of August, when the force led by Najumi issued from behind a range of hills, and moved upon Toski. The advance was checked by the 9th, 10th, and 13th battalions of Soudanese in garrison at Wady Halfa, and the 11th, which had marched from Suakim, and by two battalions of Egyptians acting with them. The enemy's force was driven from one position after another with great loss ; not more than 100 succeeded in returning to Khartoum. Najumi was among the slain. His followers made a desperate stand, and they fell to a man in fighting for him. The prisoners pressed forward to kiss his corpse before it was carried away. This crushing defeat at Toski, and the capture of Tokar on the 19th of February, 1891, conclusively proved that the Soudanese and the Egyptians, when properly dis-ciplined and led, could meet the forces of the Mahdi with good hope of being the victors.*

After the defeat at Toski, many of the prisoners elected to settle in Nubia. The Egyptian Govern-

* Full particulars of the fighting at Toski and Tokar, as well as on other occasions, are contained in Major Wingate's authoritative and well-written work, " Mahdiism and the Egyptian Soudan."

ment appropriated 500 acres to their use, and as many as 3,000 Soudanese have found new homes in the village of Deberah. It is estimated that 22,000 Soudanese have voluntarily settled in the part of Nubia which is under Egyptian rule, preferring the mild sway of the Khedive to the arbitrary one of the Mahdi.

Wady Halfa, at the foot of the second cataract, has been chosen as the scientific frontier of Egypt. It is 802 miles south of Cairo. It is defended by a series of small forts, and is garrisoned with four battalions of native infantry, two squadrons of cavalry, one mule field-battery, and one camel corps. The officers are Englishmen; the commandant is Lieut.-Colonel Kempster. After the battle of Toski the outpost was advanced twenty miles southwards to Sarras, where there is a small garrison; there is telephonic communication and a railway between the two places.

The ordinary tourist who visits Wady Halfa is animated with the desire to ascend Abousir, and to behold from that elevation the Nile rushing over and between black rocks, and forming what is styled the second cataract. Having seen this he is anxious to turn his face northwards. No bazaars like those at Assouan and Assiout tempt him to linger, nor do venerable ruins gratify his acquired taste for what is old. The village of Wady Halfa is not new, and it is as unattractive as any Nubian village; but the part where the garrison is quartered is both new and interesting.

On no part of the Nile is a prettier sight to be

enjoyed than on the right bank at Wady Halfa, which is lined with houses in which the English officers live, and where their mess-house stands. The road is well-made and well-kept. Small gardens filled with flowering shrubs surround each dwelling. An air of neatness, which is most un-common along the Nile, reigns here. The spectacle is charming and very un-Egyptian.

The barracks are as clean and comfortable as the officers' quarters. When Major von Wissmann saw this place and Sarras after my visit, nothing impressed him more than the excellent appearance of the men in their barracks and tents, as well as on parade. He was pleased with the small flower-gardens around some of the tents; he never saw them in the part of Africa with which he is familiar. Indeed, he considered that the men who were serving on the southern frontier were learning habits of neatness as well as discipline. It is true, as Major von Wissmann heard with regret, that all these soldiers do not keep up their cleanly habits after returning to their dusty and filthy villages, yet as one generation after another passes through the ranks, the improvement will not be wholly lost which was attained during the days of soldiering.

Moreover, the present Egyptian army is a very young force, and it is a small one, not exceeding 13,000 men. Besides, it is an experimental army. The system upon which it is founded is the reverse of that of the army which supplied recruits to Arabi, and was disbanded after his defeat. To be a soldier used to be dreaded by the Fellaheen as the greatest

of curses. Desertion was frequent. Compulsion
and the fear of death alone kept the men in the
ranks. When a soldier was discharged and returned
to his native village he was regarded as a miserable
creature. There was neither love of the uniform on
the part of those who wore it, nor respect on the
part of those who saw it.

When the existing force was organized by Sir
Evelyn Wood, who was the first English Sirdar, or
commander-in-chief, he treated the soldiers as he
would do those of his own country. They were not
locked up in barracks as their predecessors had been,
lest they should desert in a body ; they were not half-
starved like them, and, unlike them, they were paid.

From the days of Mehemet Ali down to those
of the Khedive Ismail the lot of the Egyptian soldier
has been harder than that of many a slave. He is
now more comfortably housed and clad, and he is far
better fed, than his brother Fellah who tills the fields.
When he goes on furlough to his native village he
is treated as a person of consequence. The most
astounding thing connected with him in the opinion
of native critics was that he should have leave
granted him ; they were unanimous in holding that
" he would never come back." However, Sir Evelyn
Wood had a confidence in his Egyptians which
proved to be well-founded. He granted 2,000
privates leave of absence, and he gave each a rail-
way-ticket to his native village, and another available
for his return on the day that his leave expired.
Not one of the 2,000 failed to answer to his name
when his furlough had ended and the roll was called.

At Toski and at Tokar the Egyptian soldiers showed that they were a credit to their country. The Soudanese battalions are as fine troops as any general officer can wish to have under his command. They are fighting men by nature. Major von Wissmann acutely remarks that the Egyptian is the better soldier for times of peace, and the Soudanese for service in the field.

He does not mean by this that the Egyptian is averse to fighting when required to do so ; but he means that in garrison the Egyptian quietly does his duty, while the Soudanese is apt to become discontented with the monotony of the life.*

In order to keep his troops in good trim Lieut.-Colonel Kempster has frequent field-days at Wady Halfa, and the training on these occasions is serviceable to the officers and men. I was present at one of the sham fights, and I gladly noted the thoroughness and effectiveness of the manœuvres. The officers had their men well in hand. The men appeared to have implicit trust in their officers. With such a force an able general could easily vanquish twice or thrice the number of the best troops of the Mahdi.

Those who have seen the admirably drilled and disciplined army of his Highness the Khedive cannot help asking why the southern frontier of Egypt should be drawn at Wady Halfa, and why it should not again extend to the Equator ? Bad

---

* Major von Wissmann's instructive remarks on the Egyptian force at Wady Halfa appeared in the Berlin *Militär-Wochenblatt,* for May 24, 1892.

management on the Egyptian side made the dwellers to the south of Wady Halfa long to be separated from Egypt. The tax-master scourged the tribes of the Soudan as grievously in the days of Ismail as the task-masters scourged the Israelites in the days of Rameses the Great. During the last ten years these tribes have been treated quite as ruthlessly by two Mahdis, and they would welcome such a rational and beneficent rule as that which now prevails in Egypt. So long as Egypt is severed from her former provinces the horrors of the slave-trade will continue, while these provinces will be debarred from making any progress in the civilization which is gradually transforming Egypt's face into a thing of beauty.

The line of the frontier was not drawn at Wady Halfa with the consent of the Egyptian Government. Orders coming from London determined the frontier line. Blundering on the part of British officers, and vacillation on the part of the Government itself, culminated in the catastrophe of Gordon's death in Khartoum. The power of the Mahdi for mischief was recognised. It was deemed unwise to fight against him. Happily he is dead, and unfortunately he has bequeathed nothing to his successor, save cruelty and a desire to heap up treasure.

A scheme is now in contemplation for constructing a narrow-gauge railway from Cairo to Wady Halfa. Its advantages have been luminously set forth by Boghos Nubar Pasha, one of the three Directors of the Egyptian Government Railways. The money is ready at hand, and the French colony favours the scheme, chiefly because it is supposed to be regarded with dislike by the representative of Great Britain. Happily the English administrators in the Khedive's service and the English Consul General and Envoy are not adverse to the project, so that it may be realized before another year has elapsed. With a railway running from Cairo to Wady Halfa the distance between the two places could be traversed in forty hours. From Wady Halfa to Khartoum the ground has been surveyed for a railway, a part of which is constructed.

The reoccupation of the Soudan by Egypt is really the simplest of all the Egyptian problems. No expedition of a large size, costing an enormous sum and foredoomed to disaster, needs to be fitted out. Let the garrison at Wady Halfa be reinforced, and let three or four thousand men be moved forward on the line surveyed for a railway, and let the rails be laid as they go. Such a force would carry necessary supplies with it, and would be in constant communication with its base. Thus the North American desert was crossed in defiance of hostile Indians. The speed might be slow, but the outlay would be small, while the ground conquered from the desert would remain in the conqueror's hand. When Dongola is reached a halt might be made till the surrounding country had been brought under the sway of his Highness the Khedive. Once pacified and occupied, the inhabitants of the Soudan would find that their lot had changed for the better. The resources of their country would be developed. Egypt as a whole would be the gainer.

The Soudanese would neither be plundered nor oppressed again. Courts of justice such as now exist in Egypt would be established for their benefit, and the poorest labourer would be able to appeal to the law for maintaining his rights or redressing his wrongs. No tyrant, bearing the abused name of Mahdi, or Saviour, would then make them suffer, and no Pasha representing the Khedive would dare to make them afraid.

In this forecast the construction of a railway is assumed as being indispensable to its verification. The dark places of the earth—and the Soudan under its present Government is one of them—are full of the habitations of cruelty. When a railway is constructed in a barbarous land, the triumph of civilization is an inevitable consequence, as the Marquess of Salisbury rightly declared in a memorable speech. It is almost impossible to settle with precision how soon the whole of Nubia and the southern land will become as peaceful as the Highlands did after Marshal Wade had covered them with roads; but it is indubitable that civilization will spread over the Soudan when the railway runs through it.

Humanity is the gainer by every addition which is made to the habitable part of the globe. The Soudan is fertile ; but it will remain as worthless as the desert so long as the Egyptians are excluded from it and a religious bigot exercises despotic and cruel control. It is alike just and excusable that the Egyptian Government should resent the loss of the provinces over which the Khedive formerly ruled. Great Britain is responsible for the prevalence of a feeling which does credit to Egyptian patriotism. There is no reason why the blunder of drawing the southern frontier at Wady Halfa should continue to give offence, and hinder Egypt from being again the granary of the world. It seems absolutely necessary that the new irrigation works upon which the progress and welfare of the Nile Valley depend should have their beginning beyond the provisional frontier, and for this reason alone it is imperative that it should be advanced southwards. When moved, as I hope it soon may be, I hold that the railway must go with it.

When the locomotive shall run as far south as is possible under Egyptian rule, it may be possible for it to continue its course on a line of rail within the British Empire. Children now living may travel in a railway-carriage, before they are very old men, from Cape Town to Cairo.

.

CHAPTER XIV.

MEN AT THE HELM.

IF any of the boats which shoot the rapids at
Assouan were as badly steered as the Egyptian ship
of state was a few years since, it would assuredly be
wrecked.

Mehemet Ali possessed that power of governing
his fellows which appears to be a gift from heaven or
elsewhere. His will was supreme, and he used his
authority without always abusing it. He often made
mistakes, which it is the irremediable misfortune of
despots to do; yet a less uncompromising ruler might
not have achieved a tithe of his success. Perhaps the
best trait in his character was his consciousness that
he was an erring mortal, and this made him address
Sir John Bowring in the following terms, " I want
good advice; I look round in search of it; my wish
is to have a council of honest men."*

His immediate successors were neither so
scrupulous nor so capable. They had a foolish
belief in themselves, and they governed Egypt after
the autocratic model of their Suzerain.

Ismail was the most unworthy of all modern men

* Report on Egypt, p. 147.

at the helm. He was over-sanguine and rash in emergencies when coolness and a calm estimate of the situation were requisite. He abounded in talent, but it was misdirected. The commonplace excuse of meaning well cannot be urged in his behalf. It is unquestionable that his one object in life was the enrichment of himself and his family. The well-being of his country appeared to be a matter of absolute indifference to him. He did not even care to solicit the advice of the Ministers of State whom he had entrusted with responsible office. His ministers were often treated as clerks whose duties consisted in executing his orders.

Till the helm was entrusted to Tewfik Pasha, no Egyptian chief of the State had manifested a true sentiment of duty to the country in which he was born. Mr. Moberly Bell, who was intimately acquainted with him, says that his character may be summed up in the word "loyal."

He was loyal to his father; he was loyal to the Great Powers whose advice he accepted; he was loyal to the people over whom he was placed. He never committed any one act, to use Mr. Moberly Bell's emphatic words, "which had not its basis in an honest wish to do what he thought right."*

Tewfik had more of the Egyptian than the Turk in his nature, whereas the founder of his family, though he successfully warred against the Turks, was from first to last much more of a Turk than an Egyptian. The distinction is quite as great as that which prevailed in bygone days between the

* "Khedives and Pashas," p. 47.

Norman and the Saxon in England, and the Celt
and the Lowlander in Scotland.   A Turk is a tyrant
at heart ; an Egyptian is a tyrant by accident.   In
Egypt, as elsewhere, unlimited power vitiates the
noblest natures.   The second Khedive entered into
an inheritance of misfortune where his virtues had full
scope for development.   When he died in the prime
of his life, he had earned the gratitude of his people
for having shown himself a conciliatory, a patriotic
and a constitutional ruler, while he had set them a
better example as a husband and father than any
predecessor.

I had a long interview with him shortly before
he was smitten with the illness which proved fatal.
As his appearance has often been minutely described,
I content myself with saying that he was above the
middle-height, and thick-set ; had rather heavy
features, and an impassive look.   However, his
features brightened when he smiled, and he smiled
frequently.   He reminded me in Abdin Palace of
General Grant in the White House.   Both were
reticent and seemed averse to commit themselves,
preferring the parts of listeners to those of con-
versers.   Yet, when President Grant began to talk
on a subject in which he was interested, his almost
Oriental gravity disappeared ; he spoke fluently
and to the point, never wasting a word or an idea.
The Khedive of Egypt, who had nothing else
in common with the great President of the
United States of America, was indisposed to speak
unless specially interested in a subject ; yet, when
his mind was touched, his tongue was loosened, and

his features were illumined with a most pleasing expression.

I made the remark to him that the educational arrangements in Cairo seemed to be very good, but that a larger outlay was required to render them almost complete. " Ah ! money is the difficulty," he replied. " I wish it could be got for so good a purpose, but my Ministers tell me there is none to spare at present."

I noted at the time that he placed the blame upon his Ministers ; his father would doubtless have said that the treasury was empty. I added that I had been greatly impressed with the admirable arrangements of the School of Arts and Handicrafts. " I am glad to hear you say so," he observed, " because I am very proud of that school. The pupils who pass through it do not worry me with requests for places in my Government." He advised me to visit the Agricultural College, which I had not then seen. He styled it one of his hobbies, and he expressed the conviction that it would render great service to his country.

No one who has a single interview with a sovereign ruler can learn much. Preconceived opinions may then be confirmed or altered, but nothing more may follow. I have stated my opinion of the second Khedive which I formed when conversing with him. I supplied material in the Second chapter for a judgment being passed upon him, and I shall supplement what I there wrote with some particulars which may enable that judgment to be founded upon a still more comprehensive basis.

Mr. Butler records that the cruelty to animals, which is as common and loathsome in Egypt as in Southern Italy, was abominated by Tewfik, and that it was his hope to effect some improvement by his example. He put an end to the barbarous ceremony of the Dôsah, or trampling the dervishes, which took place on the anniversary of the Prophet's birthday. A holy man on horseback rode over a row of living bodies. Lady Duff Gordon was present at the ceremony of August, 1866, and called it "an awful sight; so many men drunk with religious ardour."*

Mr. Butler witnessed the spectacle in 1880, and thus wrote of it: "I saw the dreadful yielding of the bodies, as thigh or ribs, spine or shoulder, felt the crushing weight of the hoofs, and I saw the writhing of the poor tortured forms. Just opposite me the horse planted his foot on the side of a poor wretch, and let it slip down between two men; the result was that he stumbled, plunged heavily forward, recovered with difficulty, and came with dreadful force on one or two bodies before my eyes."†

He related to the Khedive the impression which the nauseating spectacle had made upon him, and the Khedive intimated his abhorrence of the Dôsah, promising to do his best to get it abolished, and stating, at the same time, the difficulties which he would have to encounter and overcome. However, the order which he issued

* "Last Letters from Egypt," p. 56.
† "Court Life in Egypt," p. 42.

prohibiting it was obeyed, and since then the birthday of the Prophet has been celebrated in Egypt
without the hideous accompaniment of crushed and
mangled human beings.

The readiness of the second Khedive to sanction
and aid every good work made his premature death
the severer loss. The event was justly deplored in
the English public press, and this caused a French
paper in Cairo, *Le Bosphore*, for the 11th of January,
1892, to utter a protest against these eulogiums
on the ground that they were "outrages on his
memory." In the same number, an anonymous
correspondent is cited as the authority for the statement that the deceased Khedive had exclaimed,
after the English troops paraded before his palace,
that he was styled a sovereign in irony, and that
he was "bent under a yoke which he had to
conceal." Again, this unnamed writer says that he
heard the Khedive exclaim, after being complimented
on the splendour of an entertainment which he had
given to the Prince of Wales : "Splendid indeed!
I am compelled to offer splendid hospitality to the
conquerors of Egypt."

The French view of Tewfik is that he under-
went martyrdom at the hands of the English, and
that his heart yearned for France. Stories, which
have never been authenticated, are repeated in support of this view. It is as difficult to refute as it
is hard to believe them. It is easier to manufacture
than to substantiate them.

However, having quoted some French fictions by
way of sample, I may quote facts from an English

source, and from the pen of a man who really enjoyed Tewfik's intimate acquaintance. Very shortly after his accession, M. Tricon, the French Consul-General, remonstrated with him for remaining on good terms with his father, his reply being : " M. Tricon, I listen to you as Khedive, not as a son." When England and France were re-establishing the Dual Control, to which the Khedive was understood to be opposed, "one of Tenniel's cartoons in *Punch* represented him as disliking his ' new pair of boots.' I showed it to him. He looked at it closely, and then he said : ' Ah ! but this is a pair. Your Mr. Punch should have drawn two odd boots, one of English make, one of French make.'

" Although compelled in the early part of his reign to wear the odd pair, and to look as if he found them equally pleasant, he never concealed from me, at least, his strong English prepossessions ; and he was fond of saying : ' They make French boots too narrow ; they pinch in the toes.' This mild little joke was repeated in various forms until the abolition of the Dual Control, when I con-gratulated him upon getting into Egyptian babooshes again. ' Yes,' he added, ' but English-soled.' "*

The skill with which Tewfik had steered the ship of state was doubted during his lifetime, but it was demonstrated at his death. His son, Abbas Hilmy, on taking the helm, found that he had simply to keep the ship in the old course, and all would go well.

The earliest mention of the third Khedive is

* " Khedives and Pashas," pp. 38, 39.

that made by Mr. Butler, his tutor. His brother
and he are pronounced by him the most charming
children it is possible to imagine. Abbas was then
six years old. Mr. Butler says that both his younger
brother and he had bright pretty faces and most
winning manners, and that "Abbas Bey was remarkable for his sweetness of disposition ; Mohammed
Ali for a roguishness that soon made me christen
him 'Little Mischief.' Both had good qualities,
and it was a real pleasure to teach them."*

One of Tewfik's first acts as Khedive was to
establish the Ali School, opposite Abdin Palace. A
hundred boys, the sons of Princes and Pashas, were
educated there. He sent his two sons to this school,
where they were treated exactly as the other pupils,
and were not given their titles during class-hours.
Afterwards the two brothers went first to Geneva,
and next to Vienna, where they became pupils of
the Theresianum, the great Austrian training college
for the sons of gentlemen who are destined for a
military career.

I had the honour of a long interview with his
Highness Abbas Hilmy Pasha soon after his
accession to the throne. He is rather shorter than
his father, and seems fonder than he was of a
military uniform, usually appearing in the undress
of a General. His father preferred to appear
in a "Stambouli coat," which resembles the
European frock-coat, making no profession of love
for soldiering, though he was as keenly alive as
George III. to having vacancies in his army filled

* "Court Life in Egypt," p. 101.

by the men whom he preferred. The present
Khedive, on the other hand, has a decided liking
for the army, and perhaps he expects too much
from his soldiers. Though the Egyptian army is
well-disciplined, it must not be judged or treated
by a European standard, least of all by the standard
which prevails in Vienna, where trivial shortcomings,
as regards the uniform and accoutrements, are regarded as heinous offences.

The reigning Khedive has visited England and
Scotland ; he speaks both English and French with
accuracy and fluency, and his German is excellent.
He retains very pleasant personal impressions of
Great Britain. Though a young man, he has none of
the frivolity or indolence of youth. He discharges
his duties with punctuality and zeal, and he takes
great pains in mastering all the details of every case
with which he has to deal. He naturally would
prefer being an absolute ruler ; Muslims and
Christians in high places desire to have their own
way as strongly as others whose position is lowly.
But he is not in favour of the French supplanting
the English in Egypt. Still less does he wish to
become a puppet in the hands of the Sultan of
Turkey.

The manner in which Ismail was deposed may
be accounted, as I have remarked in the First
chapter, a Turkish victory. The attempt made by
the Sultan to limit the third Khedive's jurisdiction ended in a Turkish defeat. It is improbable
that his Highness Abbas Hilmy Pasha will forget
his indebtedness to Great Britain on this occasion.

It is certain that he has not displayed any leaning towards France, neither has he intimated a desire to exchange the patriotic policy of his father for a policy which would be applauded by the French press in Egypt and would end in utter confusion.

The Ministers in whom Tewfik placed confidence enjoy that of the reigning Khedive. Mustapha Fehmy Pasha, who presides over the Council of Ministers, has the recommendation of professing the religion of the majority. He is neither brilliant nor incompetent, neither unduly self-asserting nor a complete dummy. He clearly understands and honestly discharges his duty. An abler and a more restless man in the office which he fills might cause friction in the working of the Government machinery. An ambitious Chief Minister might be tempted to intrigue with a foreign Power in order to further his ends. The maxim of Sir Robert Walpole when in the hey-day of his fame is the appropriate one for a patriotic Prime Minister of Egypt now. *Quieta non movere*—" Let well alone." This is a serviceable maxim at certain times, and it appears to be that of his Excellency Mustapha Fehmy Pasha.

His Excellency Tigrane Pasha, the Minister of Foreign Affairs, is the ablest man in the Administration, with the exception of Jacoub Artin Pasha, the Under-Secretary for Education. Tigrane is the son-in-law of Nubar Pasha, one of the shrewdest among Egyptian public men. His earliest achievement was the press law, which he drafted in France with the assistance of French statesmen. It is as absurd to have a special law concerning the conductors of newspapers anywhere as it would be to have a special law concerning Prime Ministers. If the editor of a newspaper should make public what is indecent or treasonable, let him be tried like any other man who is guilty of open indecency or treason. The ridiculous side of the Egyptian press law is the immunity enjoyed by the worst offenders against its provisions.

It is not surprising that despots should dislike and dread an independent and honestly-conducted newspaper. Nothing is more unwelcome to them than the truth about their doings. Besides, the natural man enjoys flattery, and fair criticism is tolerated by those only whose education has reached a certain standard, and who have learned to value free discussion as the salt of existence. If such a journal as *The Times* had been placed upon Haroun Alraschid's breakfast-table every morning, he would not have been obliged to spend a part of the night in disguise, listening to gossip in a coffee-house or at a street corner, in order to learn what his subjects thought of him. Such an absolute ruler as the Sultan of Turkey or the Czar of Russia lives in an atmosphere of adulation ascending from a tribe of courtiers. The parasites of the great can say their worst without harm in a country where a free newspaper Press exists and is prized. These obvious considerations are not commonplaces throughout Europe, and the Khedive of Egypt, and his Ministers, may be pardoned for not appreciating their force and acting accordingly.

It would probably be unfair to attribute to Tigrane Pasha a personal liking for the law governing journalists which he prepared at the request of his superiors. Having strong sympathies in favour of France, he may share the French taste for Government intermeddling in the private affairs of citizens. Many forms of administration, as well as of procedure in courts of justice in Egypt, are borrowed from the French, and this is due to the better class of Egyptian statesmen having been trained in France and having their minds stored with French ideas. Tigrane Pasha is a man of culture as well as an accomplished Minister of State. He has a choice collection of pictures by French artists. If he prefer France to England, he resembles some English politicians in this respect. Personal tastes are harmless in any statesman so long as they do not affect his political action. Tigrane Pasha understands English thoroughly, but he prefers to speak French. He has no dread of the French occupying Egypt should the English retire ; and, while not openly inimical to the British occupation, he would emphatically contend, if called upon for advice, that it should end as speedily as possible.

He hopes that the Soudan will be reoccupied and governed by the Egyptians again, and in this he is in accord with his countrymen and with all who have given adequate attention to the subject. In his opinion, the unconciliatory attitude of France renders it harder for England to discuss the Egyptian question with her. I was not surprised to learn that he has a great respect for Mr. J. M. Cook, and considers that the latter has rendered marked service to Egypt. Tigrane Pasha is one of the younger Ministers and few of the elder surpass him in ability. If asked whether he might be termed "popular," I should feel it as difficult to reply in the affirmative as in the negative. An Egyptian statesman is seldom popular in the English sense of the word. Arabi Pasha did enjoy and abuse popularity; but this was due to his preaching a sort of holy war, and to his declaring that debtors need no longer pay their creditors, whom he denounced as usurers. The Egyptians accept without murmuring any Minister whom the Khedive appoints; and if they have a greater admiration for one more than another, it may turn out that the one whom they favour is a Muslim, while the other is a Christian. Islamism has the same influence in Egyptian politics that Roman Catholicism has in those of Ireland. Tigrane Pasha is a Christian.

Jacoub Artin Pasha would doubtless be Minister of Education, instead of Under-Secretary, if it were not considered expedient that the Minister should be a Muslim. Now, Artin Pasha is a Christian, and, though an authority on education and the author of an excellent work on the subject, he occupies the second place instead of the first, lest religious prejudices should be aroused. He, too, is a master of the French tongue; but he is quite as ready to speak English, which he does with fluency and ease. He is as courteous to the French as to the English, and he is held in equal esteem by the representatives of the two nationalities, who,

although rivals on the Nile, are at one in admiring
Artin Pasha. The French writer who adopted
the pseudonym of Frédolin is his strong eulogist,
and classes him with Nubar Pasha for his foresight
in having chalked out the road wherein Egypt will
walk despite the British occupation.*

Yet the Under-Secretary for Education deserves
as much praise as Tigrane Pasha from any English
writer. If questioned as to whether the country
should be instantly evacuated by the British force, he
would probably deprecate any hasty action, express
his fear lest anarchy should follow, and remark that
the old system had been destroyed, and that the new
had not been consolidated. His suave and genial
manner may conceal views which he never embodies
in words. He may be all things to all men, with
the result of no man being able to ascertain what he
really means. I think that he has such an intense
wish for his countrymen being educated, and so firm
a belief in the generation which is now passing
through school becoming infinitely superior to the
preceding one, that he may wish things to continue
as they are until that generation shall have reached
maturity, and have shown itself fitted for self-govern-
ment. Whether Artin Pasha cherish French or
English sympathies, he is a fine specimen of the ruling
class in Egypt, being polished in manner, well read,
and exhibiting the best qualities of the statesman
with the most useful traits in a man of the world.

Egypt possesses two ex-Prime Ministers, each
of whom is remarkable, and each has an invincible

* "John Bull sur le Nil," par Frédolin, p. 345.

belief that he is unique among the statesmen of the country which he adorns. One is a Muslim; the other is a Christian. The first has held office under Ismail and Tewfik, while the second was prepared for public life by serving Mehemet Ali as secretary. I have conversed with Riaz Pasha, who is the first of these two, and I enjoyed many talks with Nubar Pasha, who is the second. Both are familiar figures in modern Egyptian history, and much has been written about them. Nothing, however, has been said concerning Riaz Pasha which is better than the account given of him by Mr. Moberly Bell, and I refer the reader to it, contenting myself with summarizing some of the more instructive passages.*

His beginnings are obscure; what is certain is that Ismail discovered his capacity, and elevated him from a menial station to high office. He was Premier when Arabi was hatching rebellion; but he would not pay heed to the signs of the times. He was Minister of the Interior in Cherif's Administration, of which he was the soul. Riaz Pasha has an irreversible conviction that all his opinions are right, and that he has been expressly created to direct the affairs of the country. Mr. Moberly Bell sums up his character and conceptions in the following phrase: "I imagine that his conception of the universe is a Divine mandate, 'Let there be Riaz, and there was Riaz.'" He has the virtue of honesty, which redeems many faults, and he laboured to convince his colleagues and his sovereign that honesty and poverty were more honourable than

* "Khedives and Pashas," pp. 121, 141.

wealth and corruption. There is a tincture of Puritanism in him, and the public man who is puritanical may be more admired than beloved.

Since Joseph the Hebrew became Governor of Egypt under Pharaoh, no one has displayed greater aptitude for such an office under a Khedive than the Armenian, Nubar Pasha. He had a French training before he arrived at Cairo and became a member of Mehemet Ali's household. He writes French with the grace and point, the delicacy of touch and the polish of the most accomplished Frenchman. He knows English, and speaks it admirably ; indeed, it is difficult to name anything which he cannot do well if he should care to undertake it.

Nubar Pasha has held many offices in the Government, the Premiership being one of them. He deserves the credit of having established the International Tribunals, while their imperfections are not chargeable upon him. He wished to abolish the consular jurisdictions, and to extinguish the claims which are based upon imaginary capitulations; and if he had succeeded, then Egypt would sooner have begun preparing herself for entering the community of civilized nations. Nubar Pasha is simple in his tastes and habits, yet he lavishes hospitality in true Oriental fashion. He is very communicative, yet he shrinks from publicity being given to his views ; indeed, his modesty appears to be as wonderful as his capacity.

I shall neither offend his feelings nor betray his confidence by repeating the opinions which he uttered in my presence, and I confine myself to

remarking that the general public have been made
aware, by those who have not hesitated to reproduce
his views, of his strong disapproval of further interference by any foreign Power in the internal affairs of
Egypt. He does profess an irreconcilable objection
to the continuance of the British occupation. He
has an intense dislike to what he styles the administrative occupation of Egypt, meaning by this the
exercise of influence of the British representative
over the Egyptian Ministry. " Keep the peace in
Egypt," he would say to the commander of the
British force. " Let me preside over the Ministry,
and carry out my plans in my own way," is the
language which he might address to the British
Consul-General and Envoy.

I cannot determine whether his leanings are
towards France or England, but I feel confident it
would be a gross mistake to call him pro-Turkish.
Frédolin, whom I have already quoted, has reproduced what he styles " Nubar Pasha's profession of
faith," which runs thus : " I love the French and
France. Yet by an inexplicable fatality I have always
been at logger-heads with the French Government.
It is the French Consuls who always cut out much
trouble for me ; nevertheless, since the time of
Mehemet Ali I have always welcomed French ideas
because they are advantageous to the country."*

An Englishman, who knows him as intimately
as the French author I have just mentioned, writes
in another strain : " Nubar Pasha has strong sympathies with Germany and England. His favourite

* " John Bull sur le Nil," p. 311.

policy until recently was to render Egypt an African
Belgium; whether recent events have not altered
this may be doubted. In my own opinion he looks
to the Government of Egypt by England through
an Armenian Resident."*

Cairo is not much behind Constantinople as a
city in which intrigue is rampant, and where false
reports constitute the chief news of the day. Statesmen like Riaz Pasha and Nubar Pasha have each a
following which has no warmer wish than the return
to power of either, and the partisans of both are not
over-scrupulous in speech and conduct.

If the two united their forces, as William Pitt
and the Duke of Newcastle did in England during the
last century, the two ablest Egyptian statesmen would
then manage Egyptian affairs. Pitt was accustomed
to say: " I do everything; the Duke of Newcastle
gives everything." It is doubtful, however, whether
Riaz and Nubar could agree to divide their functions
in this manner, both being anxious to wield power
and neither having the Duke of Newcastle's sordid
longing for patronage. The Khedive is to be con-
gratulated upon having devoted and competent
advisers among the older as well as the younger
generation of statesmen. He is also fortunate in
having among his subjects such a capable officer as
Major-General Sir Edward Zohrab, Pasha.

Neither the ship of state nor any vessel of vulgar
mould can subserve its purpose unless those who
occupy subordinate offices in it are thoroughly competent and trustworthy. The progress which Egypt

* "Khedives and Pashas," p. 155.

has made during the last five years—a progress
which the French deny and the Turks envy—is
attributable to the Englishmen whom the late
Khedive attracted to his service, and whom the
present Khedive has retained. Sir Elwin Palmer, the
Financial Adviser to his Highness; Mr. Justice Scott,
the Judicial Adviser; Sir Colin Scott Moncrieff,
while Under-Secretary of State for Public Works,
and Mr. Alfred Milner, while Under-Secretary of
State for the Department of Finance, have largely
contributed to undo the mischief which followed the
maladministration in the past, and to prepare a
glorious future for Egypt.* Other Englishmen are
aiding in the good work. I have mentioned some
of them in preceding chapters; I may now add the
names of Kitchener Pasha, Sirdar of the Egyptian
army, Major Wingate, the head of the Intelligence
department, and Johnson Pasha, who most ably
commands the police. If I judge from what is
written in French newspapers published in Egypt,
the fact of these men being in office is an insult to
France. I entertain profound respect for whatever
appears in a newspaper, but I hesitate to admit the
infallibility of any journalist, and I have repeatedly
observed that the French journals in Egypt, and
those in France which deal with Egyptian affairs,
are inaccurate, if not worse.

The conductors of these journals accuse English-

---

* Sir Colin is now Under-Secretary for Scotland, and Mr. Milner
is Chairman of the Board of Inland Revenue in London. The
former has been replaced by Mr. Garstin, and the loss of the latter
to Egypt is lessened owing to Mr. Gorst having succeeded him.

men of occupying all the best posts, and refusing to promote native Egyptians, however great their merits may be. The truth is that a native Egyptian has been chosen to preside over the Post-office in Cairo, another to be the head of one of a circle in the Irrigation Department, while a third has been made Deputy-Governor of Alexandria, his promotion being chiefly due to the recommendation of the Khedive's English advisers and his office being one of the most responsible and lucrative in the land.

Authentic figures ought to be more convincing than assertions. According to the last published return, the number of Italians in the Khedive's service is 348, of French 326, and of English 174.* In the Department of Irrigation there are but seventeen English officials, while in the Department of Finance, in which the officials are numbered by the hundred, the English do not exceed half a dozen. It is true that some of the most responsible and most lucrative offices are filled by Englishmen, and it is also true that they have proved most profitable servants. Some of them, after acting for a single month, have effected savings equal to their salaries for a year. If well paid they are hard worked, and if challenged to justify their appointments they can point to a remodelled and effective army ; an overflowing treasury ; a school system as good as any in the world, and capable of boundless expansion ; public works in perfect order, which French engineers have declared to be impracticable; courts of justice of which a more civilized country might be

* " Egypt : Native Rulers and Foreign Interference," p. 309.

proud ; a police force which is not, as was formerly the case, a terror to the innocent, but one which is now feared by the criminal. Let the work which has been begun and conducted with consummate skill, continue without interference, until the younger generation of Egyptians shall have attained manhood, the reigning Khedive, who may then, as I hope, be at the helm of the ship of state, will have no reason to envy any predecessor, or to fear any rival.

CHAPTER XV.

A SURVEY AND A FORECAST.

THE antiquity of Egypt astounds the chronologist. The question which Horace Smith put, in his "Address to a Mummy," has never yet been answered :

"Antiquity appears to have begun
  Long after thy primeval race was won.
  Thou couldst develop, if that withered tongue
    Might tell us what those sightless orbs have seen,
  How the world looked when it was fresh and young,
    And the great Deluge still had left it green ;
  Or was it then so old, that History's pages
  Contained no record of its early ages ?"

In profane as in sacred history, Egypt's place is unique. It is a land of old religions, of mysteries which have never been fathomed, and of life in its most enviable form to those who command wealth and leisure. The human race cannot thrive under more favourable natural conditions than within sight of the Nile. The wretched there have been the victims of destiny cr despotism.

During countless ages Egypt has been the battle-field of antagonistic races. Its inhabitants have had to struggle for existence, not because the sun was darkened, or the soil yielded no increase, but because they were dismayed by rumours of wars or trodden underfoot by savage conquerors. The blessing of which the Valley of the Nile has known the least is the inestimable blessing of peace. Few things are older than the Egyptian question. It existed when the Pyramids were building. Joseph tried to solve it. Pharaoh may have thought that it was ended when the Israelites had departed ; if he did, he foolishly reopened it by pursuing them. Their descendants have found it active and alarming, and some of them have breathed new life into it.

Sir Archibald Alison, the respected and voluminous historian of modern Europe, delighted in speculating as to what might have happened, provided a particular event had not occurred. Those who value hypothetical history might amuse themselves by treating that of Egypt on the assumption that there had not been an exodus under one of the Pharaohs, or a British occupation under the second Khedive. Instead of indulging in speculations which are aimless, I have endeavoured to set forth facts which are indisputable. Any reader who is devoid of bias can use them to form a logical conclusion, and such a conclusion might take the following shape.

The late Miss Amelia B. Edwards acutely remarked that " the sun and soil of Egypt demand a special breed of men, and will tolerate no other ";* hence, while the land can be civilized, it cannot be entirely Europeanized. It is being civilized ; both Europe and America are enriching the dwellers in

* " A Thousand Miles up the Nile," p. 104.

the Valley of the Nile with new ideas as surely as the great river is fertilizing its banks. Would it be desirable that the regenerative process should be interrupted, and that the progress which has been made should be rendered nugatory ? The stoppage and the reaction would inevitably follow the withdrawal of British influence, resting upon material force, which is now exercised with a single-minded desire to promote the efficiency of the Egyptian Government and the happiness of the Egyptian people. Let that influence wither, and the immediate consequence would resemble what occurs when a steel ship is launched before her plates are all riveted together, and when the supports are withdrawn from a stone arch before the keystone has been inserted.

I have read the speeches of certain members of Parliament, who clearly and congenially represent the ignorance of the nation, wherein it is stated, without qualification, that England's disinterested occupation of Egypt is utterly indefensible and mischievous. Other members of Parliament who rank among statesmen have kept their unenlightened brethren in countenance by stating in substance, "Leave Egypt to its fate and France." It is undeniable that French journalists and politicians are grievously offended owing to the prospect of the Egyptians being civilized under the ægis and with the aid of Great Britain. Their friends and sympathizers in this country, who care more about humouring France than about regenerating the Egyptians, might have no compunction in acting upon the phrase, " Perish Egypt rather than that France should feel jealous !"

In considering the Egyptian question from a critical point of view, the essential element in a just judgment is impartiality. I do not mean by this the display or the affectation of indifference, but the elimination of all political prejudice. Home politics are unfitted for exportation, and those who refuse to believe this will suffer the disappointment or confusion of the wine-grower whose produce can be drunk with pleasure on the spot, but which becomes undrinkable, if not poisonous, after a long journey by rail or sea. The truth which experience teaches, but which few politicians learn, is that foreign affairs require a totally different habit of mind for their judicious treatment than the affairs of every-day life at home.

Bearing this in mind, I have treated the Egyptian question purely as a critic who has studied it carefully, and is desirous of arriving at a rational conclusion. Writing in that capacity, I cannot believe that the civilizing action of Great Britain in Egypt, even though conducted in the teeth of embittered opposition from France, necessarily implies the ruin of the British Empire. The danger of war with France, as the consequence of England's temporary occupation of Egypt, should have as little weight with an intelligent Englishman as a badly-constructed scarecrow has with a flock of intelligent rooks. The rooks may be engaged in the laudable endeavour to free a ploughed field from noxious grubs. An ignorant farmer will strive to frighten away his best friends.

The friendship of France is rightly prized by

English statesmen ; but the friendship of England is a gain to France which no sensible Frenchman can over-estimate. One-sided friendship is a contradiction in terms. If French friendship be dependent upon compliance with every French whim, then it is worthless.

All talk about the rights of France in Egypt is empty. France has never concealed a desire to acquire Egypt, but this does not constitute a claim to the country. The Great Powers have assumed the position of guardians to the Egyptians in order that Egyptian bondholders shall receive their dividends with commendable punctuality. The natives of Egypt, like the natives of India, account themselves fortunate if they can earn their daily bread and satisfy the tax-gatherer. Should they have a surplus to squander upon a marriage-feast or a funeral ceremony, they consider themselves especially favoured by fortune. The best ruler in Egypt is the ruler who taxes the people most lightly, and as the reduction of taxation is one aim of English administrators, the Egyptians are in perfect accord with them and their object. Has French influence in Egypt ever been employed to lessen the burdens of the Fellaheen ? It is frequently asserted by ill-informed and illogical politicians that the French have a title to exercise control in Egypt, because the Suez Canal was the work of Frenchmen. These men do not know how much Egypt has contributed to a work from which France has reaped glory and profit. Hitherto, the Egyptians have been heavy losers by the Canal ; happily, however, when the concession expires, their turn will come for benefiting by it. With such a prospective asset as the Suez Canal the Egyptian debt is deprived of all its terrors. The prospect has a still more glorious side. When Egypt shall become wealthy, she may become independent.

The facts which I have set forth in the preceding chapters must inspire those persons with confidence who hope for the expansion and progress of the whole land of Egypt. If its development be not checked by external interference, the country must grow in power and knowledge, and the people will gradually rise to a higher rank in civilization. They have much to learn, but they have an aptitude for acquiring knowledge which is as admirable as it is rare.

Juster and kindlier views might be disseminated and gain recognition concerning Egypt if the thousands of Europeans and Americans who visit it yearly regarded the natives with as much interest as they regard monuments and mummies. The ordinary tourist returns from the Nile to his native land cherishing the belief that most of the Egyptians are donkey-boys, or are fairly represented by them. It is as sensible to hold such a view as it would be to consider the cabmen of London and the hackmen of New York as typical Englishmen and Americans. Keepers of donkeys and drivers of cabs fill a part in the Divine economy of things; but that part is restricted in scope and insignificant in effect. There is an Egyptian community which merits study and sympathy, and the better it is known the stronger must be the feeling in its favour. The people have many virtues. They are tractable and teachable. Since the spread of British influence in the Nile Valley, the condition of the people has been greatly improved, and their best qualities have had opportunities for development.

It has long been the failing of visitors to the Morning-land to concentrate their attention on what is old and strange, and to be indifferent to the human beings who inhabit it. Lady Duff Gordon was the first to depict the poorer Egyptians at home in sympathetic terms. Thirty years ago she noted that contempt for the common people on the part of foreign visitors which is conspicuous still. Even Harriet Martineau, one of the ablest of her sex, was not superior in this respect to others far less intelligent, and Lady Duff Gordon remarks in one of her letters : " I have been reading Miss Martineau's book ; the descriptions are excellent, and it is true as far as it goes ; but there is the usual defect: to her, as to most Europeans, the people are not real people, only part of the scenery. She evidently knew and cared nothing about them, and had the feeling of most English travellers, that the differences of manners are a sort of impassable gulf ; the truth being that their feelings and passions are just like her own."*

Those who look with indifference upon living Egyptians do not regard dead ones with more respect. In no country are the remains of mortal men treated with greater indignity than in Egypt, the worst offenders being Europeans and Americans, or else they are natives partly acting in obedience to

* " Letters from Egypt," pp. 180, 181.

orders, and partly out of sheer cupidity.   Sir
Thomas Browne wrote : " The Egyptian mummies
that Cambyses or Time hath spared, avarice now
consumeth.   Mummy is become merchandize ; Miz-
raim cures wounds, and Pharaoh is sold for balsams."
To use mummies for medicine or for manuring the
ground is no desecration ; they would serve a
rational purpose in alleviating sickness, or, if returned
to kindred dust they might blossom there.   But to
expose the remains of a man or woman to public
view in the Gizeh Museum is a sickening and a sad
spectacle.   Knowledge may be increased by rifling
the sepulchres of the ancients and groping among
the cerements of the dead, but I question if a single
human being is benefited by gazing on the leathern
lineaments and limbs of ancient priests or kings.
Women, whose nakedness was carefully veiled
during life, have their unclad remains remorselessly
exhibited after death because they are mummies
who trod the earth many centuries ago.   Curiosity
ought to be satisfied when the remains have been
photographed ; they ought to be returned to the
earth after their appearance has been fixed on
paper.   There is as much sanctity in the grave as
in the church.   The visitor to Egypt who is not in
favour of cremation must be converted by the sights
there.   I consider it consolatory, as the great writer
puts it, from whom I have quoted more than once,
that " to be gnawed out of our graves, to have our
skulls made drinking-bowls, and our bones turned
into pipes, to delight and sport our enemies, are
tragical abominations escaped in burning burials."

American visitors to Egypt are accounted the best customers of Egyptian body-snatchers. They are glad to return home with a mummy ; they are proud of being able to invite their friends to see it unrolled. They bury their own dead with surpassing care, placing them in caskets within splendid tombs. It might seem as if they held with Ulysses in Hecuba, that they were recompensed for lives of struggle by reposing under noble monuments after death. A cemetery in America is generally the most beautiful adjunct to a city. Would not the highly cultured citizens of Boston shudder if told that a day might come when Mount Auburn would be treated as a mine in which shafts were sunk, and levels driven in order to discover human remains and bring them to the surface, there to be sold to strangers from beyond the sea in quest of curiosities, or else to be put on exhibition at home ?

It is true that Egyptians robbed the dead before Europeans and Americans trafficked in mummies, the temptation being the gold ornaments with which the bodies were adorned, yet they left the remains in the sepulchre where they had been deposited. Some modern Egyptians have protested against the disrespect shown to these dead bodies, Sheikh Joosuf, the pious friend of Lady Duff Gordon, being one of them. She records that, when they went together to the Tombs of the Kings, he expressed himself " shocked at the way in which the mummies are kicked about ; he said one boy told him, as an excuse, that they were not Muslims. Yoosuf rebuked him severely, and told him that it was *harám* (accursed) to do so to any of the children of Adam."*

An earlier and a greater Joseph was embalmed and "put in a coffin in Egypt." Before his death, he made the children of Israel swear that they would afterwards remove his bones. His hope doubtless was that they would be reverently laid in a tomb. If discovered now, they would be put on exhibition in a museum.

I have several times expressed the opinion in the course of this work that if Egypt were allowed to work out her own destiny under existing conditions, and with the assurance that these would not be rashly disturbed, the progress already made would be accelerated and consolidated. But the maintenance of existing conditions is the essential element in the rejuvenation of Egypt. I cited Edmond About in the Third chapter as a writer whose views concerning the country had been based upon a study of the people. He was more concerned about living Fellaheen than embalmed Pharaohs. He saw in 1867 what any competent observer must perceive now, that the people require instruction and example to develop their best qualities, and that till they have been trained under European direction their advance in civilization must either be slow or be arrested altogether. What About desired is now in process of accomplishment.

A most significant fact has not received adequate consideration. The country is increasing in population. No country which continues under-peopled

* "Letters from Egypt," p. 243.

can ever be conspicuous among the nations. In the heyday of its power and glory, the population of Egypt was reckoned at 20,000,000. Seventy years ago, when the country had declined to the despised rank of an insignificant Turkish province, the people numbered 2,514,400. A quarter of a century later, when Mehemet Ali had nearly succeeded in throwing off the Turkish yoke, the inhabitants numbered 4,456,186. The number had risen to 6,806,381 when the census was taken in 1882. A confident expectation exists among those who are best qualified to judge, that the next census will exhibit a still greater proportionate increase.

The addition to the foreign is even more marked than that to the native element. When this century was young the foreigners settled in Egypt were few and uninfluential. At present they number nearly 100,000. Many civilized nations complain of the influx of foreigners, and some either forbid their entrance or else interpose obstacles. Unhappily for Egypt, the door is open through which the scum of Southern Europe may enter. The least creditable and the most lucrative industries of the country are monopolized by Greeks and Italians. These foreigners and others place themselves under the protection of their respective Consuls, and defy the Egyptian Government to punish them if they are guilty of heinous crimes, while they refuse to pay any taxes. I have said already that a licence tax was imposed upon foreign traders a year ago ; the representative of England admitted its justice, and the English residents readily paid it, but it had to be cancelled owing to the persistent and menacing protests of France and Greece. If but £1 a head were paid by foreigners the burdensome taxation of the Fellaheen would be lightened.

While money is urgently required to enable the heavily-taxed Egyptians to breathe more freely, the call for additional expenditure upon public education and public works is not less pressing. Ominous rumours are current about the yield from agriculture diminishing. Some of the land is becoming infertile because it has been over-cropped. Too much has been extracted from the soil; too little has been returned to it. The earth, like the Fellaheen, may be over-strained, and just as the Fellaheen cannot work at their best if their labour is inadequately recompensed, so does the earth prove barren when imperfectly nourished. Mehemet Ali said to Sir John Bowring: "I have hitherto only scratched the earth with a pin or tilled it with a hoe, but I mean to go over it with a plough."* The scientific farmer would add that the addition of appropriate fertilizers is indispensable before heroic cropping can be attempted with success and safety. I anticipate, however, that the teaching of the Agricultural College near Cairo will lead to better treatment of the land throughout Egypt, and, as a consequence, to an enormously enhanced return from it.

Mehemet Ali was not more anxious that the Nile Valley should enrich the husbandman than that his army and navy should do him credit by defending him against his foes, or enabling him to

* "Autobiographical Recollections," p. 181.

attack an enemy with the expectation of triumphing. One of his disappointments was the refusal of the British Government of his day to favour him with officers for the purpose of organizing and disciplining his army and navy. He turned to France after this rebuff, and French officers were permitted to do what he desired. How far the Egyptian army and navy benefited by the training which they received is a matter of history. Frequent protests appear in French newspapers printed in Egypt against the employment of English officers by the Khedive. If their services have proved advantageous, so much the better for Egypt. Surely the present Khedive has as much right to engage Englishmen in his service as Mehemet Ali had to engage Frenchmen !

The most striking and pregnant circumstance in a survey of Egypt at the present day is the extent of, as well as the necessity for, British influence over it till a later and prouder stage in its history shall be reached. Accident has made England supreme, for the time being, in the Valley of the Nile. Much controversy and sacrifice would have been averted if she had consistently acted upon that policy of enlightened selfishness which an American states- man once asserted to be the true policy of an astute nation. Had England left the Egyptians and their foreign creditors to arrange matters between them, she might then have regarded with sublime stolidity or philosophic calm the interference of other nations in the affairs of Egypt. One of these nations would have been Germany; another would have been France; and the two would soon have quarrelled and fought.

Having interfered in Egyptian affairs, and, it may be, prevented a breach of European peace by so doing, England has incurred a moral responsibility which cannot be cancelled by the recall of her troops before all danger to the country is at an end, and all detriment to the condition of the people has been averted.   The office of guardian over the Nile Valley, and trustee for the Egyptian people, was not sought after by her.   She never intrigued to occupy a thankless office and discharge arduous duties.   Egypt is no longer England's stepping-stone to India.   The Suez Canal shortens the journey between London and Calcutta ; but if the Canal were closed, the greatest losers would be Italy, Germany, and France.   Indeed, when the several steps which preceded the British occupation of the Nile Valley are marked and measured, the hackneyed lines of Byron recur to the mind as containing a possible explanation, though they do not really explain anything :

> " Men are the sport of circumstances, when
> The circumstances seem the sport of men."

The last lesson which statesmen learn is that they have but an imperfect, if any, control over the course of events.   They blunder as easily as plain men, but they are more ingenious than plain men in disguising their blunders in fine phrases.   England might have stood aloof when the Egyptian question passed into an acute state, and waited till phrase-mongers had done their worst.   It was forgotten by some who were responsible for her policy when intervention had been decided upon that the one thing needful, in the circumstances, was promptitude in decision because time pressed, and firmness in adhering to a course of action because an emergency had occurred. What actually and unexpectedly happened can be stated in a few sentences which may be pondered with advantage.

England joined France in the Dual Control over Egyptian interests, which was an ingenious device for rendering the minimum of service to Egypt, and providing innumerable occasions for quarrel. She sided with France when the Sultan of Turkey was unhappily instigated to magnify his office by deposing the reigning Khedive. I have stated my opinion of Ismail in the opening chapter of this book, and I must add in the closing one that his worst vices and his most atrocious crimes were those which Sultans of Turkey have perpetrated without shame or punishment. When Tewfik, an excellent and amiable man and an exception among Oriental rulers, had to face a rebellion for which the Dual Control was largely responsible, then France withdrew from the theatre of war, leaving England to regain for the Khedive the authority which he had lost. Further sacrifices had to be made by her in order that Egypt might be at peace. The end was attained; but it was preceded by the bitter humiliation of failure to avert the death of Gordon, the Bayard of this age.

English statesmen wisely determined to make amends for many sad errors of judgment by restoring tranquillity to Egypt through a temporary occupation of it, and their wisdom will be further manifested should they maintain a force there till the country shall have been rendered capable of standing alone.

The lesson which emerges from the story of contemporary Egypt is so clear that none but the wilfully blind can fail to read it, and so instructive that none, except those who are constitutionally unteachable, can fail to profit by it. A few words written on the 28th of February, 1884, by Sir Evelyn Baring (now Lord Cromer) to Earl Granville embody that lesson. If these words had not been ineffectual in bygone days, the chivalrous Gordon might have been alive now. However, the dead past cannot be resuscitated; it will be a subject of congratulation if the passage which I am about to quote be taken to heart by statesmen, and be made to serve as a lamp to their feet when picking their way towards the true policy to be followed in the Valley of the Nile : "It is for her Majesty's Government to judge of the importance to be attached to public opinion in England ; but I venture to think that any attempt to settle Egyptian questions by the light of English popular feeling is sure to be productive of harm, and in this, as in other cases, it would be preferable to follow the advice of responsible authorities on the spot."*

A nation cannot blunder twice in exactly the same way. The new conditions created by the first blunder hinder the perpetration of an identical one. There is no likelihood, then, of England repeating mistakes in her Egyptian policy resembling those which are matters of unavailing regret, being deplored now as much as they have been criticised. It is still possible, however, to commit a new and crown-

---

* "The Ruin of the Soudan," by Henry Russell, p. 75.

ing blunder. This would consist in acting as if the aspirations of the Sultan of Turkey or the wounded vanity of the French people ought to receive greater consideration than the well-being of the Egyptians.

Neither Turkey nor France displays the courtesy of crediting England with a determination to fulfil her obligations. A pledge has been given that Egypt is not to be annexed to the British Empire, or permanently occupied by British troops. Some time may elapse, possibly twenty or thirty years, before the fitting time for evacuation arrives; the surest way to postpone it is to interfere with the policy of conciliation and progress which is now pursued in the Valley of the Nile. Lord Dufferin answered beforehand the complaints which he may have foreseen would proceed from France and Turkey by writing as follows in his famous report from Cairo: "Though it be our fixed determination that the new régime shall not surcharge us with the responsibility of permanently administering the country, whether directly or indirectly, it is absolutely necessary to prevent the fabric we have raised from tumbling to the ground the moment our sustaining hand is withdrawn. Such a catastrophe would be the signal for the return of confusion to this country, and renewed discord in Europe. At the present moment we are labouring in the interests of the world at large. . . . The very fact of our having endowed the country with representative institutions is a proof of our disinterestedness. It is the last thing we should have done had we desired to retain its Government in leading-strings."

Egypt had a Parliament under Mehemet Ali, and a Chamber of Notables under Arabi Pasha; but in each case the result was a burlesque upon representative government. How the system worked under Mehemet Ali may be gathered from what Mr. Augustus St. John saw when he visited Egypt in 1832 : " It is a Parliament of a very extraordinary kind. When the Pasha has anything agreeable to do, he does it himself, without consulting this wretched Council, who, he well knows, would not dare to entertain any opinion different from his ; but when application is made to him for money, or some favour is demanded, which it might be inexpedient to grant and imprudent to refuse, he suddenly feigns a high veneration for the authority of his Council, refers the applicants to them, and while he imperiously directs their decisions, shifts off the odium upon their shoulders."*

The General Assembly, composed of eighty members, which meets yearly in Cairo to deliberate upon national affairs, is a very different body from any other of the kind which has yet been established in the country. No matter of moment is determined by the Government before being submitted to it, and its representations have always been attended to because they have always been practical. As education advances, the day will draw nearer when this assembly will legislate as well as deliberate, and then a great stride will have been made towards the reconstruction of Egypt. This is one of the chief objects which England hopes to attain before she

* " Egypt and Mehemet Ali," vol. i., p. 130.

leaves Egypt to her own resources. While Turkey and France regard her action with dislike, Germany, Italy, and Austria-Hungary accord to it their moral support. Moreover, the Great Republic of the West, which has taken an ardent interest in Egyptian affairs, manifests sympathy with the conduct and the aims of England in Egypt, knowing well that the triumph of Anglo Saxon speech and freedom is the real point at issue.

The present position and purpose of England in the land of the Pharaohs cannot be better character-ized than in the words of Macaulay: "It is her peculiar glory, not that she has ruled so widely, not that she has conquered so splendidly, but that she has ruled only to bless, and conquered only to spare. Her mightiest empire is that of her morals, her language, and her laws; her proudest victories are those she has achieved over ferocity and ignorance; her most durable trophies are those she has erected in the hearts of civilized and liberated nations." Victories such as these she is now achieving in Egypt; trophies such as these she is gradually erecting in the hearts of dwellers in the grand Nile Valley. The Egyptians, who are marvellously patient, have borne unmur-muringly the cruellest oppression; but they are awakening to a sense of their dignity as human beings, and they are learning to live as free men.

The forty centuries which Bonaparte apostro-phized can now behold from the summits of the ancient Pyramids the soldiers of the only European nation upon whose neck he could not set his heel. They protect the descendants of those whom Bonaparte conquered and was ready to oppress. Many of the Fellaheen lead hard and monotonous lives ; but the majority do not toil at present as these for whom the morrow brings neither hope nor respite ; they have ceased to resemble mere beasts of burden for exacting and pitiless masters, and all of them are now aware that, whatever they honestly earn, they may retain and dispose of as they please, after their legal obligations have been fulfilled. The revolving hours have become rich in promise to them, and they no longer sadly regard death as the gate through which they may escape for ever from the torments of the insatiable, ruthless, and irresponsible tax-gatherer. These are personal and physical gains of marvellous value. Others, which are even more precious, may be in store for every class of the community.

The annals of the British Empire are tapestried with splendid and enthralling pictures of daring, abnegation, and magnificent achievement. I hope that another may yet adorn the gorgeous whole. It will display how the citizens of that empire extended the right hand of fellowship to the impoverished and oppressed Egyptians, pitying them when they were feeble, aiding them to become worthy of independence, gradually elevating them to the rank of a nation, and neither pausing nor wearying in well-doing till they transmuted the phrase " Egypt for the Egyptians," which had often been uttered in jest or derision, into one of the grandest, most significant and inspiriting facts in modern history.

INDEX

THE END.

www.ingramcontent.com/pod-product-compliance
Lightning Source LLC
Chambersburg PA
CBHW021118270326
41929CB00009B/946